Pay to Play

Pay to Play

Race and the Perils of the College Sports Industrial Complex

Lori Latrice Martin, PhD
Kenneth J. Fasching-Varner, PhD
and Nicholas D. Hartlep, PhD

PRAEGER™

An Imprint of ABC-CLIO, LLC
Santa Barbara, California • Denver, Colorado

Library of Congress Cataloging-in-Publication Data

Pay to Play: Race and the Perils of the College Sports Industrial Complex

Library of Congress Cataloging in Publication Control Number: 2017003232

ISBN: 978-1-4408-4315-0
EISBN: 978-1-4408-4316-7

21 20 19 18 17   1 2 3 4 5

This book is also available as an eBook.

Praeger
An Imprint of ABC-CLIO, LLC

ABC-CLIO, LLC
130 Cremona Drive, P.O. Box 1911
Santa Barbara, California 93116-1911
www.abc-clio.com

This book is printed on acid-free paper ∞

Manufactured in the United States of America

In memory of Dr. Willie L. Bryant

Contents

Acknowledgments

The authors wish to thank the following individuals and organizations for their continued support: Jim Ciment at Praeger, Lee and Edith Burns, Derrick Martin Jr., Emir Sykes, Raymond A. Jetson, Jeremiah Anthony Rogers, Tat Yau, Lauren Crump, Melinda Jackson, Tifanie Pulley, Roland Mitchell, LSU Curriculum Theory Project, LSU Department of Sociology, LSU African and African American Studies Program, Stephen Finley, Jahaan Chandler, Danielle Thomas, Landon Douglas, Hayward Derrick Horton, Mark Naison, Henry Louis Taylor, Kwando and Imani Kinshasa, Teresa A. Booker, David I. Rudder, Reggie and LaDonna Sanders, McKinley and Sue Johnson, Andre Sigmone, Christopher and Sonya Williams, Walter Martin, Modrall Lathers, Lisa Freeman, Sarah Corie, Emily and John Thornton, Lee Burns Jr., Mahima Christian, John Edward Clayton Thornton, Rachel Nichols, Michael Jerome Thornton, Constance Slaughter Harvey, Alice Crowe Bell, Alicia Crowe, Frances Pratt, Rockland County Ministerial Alliance, Barbara Ann and Lewis Johnson, Sidney Rand, Ray Graham, Dione Cooper Footman, Norma Crowder, Larry Mathews, Patricia Bullock, Mary White, Antoinette Bennett, Alison Satake, and Dorothea Swann.

CHAPTER ONE

Amateur Athletes and the American Way

Love them or hate them; win, lose, or draw, sports are an important social institution. Individuals engaged in physical competitions, who are motivated by intrinsic and extrinsic rewards, represent many core American values, among which are fairness, justice, equality, hard work, success, and freedom. Unfortunately, sports provide some of the most convincing evidence of the persistent gap between ideal and real culture, or the persistent gap between what we say and what we do. For much of the nation's history, members of the dominant racial group in America kept nonwhites and women from competition for fear that the success of the minority groups would embolden disadvantaged groups and challenge dominant racial and gender ideology. Although black athletes dominated sports such as boxing, cycling, and horse racing in the late 1800s and the early 1900s, they were soon excluded from these sports or seriously limited in their ability to earn a living or compete at the college level. The exclusion of black athletes from sports where they are now the numerical majority is hard for many to imagine, but it is as much a fact of American history as it is an important part of the history of sports. Despite the contradictions, many Americans continue to see sports as an important part of everyday life, and evidence of the significance of sports in the lives of everyday Americans is all around.

Sports metaphors are common in many areas of public and private life, including in politics and religion. Some of the most recognizable people in pop culture, and in the broader society, are athletes—and not just professional athletes, but increasingly college athletes in elite programs. Amateur athletes are a source of inspiration and entertainment. They are a source of inspiration for many because many Americans believe the ideal amateur athlete is one who possesses natural talents, works hard, demonstrates leadership skills, and works well as a team member. At the same time, amateur athletes provide fans the opportunity to escape from their everyday lives. High school and college sporting events, for example, help create a sense of community. In many places, people plan their workday, vacations, meetings, even their weddings, around Friday night high school games and Saturday college football games. Whether a business in a college town lives or dies often depends upon the failure or success of the neighboring athletic programs. Second only to professional sports, America's near obsession with college sports is enduring, and in some media markets where a professional sports team does not exist, college sport is king.

About 350 colleges and universities in the United States are designated Division I programs in the National Collegiate Athletic Association (NCAA). Of the three divisions within the NCAA, schools in Division I have the largest budgets and offer some of the largest scholarships. The racial and ethnic composition of the players has changed over time but remains fairly consistent for both male and female athletes. During the 1991–1992 season, 66 percent of male athletes were white, 27 percent were black, less than 3 percent were Latino, and less than 1 percent were Asian or American Indian/Alaska Native. Almost 80 percent of Division I female athletes identified their race as white, compared to 13 percent of black females, 2.2 percent identified as Latino and less than 2 percent identified as either Asian or American Indian/Alaska Native.

By the turn the of the 20th to 21st century, 62 percent of Division I male athletes were white, compared to 24.3 percent black, 3.3 percent Latino, 0.4 percent as American Indian/Alaskan Native, and 1.4 percent Asian. Seventy percent of Division I female athletes identified as white, compared to about 15 percent black, 2.6 Latino, 0.4 percent American Indian/Alaskan Native, and 1.4 percent Asian.

In the case of college basketball, between the 1991–1992 and the 2013–2014 seasons, the percentage of black players in Division I basketball declined slightly from 61.8 to 57.6 percent. The percentage of white players also declined from 34.5 to 27.1 percent. The percentages for Latino and Asian players were almost identical in both years.[1]

According to a 2014 report Race and Gender Report Card for College Sports, nearly 60 percent of Division I basketball players were identified as black, 27 percent identified as white, 1.7 percent as Latino, 0.4 percent as

Asian, and about 6 percent as "non-resident aliens."[2] Almost half of Division I football players during the 2013–2014 season identified as black. A little over 41 percent of players in Division I football identified as white. Less than 3 percent of student-athletes playing Division I football identified as Latino, and less than 2 percent identified as Asian. Less than 1 percent of players were international players.[3]

More than 80 percent of Division I baseball players identified their race as white, compared to less than 5 percent as black, 6.5 percent as Latino, 0.9 percent as Asian, and 0.8 percent as international. The percentage of white players in the sport was 90 percent during the 1991–1992 season, with 4.3 percent for blacks, 3.9 percent for Latinos, and 0.7 percent for Asians. No numbers were recorded for international students.[4]

Racial disparities are not relegated to elite male programs. Racial differences in college sport participation are evident in women's sports too. The percentage of black players in Division I women's basketball during the 2013–2014 season was more than half; over a third of players were white; about 2 percent identified their ethnicity as Latino; and 1 percent identified as Asian. About 4 percent of athletes were international students. During the 1999–2000 season, the earliest available, 54.6 percent of players identified as white, compared to 35.7 percent as black, 1.5 percent Latino, 0.7 percent Asian, and 2.4 percent international. Division I women's basketball went from predominantly white to black during that time period. Of particular note is the 2010–2011 season, when 47.4 percent of players identified as black compared to only 39.3 percent as white.[5]

Although the percentages of black players in Division I sports are substantially higher in football, men's basketball, and women's basketball, the percentages of blacks in positions with decision-making authority are not. In men's Division I basketball, about one-fifth of all head coaches were African American, which was slightly down 1 percentage point from the findings for the 2012–2013 season, and down slightly more from the all-time high percentage reported in the 2005–2006 season. In all, less than a quarter of men's basketball coaches were coaches of color.[6]

In Division I women's basketball, 10.6 percent of head coaches identified as black women, and less than 4 percent identified as black men, during the 2013–2014 season. The percentages of black college coaches in Division I women's basketball decreased from a combined percentage of 20.6 percent during the 2012–2013 season. "The 10.6 percent stood in stark contrast to the 51.1 percent of the African American women student-athletes who played basketball."[7]

The Race and Gender Report Card for College Sports in 2014 also found that almost 90 percent of athletic directors were held by individuals identifying as white for Division I sports, and the percentages for whites holding similar positions in Division II and III schools was even higher. About 8 percent of athletic directors in Division I sports identified as black; less than 3 percent, as Latino; and less than 1 percent, as Asian/Pacific Islander.

Similar trends were observed for the position of associate athletic director, assistant athletic director, faculty athletics representative, and even sports information director. Overall, college sports received a C for race and gender hiring practices, which is lower than the C+ earned last year. Division I assistant coaches for men's teams earned the highest grade possible.[8]

Although college sports are not as racially diverse as some may have expected, sports are nonetheless very profitable. Economic impact studies appear throughout the year to demonstrate how much money particular athletic events bring to a community, a city, an institution, and even to a nation. College sports are not different. The sacrifice a student-athlete makes to earn a spot on the national stage is part of a multibillion-dollar industry. Researchers conducted a study of the economic impact of the Fiesta Bowl Festival during the 2010–2011 season. The Fiesta Bowl Festival, which took place in Glendale, Arizona, included the Tostitos BCS National Championship Game, the Tostitos Fiesta Bowl, and the Insight Bowl. The researchers estimated that visitors at the BCS championship contributed about $188 million to the economy. Visitors at the Tostitos Fiesta Bowl spent about $85 million. The total economic impact for all three events was over $320 million. "It is conservatively estimated based on extrapolation of our research data and analyses that the Fiesta Bowl and its events have generated more than $1 billion in the past five-year cycle."[9]

Another example of the economic impact of college sports on various economies is found in college basketball and the madness that is the month of March. An article from NBC News documented what a so-called "Cinderella run" in Division I college basketball tournament play means in real dollars. A "Cinderella run" is a term used to describe the improbable success of a team with relatively low ranking or a relatively unknown athletic program in a national championship that beats the odds and takes down a more highly ranked team or a team with a storied athletic tradition. The team that makes the "Cinderella run" often captures the attention of die-hard and occasional fans alike. In the case of women's Division I basketball, few teams have dominated as much as the University of Connecticut's since the mid-1990s, when the women's team won the first of 10 national championships. "Those championships have not only boosted Huskies pride, they've helped to draw billions of dollars in public funds and alumni donations to upgrade UConn's academic infrastructure and the school's stature." A number of basketball programs have enjoyed the economic rewards of a "Cinderella run," lasting longer into March Madness than anyone anticipated.[10]

NBC News also reported the benefits associated with participating in the NCAA basketball tournament and doing well. Colleges and universities may receive contributions to offset the costs associated with capital improvements, but they are also likely to see increases in sponsorships from large corporations, ticket sales, licensing deals, and freshman and transfer applications, as well as greater student retention, due to all the media attention, which is valued in the hundreds of millions of dollars.[11]

Relatively unknown Division I basketball programs saw almost immediate economic benefits for their unexpected success in the tournament. In 2010, Butler University made it to the championship game before losing a close game to Duke University. Corporate sponsorship grew the following year, and licensing increased by more than 300 percent.[12]

George Mason University saw similar gains four years prior to Butler's run. The team upset Michigan State and North Carolina, among others, before losing to Florida in the semifinals. After their remarkable season, revenue increased from about $530 million to more than $630 million. George Washington University also saw an increase in fund-raising, from $19.6 million to nearly $24 million. The university even exceeded its capital campaign goals by more than $30 million. In 2006, George Mason University had less than 40 licensees. After the appearance in the Final Four, George Mason had 53, which translated into a $100,000 increase in licensing revenue.[13] After the team appeared on the cover of *Sports Illustrated*, the university estimated it received nearly $700 million in free publicity.[14]

A recent report from CNN Money attempts to assign a numerical value to college sports. CNN Money projects that the profits will be even greater with the move to a new football playoff system. According to the January 2015 article, the University of Texas had the biggest profit of any program during the previous season, earning $74 million. The University of Michigan earned over $64 million. In all, "64 schools in the five major conferences received a total of $2.8 billion in revenue last year. Most of the revenue came from broadcasting rights and ticket sales. And since these teams don't have to pay their players, they keep nearly half of that revenue—a profit margin that would make any professional team owner green with envy."[15] ESPN has already agreed to pay over $7 billion to broadcast the new playoffs for more than 10 years. "Most profits from the playoffs will be split roughly evenly between members of the five major conferences, regardless of whether a school makes the playoffs."[16]

As the revenue from college sports increases, controversies about whether student-athletes should share in some of the profits also appear to increase—in sports media, the popular press, and among fans and non-fans alike. The current controversy surrounding whether to pay college athletes in elite programs, especially in high-revenue-generating sports, is gaining momentum after two key recent events: the O'Bannon case and the case involving the Northwestern University football team. The O'Bannon case was filed by former UCLA standout, Ed O'Bannon and other athletes to force the NCAA and Electronic Arts (EA) Sports to compensate current and former players for the use of their likeness in such media as video games. The Northwestern University football team fought to unionize. A number of questions arise. Why now? Why is the issue so controversial? Why is there so much resistance? Some would argue that college athletes are already paid through scholarships and special treatment received from others. Others would argue that athletes in elite programs will earn more money than they can handle over the course of their careers and that payment during their time as a college athlete is moot. A long list of professions are deemed more worthy of high salaries than athlete, so paying student-athletes is problematic for many. Still others say figuring out how to pay college athletes is just too hard and will negatively impact low- and non-revenue-generating sports. It is hard to imagine that in a capitalist society large numbers of people would object to compensating anyone at fair market value, but that is arguably what is happening in the case of athletes in high-revenue-generating college sports. Historically, the unequal treatment of selected groups is justified by portraying the group on the receiving end of the unequal treatment as "others," as undesirable and undeserving. Black male athletes are arguably the most recognizable symbols of the college sport industrial complex, and black males in general are viewed by far too many in the dominant group as undesirable and undeserving "others." It is no wonder then that there are such great objections and much debate surrounding whether to pay student-athletes in high-revenue-generating college sports.

What is missing from the conversation is consideration of the history of the commodification and exploitation of black bodies and the failure to see blacks in general, and black student-athletes in particular, as total persons. We miss the role and consequently the perceived threat black student-athletes in elite programs present to white masculinity and the overall racial social order.

Pay to Play: Race and the Perils of the College Sports Industrial Complex addresses the controversies involving paying amateur athletes, with a particular emphasis on college athletes in top-tier, high-revenue-generating sports, and places the controversies within proper historical and contemporary contexts.

Everyone seems to have an opinion about whether college athletes should be paid. Race and racism seldom enter the conversation because many Americans believe sports are the only place where race does not matter. The book tackles the issue of race and the controversy surrounding whether colleges must pay to play head-on, focusing on the historic and contemporary roles race and racism play in shaping our society and our social institutions, including sports. It highlights how race and racism are often used to criminalize certain subpopulations, including young black males. Young black males are overrepresented in high- revenue-generating college sports, such as football and men's basketball, so it is not surprising that black male student-athletes are also criminalized and considered as members of an out-group relative to the dominant racial group that makes up the majority of the student population, administration, and so on at the predominantly white institutions of higher learning (PWIs) the black male student-athletes attend. The criminalization of black males, including black male student-athletes, in conjunction with treating black male student-athletes as "others," has many implications, including treating black male student-athletes more like commodities and less like students. Just as the criminalization of blackness and treatment of blacks as "others" provided justification for the ownership of people of African ancestry in America, and later for their treatment as second-class citizens, the criminalization of blackness and the treatment of blacks as "others"—carrying distinguishing physical and cultural characteristics that are deemed inferior relative to members of the dominant group who are deemed more virtuous—is used to justify the unfair treatment of college athletes in high-revenue-generating sports, especially those where black male student-athletes are in the numerical majority.

The process by which members of the dominant group came to associate blacks with criminality, see them as others, and associate them with particular sports can best be understood as a result of a process of racial socialization, which is discussed in detail in Chapter 6. Although racial socialization is often understood as a common feature in the relationship between parents of color and their biological children about the inevitability of unfair treatment based upon race, racial socialization can include so much more, particularly given the fact that race is such a dominant force and organizing principle in American society. Volumes of research point to how people are grouped by race and how racial groups are ranked. The racial group with the greatest access to wealth, status, and power are at the highest levels of our racialized social structure. Individuals with less access to these valued resources are at relatively lower levels of the hierarchical system. The ranking of racial groups along the social ladder is based on a number of factors, including the ability of the dominant group to use its power and privilege to relegate members of subordinate groups to relatively lower levels, even in the face of resistance.

In America, the enslavement of African Americans and their continued unequal treatment relative to other groups laid the foundation for the current racial arrangement. To maintain the racial status quo, a racial ideology was developed and communicated to teach whites and people of color the ways of society. The process of racial socialization involves communicating, perpetuating, and transforming ideas about who and what is considered black and who and what is considered white, including in sports. Racial socialization is not a static process. Additionally, one thing that remains unchanged is the fact that race and racism are central to our understanding of how our society is ordered, how our institutions operate, and how ideas about what it means to be black or white in our society are maintained. Consequently, claims of a post-racial society notwithstanding, ideas about what it means to be black or white in our society don't die or fade away; rather, they are merely being reinvented, repackaged, and reproduced in an effort to yield the desired outcome, which is the maintenance of an ongoing racialized social system where whites are dominant and blacks and other racial minority groups are subordinate in every area of society, including in sports.

The bulk of research on racial socialization focuses on the family, and parenting in particular, as mentioned previously. Less attention is devoted to institutions such as sports as agents of racial socialization. Although there is an abundance of research on race and sports, few studies specifically tackle racial socialization as the set of processes by which members of the dominant racial group and members of a racial minority group come to "know" their place in the social structure and within the institutions, or the ways in which certain racial groups are criminalized, treated as "others," and experience unequal treatment. This is a significant gap, particularly at a time when much of American society is celebrating our designation as a colorblind society. Through sports, ideas are communicated as to what is acceptable participation and behavior for members of various racial and ethnic groups. Sports are among the most ideal places to convey such ideas and messages, because most players and spectators are focused on the excitement and the emotion of the individual or team and are unaware of the broader and larger context within which the game is taking place. Fans often become so engrossed in the contests that it is hard for them to see the players as anything but free beings with otherworldly talents.

Additionally, the annual salaries that some players receive far exceed what some American workers will earn over the course of a lifetime, and the scholarships student-athletes receive often mean a relatively debt-free college experience, whereas far too many non-student-athletes find themselves saddled with tens of thousands of dollars in debt.

The significance and influence of sports in our lives is quite clear. Millions share in the experience of the Super Bowl—if only for the commercials. Each weekend and on some weekdays, millions of parents and children head to sporting events in their local communities, which are sponsored by local business, religious institutions, and even subsidized by local government. Sport is an important social institution and an important agent of socialization, particularly racial socialization.

Matters of race must be viewed as central to these processes. Scholars must explore the methodological and theoretical implications of understanding the multilevel and multidimensional nature of racial socialization in sports, which is addressed in *Pay to Play*. Our approach allows scholars to adequately account for the significance of race in our society and in sports, particularly in controversies involving sports where blacks are in the numerical majority, such as in high-revenue-generating college sports like football and men's basketball.

Understanding racial socialization as the process by which blacks and whites learn what is expected of them in order to maintain the racial status quo and the myth of white supremacy and black inferiority means that we need to look at race and sports from a critical perspective. It requires looking beyond generalized theories and perspectives about socialization to provide a framework for assessing change over time and identifying seemingly race-neutral tactics that have meaningful consequences for individuals.

It is quite clear that in contemporary times certain sports have come to be associated with certain racial groups. Some maintain the belief that certain racial groups are inherently better than other racial groups at particular sports; that great athletes are created at birth and not made over time. The idea that biology equals sports destiny is still with us. Although there are a host of theories, perspectives, and paradigms in the social sciences, particularly in sociology, arguing for the continuing significance of race in our society, far too few of these ideas have found their way into scholarly discussions about sports and to recent controversies, such as whether to adequately compensate student-athletes in high-revenue-generating sports.

Pay to Play breaks new ground by linking the rise of the black athlete at predominantly white colleges and universities with perceptions about black bodies as commodities, and the unwillingness (or inability) to see black athletes as total persons to deepen our understanding about the controversies surrounding whether to pay college athletes in high-revenue-generating sports. Our book uniquely explores issues of race, stereotypes, and identity and the controversy over whether to play college athletes in elite athletic programs. We begin in Chapter 2 with a discussion about the creation of the amateur athlete in America by providing a social and historical analysis about the evolution of amateurism in the United States. The chapter includes a discussion about the Muscular Christianity movement and the movement's connection to the eugenics movement, the Young Men's Christian Association (YMCA), and efforts to redefine masculinity. The chapter also includes a discussion about muscular assimilation campaigns and the lasting effects of all of the above.

In Chapter 3, we explore the forced separation of racial groups in amateur sports in America from the period before the Civil War through the 1960s in order to illustrate the various ways that sports reflected and constructed race in American society overtime. Unlike other discussions about the history of racial segregation in amateur sports, we address the inhumane treatment of and criminalization of black athletes and the impact of integration on amateur athletic programs, especially teams at historically black colleges and universities (HBCUs).

Chapter 4 chronicles the integration of black male athletes at predominantly white colleges and universities. Chapter 5 includes a discussion about the use of black male athletes to sell just about everything in the global marketplace and the stereotypes that are perpetuated in doing so. Chapter 6 examines efforts to unionize college athletes, with a special focus on football players at Northwestern. The chapter also analyzes the history and the implications of the O'Bannon case. In Chapter 7, we lay out an argument as to why college athletes must receive adequate compensation for their labor. We include the results of a study where we asked current student-athletes, former student-athletes, and non-student-athletes to share their views on a host of issues, including whether student-athletes in high-revenue-generating sports should receive compensation beyond room and board, tuition, and books, and whether race is a factor in the controversies about paying elite college athletes. In the final chapter, Chapter 8, we offer rules for transforming amateur athletics.

CHAPTER TWO

Creation of the Amateur Athlete in America

Sports do not exist in a vacuum. Sports reflect society and society reflects sports. It is not surprising then that there is a deep connection between sports and other social institutions, such as the family, education, and even religion. In some cases, a great deal of family time is centered on sport participation and sport engagement. Parents often introduce their children to sports at an early age by signing them up for club sports and taking their sons and daughters to amateur and professional events. Family time may also be spent watching games in person or on television. Not coincidentally, sports participation and loyalty to certain teams is passed down from generation to generation much like family recipes and treasured family heirlooms. Parents, siblings, and other family members play important roles in socializing young boys and girls into learning their appropriate gender roles through sports. For example, parents are more likely to sign their male children up for contact sports like tackle football while enrolling their female children in dance, cheerleading, or soccer.

Schools not only provide compulsory physical education but may also offer opportunities for students to participate in competitive physical activities. School-sponsored sports may help generate social capital. They can also be an important avenue for students to move from playing at the high school level to playing at the college level and earning a relatively debt-free college education. The connection between religion and sports is complex and may be less obvious than the connections between sports and the family or education.

The Catholic Youth Organization (CYO) provides many opportunities for young people to participate in sports. The Young Men's Christian Association (YMCA) is also a faith-based entity connecting religion and sport. Many scholars have written about the significance of sports in the lives of Americans and have called upon religious institutions to leave the sidelines and get into the game. The Catholic Church and the YMCA have been the subject of a lot of research, the extent of which, however, is limited in important ways.

Many contemporary discussions about sports and religion tend to focus on individual athletes and the degree to which the athletes embrace—or reject—a wide range of religious beliefs. Few die-hard sports fans can articulate the true marriage between religion and sports, dating back many centuries, and the intersections of race, religion, and sports. In this chapter we examine the linkages between sports and religion that laid the groundwork for understanding the hypermasculinity, misogyny, white hegemony, and commodification of black bodies in contemporary amateur—and professional—sports. In order to understand why compensating athletes—a majority of whom are black males—in elite college programs is so controversial, we must first understand the context in which amateurism evolved in the United States. Pseudo-science, scientific racism, and eugenics played important roles in providing an empirical justification for seeing people with membership in different racial groups as inferior to the dominant racial group in America and around the globe; it also provided a justification for treating such groups unequally. The unequal treatment included the view that people of color, blacks in particular and especially black males, were more like animals than members of the same species to which whites belonged, and therefore could be treated in dehumanizing ways and exploited for the benefit of everyone but themselves. This idea was not limited to eugenics, and it had lasting ramification even for today's black athletes, particularly those in high-profile, high-revenue-generating sports in elite college programs.

We therefore begin our discussion with a movement that had a tremendous impact on the development of amateur athletes in America: the Muscular Christianity movement. The movement linked piety with athletic excellence. The Muscular Christianity movement provided a justification for another important movement in the early part of the 20th century—the eugenics movement and newly born American imperialism. The dominance of the aforementioned movements and the correspondent dominant ideologies drove many, especially blacks, to engage in a series of campaigns collectively referred to as muscular assimilation. The chapter concludes with a discussion about the lingering effects of responses to the fear of the feminization of Christianity and threats to white supremacy and white male domination.

Muscular Christianity Movement

The term "Muscular Christianity" refers to an idea that emerged in Europe in the middle of the 19th century and focused on a commitment to good physical health and a brand of masculinity that reflected the superiority of white males. The Muscular Christianity movement was part of a larger movement, referred to as the Broad Church Movement,[1] that began around the mid-1800s and consisted of several components, of which Muscular Christianity was the most influential. The Broad Church movement represented the most liberal element of the Church of England. The liberal view of the Church followed a period where evangelicals were losing influence on society because they held tightly to traditional sources of authority and neglected general learning.[2] Moreover, the church was criticized for being good faith followers but lacking understanding and displaying a general ignorance about the world in which they lived. Prominent people, like preachers Frederick Robertson and John Sterling left the church in droves.[3] The Broad Church Movement focused on two broad themes: liberty and learning.[4]

By 1860, all liberals within the Church of England were considered part of the Broad Movement, although there were varying degrees of liberalism. The movement could best be described as a loose association of two distinct groups, one of which was more critical of the church than the other. This group was also more theoretical in analysis of the Church of England and relied more on formal logic than the second group. The second group agreed that facts were important, but were much more concerned with principle. Although the first group was more Aristotle-like, the second group was more Platonic and related to God in much more personal terms than others. Both welcomed scientific advancements and textual critiques of the Bible. The Platonic-like wing of the Broad Church movement was so called because it represented the ruling class, one of the regimes famously described in *The Republic*, which represented the values and beliefs of the most privileged class. It was also considered less hostile to tradition and church authority than their peers.[5] The groups were united in their support for truth telling and their disdain for terrorism. Through both groups, "the Church gradually regained contact with the modern forces in the world."[6]

Charles Kingsley, a church priest of the Church of England and a professor, and Thomas Hughes, an English lawyer and judge, are credited with ushering in the Muscular Christianity movement. Kingsley's work drew from a popular thesis in the Christian church at the time: "the thesis that all things advance steadily from worse to better."[7] Kingsley popularized the image of the British hero who always won and never missed an opportunity to share the doctrines of the Church of England.

Hughes developed an influential concept within the movement that addressed moral earnestness. He viewed individuals as inherently flawed and saw the role of educators to teach students how to create their own commitment to what is just, good, and right. Through his literary work, and in his version of Muscular Christianity, Hughes contended that moral struggles about what is right and wrong happen over the life course, and sports provide many opportunities for positive character development. His characters were continuously engaged in struggles between good and evil. The characters in his work were involved in battles that required them to use their mind and their bodies.[8] Hughes was especially disheartened by the prevailing idea of his day that Christianity was not viewed as a particular strong or masculine religion.[9] Hughes argued this perspective could not be further from the truth because the core values of the Christian faith required followers "to fight with their bodies, minds and spirits against whatever is false."[10] Hughes went so far as to say that some of the greatest battles in history involved Christians—who fought with God's help.[11] The ability to defeat someone in a sport like boxing and still be a moral being and a Christian after the bout is what Muscular Christianity was all about.

Hughes saw many connections between ancient Greek games and the Church. Ancient games, said Hughes, brought various social classes together, which created greater social cohesion, community, and understanding. The problem arose when some classes, like farmers, turned to other forms of amusement due in part to increased leisure time and financial resources, thus creating class divisions. The significance of games, for Hughes, could not be underestimated. Games strengthened the body, and both the mind and the body required attention. The body was viewed as divine gift, and God would judge each individual based upon the extent to which his or her body was cared for.[12] There was a connectedness between the mind and body to the extent that they "reacted upon one another, [and] the man who exercised properly would be able to do far better mental work."[13] Hughes and the entire Muscular Christianity movement were not without critics. Their perspective represented an oversimplification of Christianity.

As mass immigration from southern, central, and Eastern Europe; urbanization; industrialization; and increased social problems led to the spread of Muscular Christianity across the Atlantic, members of the dominant racial group in America sought to address the social upheaval in the United States. At the same time, other Christians did not see the connectedness between religion and recreation, including many blacks in the United States. W. E. B. Du Bois, one of the leading African American intellectuals of the late 19th and early 20th centuries, weighed in on the issue. Du Bois cautioned black churches viewing amusement as a distraction from one's religious duties. Although acknowledging that leisure was not on the top of the list of social justice issues for blacks at the start of the 20th century, he did think it was important enough to address. He noted that the church was the center of black life. He also argued that the black church in many ways played a more significant role in black society than families and schools because black families were callously disrupted during the enslavement era, and blacks were in many cases forbidden from learning to read or write. Because blacks were also excluded from most mainstream institutions, or restricted in their membership and their roles, the black church became the place blacks turned to for just about everything. Du Bois said,

> The Negro Church is not simply an organism for the propagation of religion; it is the center of the social, intellectual, and religious life of an organized group of individuals. It provides social discourse, it provides amusement of various kinds, it serves as a newspaper and intelligence bureau, it supplants the theatre, it directs the picnic and excursion, it furnishes the music, it introduces the stranger to the community, it serves as lyceum, library, and lecture bureau—it is . . . the central organ of the organized life of the American Negro for amusement, relaxation, instruction, and religion.[14]

Du Bois observed that the black church was derelict in its duties "to recognize for their children the God-given right to play; to recognize that there is a perfectly natural and legitimate demand for amusement on the part of young people, and that no people can afford to laugh at, sneer at, or forcibly repress the natural joyousness and pleasure-seeking propensity of young womanhood and young manhood."[15] Du Bois warned what might happen if the black church did not become more active in the recreation of black youth and pointed to local Christian associations, like the Young Men's Christian Association, who were already recruiting Christians and non-Christians like.

Young Men's Christian Association and the Muscular Christianity Movement

Few institutions embodied Muscular Christianity, like the Young Men's Christian Association (YMCA), first in Europe and then in the United States. For many years, the roles the YMCA and British sports played in the development and popularization of amateur sports in America were understudied.[16] For a time, the YMCA did not embrace sports because the founders were of the belief that such activities promoted vanity. "Physical development could make a man unwisely vain, as could his desire for sporting accouterments, such as cycling uniforms and badges. Similarly the temptation could arise to display person prowess, simply for the sake of self-gratification."[17] There were also concerns about other activities considered immoral at the time, namely "unwelcome social mixing between the same sexes" and gambling, among others.[18] Football, swimming, and billiards were among the sports viewed as particularly troublesome and viewed as "unsuitable pastime[s] for true Christians."[19] In short, sporting activities were considered distractions from the organization's mission to spread the Gospel.

YMCA officials changed their perspectives about sports upon coming to the realization that sports could attract and retain men in a way religion alone could not accomplish. The addition of a gym in the YMCA in Sutherland, in the United Kingdom, for example, yielded the desired effect of attracting young men. After reeling in the new members, the young men were then instructed in religious and physical education.[20] The YMCA's approach was adopted—albeit unofficially—by the Church of England in the 1890s. In 1894, the Church created an entity to examine the origins of social problems plaguing the residents in a neighborhood in Sutherland. Among the issues identified were alcoholism, betting, and unemployment. To address the issues, a member of the local clergy recommended sporting activities, which served as an acknowledgment of the need to provide physical recreation. The YMCA echoed the creed of Muscular Christianity, which stressed the connectedness between the body and the mind. For the early YMCA, the body was viewed as a divine gift "to be prized and preserved. Exercise ensured young men's bodies were made fitting temples of God's Holy Spirit. It was God's purpose that man should enjoy health."[21]

The influence of the YMCA was evident not only in England but in the United States as well. The College YMCA played a particularly significant role in the development of the culture of Muscular Christianity on American campuses, as the association did throughout England. Beginning in 1877, YMCA chapters sprang up on campuses across the nation and were among the most influential examples of the role of religion in the lives of college students. Within five years, there were nearly 200 YMCA chapters on college campuses. In all, there were about 8500 members.[22] The number of chapters grew exponentially. By 1902, there were nearly 700 chapters and almost 4200 members. About one-quarter of all male college students were members of a YMCA chapter by 1914. "One of the most interesting dimensions of YMCA work in colleges and universities between 1890 and 1914 was its intersection with a concomitant movement for muscular Christianity within American Protestantism," said author David Setran.[23] The college YMCA was not only influenced by the Muscular Christianity movement but also influenced the secularization of society and the creation of "a vision of Christian faith devoted primarily to aggressive action and divorced from concrete structures of belief."[24]

The story of the College YMCA is as much a story about the Muscular Christianity movement as it is a story about "the masculinity crisis" in America during the early part of the 20th century.[25] The Muscular Christianity movement was not just about connecting the mind, body, and the soul; it was also about staving off what some feared was the feminization of Christianity. There was an expressed desire to show the connectedness between one's Christian faith and expressions of masculinity. The Christian Church in America was not alone in its concerns; there was a much broader concern about the general feminization of culture in America. Historically, middle- and upper-class white males represented the ideal male, so painstaking efforts were taken to draw men to Christianity by focusing more on the masculine attributes of Christ and other important figures, including men from athletics and the military.[26]

Marketing Manhood: From the Pulpit to the President

The Industrial Revolution fundamentally changed American life. In some ways the shift from a largely agricultural society to an industrial society improved the quality of life for some and hurt the quality of life for others. The societal shift changed both work and play. Fewer people were engaged in the labor-intensive work associated with such professions as farming and with the average American's idea of masculinity. Concerns grew that men were becoming more dependent and less self-reliant than in previous eras that grew under mid-19th-century capitalism. Corporate capitalism did not value the business owner, but rather the other-directed team player, according to Setran.[27] The myth of the self-made man was quickly becoming a distant memory. Americans in general—and white males in particular—were less involved in the economy as producers and were more involved as consumers.[28] The so-called "over-civilization" of white males—if left unchecked—would lead to "race suicide, marked by a loss of white male vitality and the potential for muscular, working-class immigrants to stage a cultural revolt against an effete native stock," claimed Setran in his work on the history of the YMCA.[29] The church was not immune.

Historically, women outnumbered male churchgoers across denominations, but the association of femininity with piety and masculinity with economic prosperity resolved the gender issue. Once corporate capitalism became more dominant, said Setran, "a feminized Protestantism was no longer needed to balance unmitigated male aggressive competition. Instead, this form of refined and pious religion now appeared to detract from an already fragile sense of masculinity."[30] To reverse course, leaders in the Protestant Church in America made conscious efforts to emphasize "the muscular and strenuous components of the Christian faith over its more refined elements."[31] Theodore Roosevelt's Rough Rider image embodied hypermasculinity in the early 1900s.

Roosevelt once wrote about a personal experience that taught him an important lesson about physical strength and shaped his life personally and professionally for many decades. He described himself as a sickly child at a time when he was bullied by a group of boys. The defeat at the hands of these boys—who were stronger and tougher than Roosevelt—led Roosevelt to participate in a training regiment, which included boxing, to prepare his mind and body in case he was threatened again. From that day forth, Roosevelt lived, governed, and talked about the importance of a strenuous life. He boxed as a student at Harvard College and was also on the rowing team. Within a few years after graduating from Harvard College, Roosevelt began a very successful political career. Early into his political career, his wife died, and he lived on a ranch in the Dakota Territory for a couple of years, interacting with many cowhands. The lessons he learned and events he witnessed would not only shape his life but also shape the nation and our understanding of masculinity and femininity for generations.

Roosevelt held positions with the U.S. Civil Service Commission and New York City's Police Commission. He was also assistant secretary of the Navy and led the First U.S. Volunteer Calvary during the Spanish American War. The regiment—more commonly known as the Rough Riders—contributed to Roosevelt's legacy as an American hero. His charge up San Juan Hill was covered widely by the mainstream press and helped propel Roosevelt to the office of Governor of New York and later to vice president of the United States. After McKinley was assassinated, Roosevelt became president. At a time of immense social and cultural change, Roosevelt's gospel of hypermasculinity was what many American males felt they needed—and the nation needed—at the time.

Roosevelt was a rising star in the nation at the same time that the nation was experiencing cultural shifts. His main goal was "to bring cultural stability to a nation he believed was being pulled apart over issues of identity. Modern women's identities seemed particularly in upheaval."[32] Demands for the right to vote, the presence of white working-class women employed outside of the home, and an increased use of birth control were viewed as serious threats to white men and American culture.

Like many Protestant leaders, Roosevelt also made the argument that industrialization, urbanization, and immigration created a perfect storm that threatened the nation's global stance and white male dominance on the home front. Increasingly, forces beyond the control of the individual called into question "the Victorian notion of success stemming from individual self-determination and self-restrain."[33]

To maintain the gender status quo, Roosevelt evoked the frontier myth and was very good at applying it to perpetuate ideas about masculinity and femininity. Roosevelt saw the frontier as one of the greatest metaphors for daily living, an area brimming with opportunities for pioneering spirits. It was a haven from the hustle and bustle of urban environments. Furthermore, the frontier represented "the tension between opposing ideals—savagery and civilization, individualism and community, progress and regression, masculinity, and femininity—that compel people to strive for equilibrium."[34] Just as there was a need to tame and control the frontier, there was a need to control the current challenges then facing the nation, such as the economic panics and calls for greater equity and equality from historically disadvantaged groups. Institutions such as Harvard University shared Roosevelt's worldview and desire for the nation, and advocated for a reimagining of the white male through sports.[35]

For a number of reasons, institutions like Harvard University and the College YMCA played an important role in defining masculinity during the latter part of the 19th century and the early part of the 20th century. The College YMCA understood that young people benefited from exposure to positive role models and could be influenced by role models exemplifying the brand of masculine faith being promoted. The leadership "worked to emphasize and redefine the person of Jesus."[36] "Muscular Christians within the organization rejected the depiction of the passive, peaceful, and otherworldly Jesus of Sunday school lore. By contrast, they pointed out the Jesus described in the Bible was a muscular carpenter with a strong physique, honed through his rugged and nomadic lifestyle and his life of active service to others."[37]

The book *The Manhood of the Master,* by Harry E. Fosdick, an American pastor, played an important role in socializing both males and females and helping men to "reclaim their correct masculine moral posture, seeking not an internal balance of masculine and feminine ideals as much as a mutual interdependence with women who would correct the potential abuses of the male code. The key to such a life was for men to follow the masculine Jesus into active and aggressive service while women followed the Savior who was meek and mild."[38] Fosdick's book was widely used in the college YMCA. The YMCA also hired leaders, like Amos Alonzo Stagg, who embodied their vision of masculinity. "Stagg's willingness to define religious work in terms of active service was perhaps the hallmark of the muscular Christian vision and the clear path of the campus YMCA."[39] The emphasis on physical activity eventually changed the YMCA in many ways, including how the organization determined eligibility for membership. A profession of Christian faith was no longer prerequisite for membership by the early part of the 20th century.

Muscular Christianity ushered in the secularization of colleges and universities across the nation. Roosevelt even praised the YMCA for their work and attributed the organization's success in promoting manhood to a willingness "not to dwarf any of the impulses of the young, vigorous man, but to guide him aright. It has not sought to make his development one-sided, not to prevent his being a man, but that he is the fullest sense of a man, a good man. The movement's alignment with the forces of Muscular Christianity could have received no greater endorsement."[40] It was ultimately the association's willingness to move more toward Muscular Christianity and engagement with the broader community that led to the secularization of many colleges and universities.

Muscular Christianity and the Well-Born Movement

The Muscular Christianity movement was not surprisingly tied to eugenics and the eugenics movement. Underlying concerns about the threats to American identity—white male identity—were concerns about "race suicide." Advocating for a faith that white males would feel comfortable following was not enough to address the threat of miscegenation—the mixing of the races through sexual activity—and intermarriage with members of the so-called lower races of the white population. "Scientific breeding, known by the scientific-sounding name of eugenics, put down strong roots in the United States as well as other countries, eventually taking its most repugnant form in Nazi Germany. At first, the idea was to select the healthiest stock. Within a short period of time, strong genes became identified with the white race."[41]

Eugenics helped rationalize the unequal treatment of people of color and immigrants from southern, eastern, and Central Europe. W. W. Hastings, the head of a physical education school in Michigan, explicitly laid out the linkages between Muscular Christianity, eugenics, and sports. Sports, Hastings claimed, provided opportunities for athletically gifted young men to show their potential as leaders.[42] Outside of sports, one of the few places such skills sets could emerge was during times of war. Sports served as proxies for wars. Competitions created opportunities to create "a new breed of natural leaders on the basis of genetic inheritance as well as the young men's own hard work and self-discipline. The expectation was that this new generation of leaders would carry out its duties and obligations so successfully that the rest of the population would naturally embrace their new brand of meritocratic leadership."[43] The role of women—white women specifically—was to give birth to and to care for the next generation.

The relationship between Muscular Christianity, eugenics, and sports was especially evident in the sport of football. The game was successful in "toughening" privileged males, and football allowed for the testing of new ideas about sanitation, nutrition, and medicine. Football also showed individuals from various social classes "that the quality of human health was not a consequence of . . . preordained fate but rather the result of behavior."[44] Football was perceived to develop character because it required dedication and a strong work ethic, and required the use of physical and intellectual abilities. Additionally, football was simultaneously very profitable for colleges and universities.

Perelman argued, "The mind-set of Muscular Christianity was almost perfectly suited to the justification of imperialism, especially when buttressed by eugenics. The imperial mission was to civilize heathens around the world."[45] Training for football was akin to training for war, some argued: preparing a football team is similar to preparing a group for combat. Discipline is required of soldiers and football players. It is not surprising that the father of football, Walter Camp, was also a military advisor during the First World War.

Eugenics originated in the early 1880s. The term—which means "well-born"—was coined by Sir Francis Galton, a British statistician, Galton focused on understanding genetics for the purpose of improving the overall health of individuals with above-average intelligence so they could reproduce and improve the human race. In this regard, Galton was considered a positive eugenicist, whereas others were considered negative eugenicists. Negative eugenics created and capitalized on the fear that the white race was deteriorating due to the presence and higher birthrates of less desirable races.

Eugenics borrowed from the work of Gregor Mendel, who studied pea plants and crossbreeding, which gave us the concept of genes and opened up genetics as a field of study.[46] Germany and the United States were the centers of negative eugenics for much of the movement. The Eugenics Record Office in New York played a particularly important role. It was here that biologist Charles Davenport developed his ideas from the agricultural model that focused upon reproduction as a means of ensuring the strongest more desirable and most capable members of a species.[47] Scientific methods were used to justify human behavior. "For Americans who feared the potential degradation of their race and culture, eugenics offered a convenient and scientifically plausible response to those fears."[48] It was not a coincidence that the eugenics movement rose to popularity when it did. The movement began in the United States after the First World War, which had contributed to increased fear about foreigners. At the same time, immigration to the United States was on the rise.[49] The American Eugenics Society grew rapidly—promoting better breeding and preventing "poor" breeding at any cost, including the forced sterilization of certain segments of the population.

As late as 2014, the victims of state-sponsored sterilization were still seeking compensation in states such as North Carolina. It is estimated that the eugenics board was responsible for the forced sterilization of more than 7500 people over a more than 40-year period, which began in 1929 and ended only in 1974. The efforts of the eugenics board were described as one of the most forceful compulsory sterilization programs in the United States, whose victims, according to proponents of eugenics in North Carolina and beyond, were deemed physically or mentally unfit to reproduce.[50]

Eugenics was particularly appealing to progressives because it was compatible with their general distain for a laissez-faire attitude and preference for "social science, social scientific expertise and right governance."[51] Thomas Leonard claimed that Progressives were drawn to eugenics—also known as scientific racism—by the same factors that drew them to attempts to legislate behavior. Progressives and eugenics followers both believed interference was necessary to bring about desired change. At the heart of the justification for such interventions were statistical data. Data served to legitimate efforts to control subordinate groups and to do so with the full faith and trust of the federal government.[52]

The sterilization of individuals deemed unfit was one consequence of such fears; another was miscegenation laws, like Virginia's Racial Integrity

Act. This discriminatory act made it a felony for anyone to misrepresent his or her race. Anyone found guilty of "the willful making of a false registration or birth certificate shall be punished by confinement in the penitentiary for one year."[53] The state would not even issue a marriage license unless the race of the man and woman were verified. "If there is reasonable cause to disbelieve that applicants are of pure white race, when that fact is stated, the clerk or deputy clerk shall withhold the granting of the license until satisfactory proof is produced that both applicants are 'white persons' as provided for in this act."[54]

Efforts to avoid the disappearance of the white race—both demographically and in terms of power and influence—were also apparent not only with respect to miscegenation laws such as the Virginia Act but also in the forced sterilization of many people considered to be a drain on humanity. According to Lutz Kaelber at the University of Vermont, over 30 states in the country adopted sterilization laws. The laws were responsible for over 60,000 sterilizations of individuals who were deemed "mentally disabled or ill, or belonged to socially disadvantaged groups living on the margins of society."[55] Although most states stopped the practice by the mid-1940s, some sterilized residents though the 1970s.[56] Moreover, there is evidence that state-sponsored sterilization is ongoing. A recent investigation in a California prison found that female inmates were forcibly sterilized between 2006 and 2010. "The doctor who was paid nearly $150,000 to perform sterilizations, James Heinrich," described the sterilizations as "a wise investment." He added, "over a 10-year period, that isn't a huge amount of money . . . compared to what you save in welfare paying for these unwanted children—as they procreated more."[57]

The fall of eugenics eventually occurred during the progressive era. American eugenics declined in the 1930s in large part because eugenics was associated with the Nazi regime. Additionally, the Catholic Church, which exerted a great deal of influence worldwide, opposed eugenics. Leonard contended the Catholic Church was against the eugenics movement because it attempted to interfere with conception and because many Catholic followers were considered unfit and undesirable by the movement's standards. Moreover, public policies—such as the discriminatory immigration law passed in 1921—cut off immigration from countries that were considered the source of many of America's social problems, and therefore did the work that adherents to the "scientific" racist movement would have undertaken.[58]

Eugenics may have declined in the 1930s, but some scholars claim it is very much alive and has simply taken on new language and been framed differently. There is less overt talk about fears of "race suicide" and more discussion about the need for genetic testing and screening as a cost-saving measure, for example, or as a means of giving parents more information to make informed decisions when considering their family planning options. Under the new eugenics, "We now have researchers with the scientific know-how working with Wall Street–backed corporations to develop the new weapon in the struggle to rid the world of people with developmental disabilities."[59] Not everyone shares these views about the new eugenics movement. Such positions are based on emotions and not "based on sound science and reasoning."[60] Eugenics—old and new—is commonly understood largely from the lens of negative eugenics, which is associated with notions of white supremacy, Social Darwinism, and the like. Rather, Entine, writing in a piece for *Forbes* magazine in 2014, says, "We are in the second age of eugenics," where the emphasis is on "the positive impact that family planning and genetic screening have already had on society."[61] The New Age eugenics is described by a desire to "eliminate disease, to live longer and healthier, with greater intelligence and a better adjustment to the conditions of society. It arises whenever the humanitarian desire for happiness and social betterment combines with an emphasis on heredity as the essence of human nature. It is the aim to control, the denial of fatalism, and the rejection of chance. The dream of engineering ourselves, of reducing suffering now and forever."[62]

Atlas Sports Genetics developed a test to determine a child's athletic aptitude, which parents can purchase for less than $150. "To predict a child's natural athletic strengths. The process is simple. Swab inside the child's cheek and along the gums to collect DNA and return it to a lab for analysis of ACTN3, one gene among more than 20,000 human genomes."[63] The purpose of the test is to provide parents with scientific evidence to determine "whether a person would be best at speed and power sports like sprinting or football, or endurance sports like distance running, or a combination of the two."[64]

The company is targeting infants and children from pre-kindergarten to third grade, and the test is already available in Australia and has been implemented in Europe and Japan. Within two or three weeks, parents know "what paths to follow so the child reaches his or her potential."[65] Success in amateur athletics creates pathways to college scholarships, access to select social networks, and so on. For historically disadvantaged minority groups, success in amateur athletics was rooted in a much larger desire—for people of color to overcome discrimination. Blacks hoped that their success in sports would convince members of the dominant racial group that blacks were capable of succeeding in all areas of social life. Scholars refer to the aforementioned process as "muscular assimilation."

Muscular Assimilation

People of the African diaspora struggled with the issue of how they would eventually become part of the mainstream American society.[66] During the Antebellum Era, blacks wondered what would happen to them in a new nation. Some believed that fighting in the Revolutionary War would prove to slaveholders, and others, how loyal and deserving they were and how worthy they were of equal treatment. Despite their valiant efforts, blacks were not granted citizenship or treated as equals. The enslavement system remained for many more generations. As the nation eventually moved toward the Civil War, debates ensued about what would become of the millions of formerly enslaved blacks now living in various parts of the United States. Some blacks supported emigration to the Caribbean or portions of Africa, whereas others believed the United States was the best place for former slaves to succeed. After the adoption of the Thirteenth, Fourteenth, and Fifteenth Amendments, blacks were still treated as second-class citizens, and their incorporation into the broader society was limited by laws that ensured that people of African ancestry would always know their place—at the bottom of the social ladder. Whereas millions of immigrants from southern, Central, and eastern Europe—who were formerly considered inferior sub-races of the white population—were given opportunities to assimilate into society through the public school system and the suburbanization of white America, blacks and other people of color were deemed too different and incapable of being assimilated. People of African ancestry faced many challenges in overcoming discrimination. Brave black men and women participated in virtually every war the United States ever fought. Each time they fought, they were fighting a double campaign: one against the stated cause and the other for equal treatment. Black soldiers fought a Double-V campaign in the first part of the 20th century, battling against discrimination at home and abroad. Many believed that their efforts would lead the dominant white group to see their sacrifices and finally see blacks as equals; alas, this was not the case. At each of these historic moments, black people tried to demonstrate patriotism in order to convince a white group in denial of what black people already knew—that they were equal partners in what is fondly referred to as "the American experiment" and should be treated as such.

Many scholars have tried to explain the inability and unwillingness to assimilate blacks into American society and the various ways that blacks have used certain characteristics, especially social class position, to strategically assimilate—as per the writings of Karyn Lacy—or to resist assimilation altogether through what is called multi-class identity.[67]

Efforts to assimilate into mainstream society are made all the more complex by the intersections of race and class. Blacks have membership in the same social classes as whites, but their race still matters. Race is a highly visible marker and much easier to detect than class. Blacks, regardless of their class position, may feel they share the common goal of creating a better space for their fellow blacks to live, work, and play, where class is not an issue.[68]

Unfortunately, the effort to work across class identities has less to do with race than with meeting a set of criteria established by developers and local governments aimed at creating spaces that are economically heterogeneous, even if that means some residents must enter buildings through "a poor door."

Karyn Lacy, on the other hand, set forth an interesting theory that blacks assimilate strategically when it comes to negotiating their class and racial identities. Lacy argued that blacks culturally assimilated, walking into doors and opening windows of opportunity that were previously closed to them, following the many legislative victories of the Civil Rights Movement. Increases in salaries and wages, as well as a narrowing of the racial wage gap, support her claims. Yet even now structural assimilation eludes many blacks. Consequently, blacks are still not welcomed into traditionally white spaces (e.g., white neighborhoods, predominantly white social clubs, and other social spaces).[69]

In her work, Lacy answers the question as to how blacks negotiate the boundaries between their class and racial identifies, particularly blacks with membership in the middle class. She makes the case that they work to gain entry into predominantly white schools, jobs, and living spaces, but in all things social maintain membership in institutions reflective of their racial and class position. Blacks engaged in a process of strategic assimilation might send their children to predominantly white colleges and universities and work in middle-management positions where there are no other people of color; they might live in neighborhoods where many of their neighbors are white, but attend religious services where most of the congregation is black and middle class; and they might belong to fraternal orders that are also comprised almost entirely of black middle-class individuals. Maintaining membership in historically black institutions that are also middle class may also serve as a coping mechanism for helping blacks in the middle class deal with the prejudice, discrimination, and racism they undoubtedly experience in their everyday lives.[70]

Muscular assimilation is yet another variation on perspectives aimed at enhancing our understanding of efforts on the part of blacks to overcome discrimination, compete on a level playing field, and receive all of the promises America's founding documents profess, as well as to understand white resistance. Wiggins and Miller discuss muscular assimilation in their book *Unlevel Playing Field*. The black press played an important role in the attempt at muscular assimilation. "African American sportswriters, including those who wrote for the *Crisis* and *Opportunity*, consistently celebrated black achievement in sport while at the same time denouncing racism and discrimination in the realm of athletics."[71]

The ultimate goal was to show that "if sportsmanship and fair play could be achieved in national pastimes, then ideally such notions could be extended to all walks of life. Such programs for racial reform were devised to bring about the demise of Jim Crow, and African American commentators on sport were exceedingly articulate about the ways they hoped to use the playing fields as a platform for social mobility and to enlist athletic triumph in the quest for equal opportunity in America."[72]

Muscular assimilation had its origins between World War I and World War II "as a means of making claims about American democracy and at the same time expressing enormous pride in black cultural achievement."[73] The campaign was not restricted to professional sports "but also by local activists, who sought to establish municipal playgrounds, recreation areas, and robust high school athletic programs."[74] William Henry Lewis was an important symbol of the muscular assimilation campaign. Lewis was a star player on Harvard's football and was most beloved by many in the black community because he made the race "proud of him because in all his success he stands for us, and the higher he goes in the physical field of athletics or the mental field of law or literature, he must necessarily open the way for others, and lift us all up at the same time."[75] The campaign relied not only on the successes of individuals but on those of institutions. "The image of the African American athlete and, more important, the integrity of black higher education needed to be carefully guarded. . . . After all, muscular assimilation was a strategy, just as parallel institutions were a necessity—until the day, yet to come, when black Americans could compete with whites on a level playing field."[76] That day still eludes us all, and Wiggins and Miller explained why. There is still a perception "that black success in sports is exceptional or, even worse, that it derives from some natural ability. It is still the case that an African American man or woman walking through a college or university campus is sometimes mistaken for a member of a varsity team, or for a coach. This attitude may attest to the ways muscular assimilation was a triumphant campaign at one level, but also too narrowly cast to transform prevailing notions of racial difference."[77] At the heart of muscular assimilation are ideas of race, religion, masculinity, and femininity.

During the second half of the 20th century a variety of groups worked to restore balance to a social order they viewed as severely damaged by second-wave feminists. The first wave of feminism defined the desire to secure the vote for women and ended with the adoption of Twentieth Amendment. The second wave of feminism, which took place in the 1960s and 1970s, focused on expanding employment opportunities and reproductive rights for women; but it is criticized for ignoring the unique experiences of women of color, who always worked outside of the home and were subject to control of their reproductive freedom dating back to the days of slavery in America whereby the enslavement system depended upon black women as producers and as reproducers. These groups, according to scholar, Dr. Stephen Finley, included the GodMen, Promise Keepers, and the Nation of Islam. Each group called upon hundreds of thousands of men to reclaim their rightful place in American society, and in the world.[78]

Finley offers a definition for understanding masculinity that takes into consideration the role of "race and gender" and "race and place" not only as a mere critique of conventional definitions but to fully understand how the concept shaped ideas about black masculinity and femininity. Finley noted that masculinity is not just about the presence of a certain set of secondary sexual characteristics but more importantly masculinity is about the social meanings that we attach to such personal characteristics. Many of the social characteristics we associate with masculinity are also closely aligned—and not surprisingly so—with many of the characteristics we associate with sports. These characteristics include "physical strength, assertiveness and aggressiveness, competitiveness, emotion distance, and rationality."[79]

Association with the above-named traits was—and still is—used to justify white male dominance throughout society. "The ideology of masculinity serves to buttress the activities and social position of the dominant group (i.e., men and white men, in particular) and to reproduce that position in subsequent generations."[80] Theological and religious justifications were used historically to justify white male dominance, and such justifications are still used today, argued Finley.

Finley focused on hegemonic masculinity—"the notion of masculinity that is deployed not only to legitimate patriarchal rule of men over women but also of white men over men of color"[81]—and the problem of masculinity in American religion and many of the issues raised are applicable to other social institutions, including sports. In fact, Finley made the case that the Muscular Christian movement was not only a reaction to a perceived threat from white women but also from men of color who were "gaining power positions that were traditionally held by white men."[82]

The historic exclusion of black men, for example, has led to what Finley described as "over-exaggerated performances of masculinity" in predominantly black churches and, we argue, in other areas of public and private life.[83] Examples of what some scholars call hypermasculinity involve efforts by black men to dominate other black men, black women, and the environment through an emphasis on the physical and in some instances through the use and/or display of guns. The purpose of such actions are to "restore respectability to black men that was believed to have been taken away by white men through the practices of slavery, raping black women, lynching, and social exclusion."[84]

Part of the problem in one of the world's most practiced religions, Christianity, is that religion moved from many areas of public life where men occupied positions of prestige and became increasing privatized and individualized, argued Finley.[85] In an effort to redefine masculinity in a way that does not promote the privilege of white males and the subordination of women and people of color, Finley called for an approach to reconstructing manhood that is reminiscent of what sociologists refer to as cultural relativism. Unlike ethnocentrism, cultural relativism is not based upon judgment. An individual or group does not use its own standards for judging what is good or bad in evaluating others; rather, difference is, if not celebrated, then tolerated and placed within an appropriate historical, cultural, political, and social context. He embraced efforts to "challenge the assumptions that issues with men are generically human rather than specifically male . . . to understand and dislodge notions of maleness as universally human and to see men and men's issues as particularities."

The battle over how to define manhood in American society may have originated—at least in part—in the Muscular Christianity movement, but it found a home outside of religion in general and outside of Christianity specifically. It founds its way to the public discourse, public policy, and the personal lives of all Americans. The use of sports to define manhood and womanhood and to define who and what is valued may have its roots in the mid-19th century, but there is evidence of it at work throughout the 20th century. Sports do not operate in a vacuum: sports influence society and society influences sport. The desire for white male dominance throughout American society is perhaps best illustrated in efforts to limit the ability of people of color to compete against whites in physical contests that would undoubtedly shine a light on all of the shortcomings, contradictions, and inconsistencies inherent in the dominant hegemonic definition of masculinity, which historically has meant white, heterosexual, and born male. Efforts to keep blacks from competing against whites in male-dominated sports from cycling to horseracing, to boxing provide a few historic examples. Congress went so far as to ban the showing of fight films during Jack Johnson's reign as the first black heavyweight champion of the world because his victories empowered people of color globally and undermined the idea of white superiority and black inferiority. Moreover, the creation of parallel institutions for amateur black athletes, including athletic programs at historically black colleges and universities and segregated high school programs, created opportunities for ways of understanding nonhegemonic masculinity. Later, with the integration of amateur sports, particularly at the college level, we see what happens when hegemonic masculinity meets nonhegemonic masculinity to produce a hypermasculinity that those in positions of power and influence attempt to both exploit and control. In the next chapter, we examine efforts to perpetuate the myth of white supremacy and white male dominance in amateur sports through the forced separation of athletes by race.

CHAPTER THREE

Racial Segregation and Amateur Athletics

Sports are much more than individual contests: they are politically and socially constructed and are best understood as social institutions. Sports affect society and society affects sports. It is not surprising—nor is it a coincidence, therefore—that race and racism played (and continue to play) important roles in American sports. Race and racism are two of the pillars upon which the American social structure was erected. Efforts to classify human beings on the basis of skin color and skin tone precede the ratification of several important founding documents. From the arrival of the first settlement of people of African ancestry to the United States in 1619 to the sentencing of the first black man to servitude for life shortly thereafter, to the present day, race and racism matter. Spreading the gospel of white supremacy and black inferiority was critical to ensuring the cultural, economic, and political survival of the new nation. Miscegenation laws and Black Codes after the Civil War were just some of the ways people in positions of power maintained social and physical distance between blacks and whites. Threats of physical violence, as well as actual violence, also played important roles in securing the privileged positions of members of the dominant racial group and the relatively disadvantaged positions of people of color. Blacks and whites were forced to separate in virtually every area of public and private life, including in houses of worship, burial grounds, schools, and in sports.

In this chapter, we examine racial segregation in amateur sports from Antebellum America through the modern-day civil rights movement to illustrate the various ways that sports reflected and constructed race in

American society over time. Unlike other treatments of the history of racial segregation in amateur sports, we focus on the dehumanization and criminalization of black male and black female athletes over time and the impact of integration of amateur teams, particularly on athletic teams at historically black colleges and universities (HBCUs).

Race and Amateur Sports Prior to the 1940s

The first settlement of people of African ancestry occurred in Jamestown, in the colony of Virginia, in 1619. Over time a system of exploitation, which was supported by state-sanctioned violence, emerged. Millions of people of African ancestry would make the painful and deadly voyage across the Atlantic or be born directly into what would become America's peculiar institution of slavery. Private practices and laws were soon established that gave varying protections to whites, but not to people of color. Laws determining the status of children born to slaves were soon on the books. Black indentured servants would eventually become slaves for life. Whites with wealth, status, and power controlled virtually every aspect of black life. The oppressive system of slavery relied on the myth of white superiority and black inferiority. It was important for the dominant racial group to create a narrative that would justify the subjugation, subordination, dehumanization, criminalization, and sexual exploitation of people of color. The justification of such inhuman practices required misrepresentation of the histories and the realities of people of black Africans. It required the stereotyping of black men, women, and children in ways that created, communicated, and transmitted myths about white purity and white virtuosity. The system of slavery relied on the perception that the mere existence of people of color, blacks in particular, was a problem: it was the white man's burden. To maintain the system of oppression, virtually every aspect of black life was controlled. Enslaved populations throughout the original thirteen colonies, and in lands acquired thereafter, were not only exploited for their labor, but many were also forced provide entertainment for wealthy white elites and others. Labor and recreation were, at times, one and the same.[1]

Corn shucking also played an important role in defining black masculinity. Within the context of slavery, there were few opportunities for enslaved black males to demonstrate control over their own bodies or to shape their identity. Corn shucking provided such an opportunity.[2] Killing hogs, picking cotton, arm wrestling, rolling logs, and sugar grinding were among the other ways males slaves demonstrated their social and physical skills within the confines of the slavery environment.[3] According to

Errol Alexander, author of *The Rattling of the Chains*, the winners of these competitions, which married entertainment and work, received benefits, especially those which other slaves did not, including various material and/ or food items. The stage was set for the unequal treatment of male slaves who demonstrated excellence in areas of amusement relative to people of color who did not.[4] Competitions between slaves from different plantations were not uncommon, particularly during the fall, when such crops as corn were harvested and sold so that landowners could pay their debts. The competitions' manifest function was to increase the output of the forced laborers. The competitions also provided for opportunities for slaves to interact with people in bondage from neighboring areas.[5]

Horse racing was another activity slaves were permitted to participate in and excelled. European settlers brought their fondness for the sport with them to the so-called New World. President Andrew Jackson not only brought horses with him to the White House, but he also brought black jockeys too.[6] Horse racing was very popular in the southern United States, so it is not surprising that the first black jockeys were slaves.[7] Slaves were responsible for the upkeep of the animals and the stables. Slaves also developed the skill sets required for success in horse racing, namely, the ability to control and connect with the animals.[8]

A slave by the name of Hercules, as an example, trained horses in Charleston, South Carolina, for a prominent family, the Sinklers . He was hired out to local breeders and had a reputation for turning horses with well-known losing streaks into winners.[9] Although still living in bondage, black jockeys were allowed more geographical mobility than other slaves because as jockeys they could travel to and from races and manage their operations.[10] Although it may seem that the small-statured black jockeys was at odds with the stereotype of the strong black male body, the success of the black jockeys actually contradicted the idea that whites were superior to blacks in every arena of life.

Sparks described horse racing in antebellum Charleston, South Carolina. Citing sports as a reflection of past societies and human interactions, he described how horses were symbols of wealth and prestige.[11] Races began in the 1600s,[12] and the love for horses and horse racing continued for centuries. Sparks argued horses were symbols of wealth, status, and prestige. Riding atop a horse was viewed as symbolic of one's position above others with lower social class positions.[13]

Gambling was as much a part of horse racing as the horses themselves. The very public events served not only as political contests, but also as a means of social control. Horse races in the 19th century in particular "had many lessons to teach the lower classes."[14]

The horse, according to a writer in 1850,

> is content to lose his own identity, to live, and move by the well of another—
> he receives the chastisements of his master, and immediately amends his
> ways. In a word, how truly may it be said that he loves him that is set in
> authority over him and serves him faithfully all the days of his life. . . . What
> a contrast is this to human contact! He lamented. He advised others, and
> here he spoke to the slaves and plain folk, to learn from his docility and
> obedience THE WHOLE DUTY OF MAN! If only the entire society could
> be as easily managed as a race, and if only slaves could be controlled as eas-
> ily as a horse! They could, of course, be bought and sold like horses, and
> were, in fact, sold between races at the track.[15]

Horse racing declined in the South with the as the advent of the Civil
War and its devastating effects on the region economically, politically, and
socially.[16] In the post–Civil War era, black jockeys headed northward to
such places as New York, New Jersey, and Pennsylvania, where they could
make a living in the sport as free men.[17] Oliver Lewis, William Walker,
Isaac Murphy, Alonzo Clayton, James Perkins, Willie Simms, and Jimmy
Winkfield were among the black jockeys who "took center stage at the
newly organized Kentucky Derby," until the early part of the 1900s, when
"racism, coupled with the economic recessions of the period, shrunk the
demand for black jockeys as racetracks closed and attendance fell. With
intensified competition for mounts, violence on the tracks against black
jockeys by white jockeys prevailed without recourse. Violence against black
athletes and against blacks more generally, as well as their exclusion from
many areas of public life was exacerbated in many ways."[18]

Slave owners did not organize all activities that we might consider recreation, amusement, play, or sport. Slaves organized footraces and boxing
matches, for example,[19] although the latter, for the most part, provided
entertainment for white spectators.[20] Tom Molineaux, one of the most
famous American boxers of the period, came from a family of boxers.

Born into slavery in Maryland in 1784, Molineaux eventually moved to
Richmond, Virginia, with his owner. He was a handyman and became the
chief handyman at the time of his father's death. Molineaux continued to
train before and after his father's death, and he gained great fame after beat-
ing another black boxer, Black Abe, from a neighboring plantation. He
earned $100 for his master and, according to some accounts, also earned
his freedom. Tom Molineaux left the South for New York, where he loaded
and unloaded cargo on the docks and worked as a porter. Eventually,

Molineaux became a semi-professional boxer in the States and later sojourned to England to fight at the highest levels of professional boxing in the world.[21]

Boxing and racing were not the only sports played prior to the 1950s. As early as the 1860s, Americans were introduced to the football.[22] The first game was played in New Jersey in 1869 between Princeton and Rutgers. The playing field was much larger than it is today; there were almost twice as many players and no officials.[23] Soon other colleges and universities fielded football teams. Many things about the game changed over time. Drawing from the sports of rugby and soccer, Walter Camp, an influential figure in American football and former leader of the American Football Rules Committee, created a set of rules that are still recognizable in the sport of football today. Camp's rules included 11 players. Unlike rugby and soccer, the sport of football also included a quarterback and a center. The soccer-like ball was replaced by an egg-shaped ball in the mid-1870s; soon after, goal posts were added, and the number of players on each team was reduced. After the first-down rule was included, the sport became ever more popular on college and university campuses. By the start of the 20th century, there were about 250 college football teams. Blacks were not routinely welcomed at predominantly white colleges and universities. With few exceptions, black football players played for HBCUs. Among the exceptions were William Henry Lewis, William Tecumseh Sherman Jackson, and George Jewett.

The black press made note of the graduation of Forbes, Jackson, and Lewis from Amherst College. An article from *Plaindealer*, a black newspaper based in Detroit, Michigan, published an article about the historic graduation on July 15, 1892. In the article it is acknowledged that the graduation of Forbes, Jackson, and Lewis was not the first time that a black person graduated from a New England college, but it was the first time that several black people graduated within the same class. It was also rare that Lewis was captain of the team. Lewis was invited to address the graduating class, which the article described as a great honor that only highly regarded students could ever achieve. Lewis, according to the article, was a prize-winning orator. Even when he did not win, his abilities were rewarded. On one occasion, a judge in an oratory competition gave Lewis $100 in spite of his losing, to help defray the cost of attending law school. Concerns about the black graduates arose, according to the account in *Plaindealer*, when it was time for the senior promenade. There was apprehension about what might happen when the black guests of Forbes, Jackson, and Lewis arrived and interacted with their white classmates and guests. The newspaper reported that there were no issues, as the black women that accompanied Forbes, Jackson, and Lewis were both refined and cultivated.

William Henry Lewis, a native of Virginia, attended Virginia Normal and Collegiate Institute. The son of former slaves, Lewis transferred to Amherst College and later attended Harvard Law School.[24] Lewis played football at Amherst and Harvard. Physical activity was a requirement for every student. He took up the game of football for the first time as a student at Amherst College, where he excelled both in the classroom and on the field. Lewis spent three years playing for Amherst and two for Harvard as center. When Lewis took the field, William Tecumseh Sherman Jackson, a black male, was already excelling in the position of halfback.[25] George Washington Forbes was one of three black players on the team and one of very few blacks enrolled in colleges in the North.[26] He "left a little known legacy to college football."[27] He founded a newspaper, *Boston Courant*, and challenged one of the most respected black leaders of his day, Booker T. Washington, for what Forbes and others thought was a far too accommodating approach to addressing racial tensions in America, one that sold the basic human and civil rights of black people for property and economic opportunity when and if whites allowed it to occur. Forbes played an important role in contributing to a climate that not only challenged Washington's thinking but also set the wheels in motion for the establishment of the nation's oldest civil rights organization, the National Association for the Advancement of Colored People (NAACP). Calls arose at Harvard and across the nation to ban football because it was considered such a violent sport. "Lewis proposed a neutral zone rule, which required teams to be kept apart by the width of the football before the start of each play. At the time, players could crowd the imaginary, hair-thin line of scrimmage that supposedly separated the teams, but in truth hid a lot of slugging and holding from the officials."[28] By 1906, "college football enacted the neutral zone rule."[29] Lewis also wrote one of the first books on college football.[30]

Additionally, *Cleveland Gazette* detailed Lewis's contributions to the legal profession in an article announcing his appointment as assistant U.S. district attorney for Boston. Lewis represented Cambridge in the legislature in 1900, 1901, and 1902, before he was defeated. President Theodore Roosevelt suggested Lewis for the position: he and Lewis were connected through Harvard athletics. Previously, Lewis had been a candidate for the position under President McKinley, and Lewis's talents even brought him before the U.S. Supreme Court.

George Jewett is remembered as a "Renaissance man."[31] Jewett was not only a great athlete, but he was also at the top of his graduating class, captain of his high school debate team, and fluent in four languages.[32] Jewett began his career at the University of Michigan in 1890 with the goal of becoming a doctor. "Jewett was Michigan's first black football player and ultimately one of its greatest stars. In just two seasons, 1890 and 1892, he started as both a fullback and halfback, and was Michigan's top scorer, rusher, and kicker during his reign."[33] Despite Jewett's achievements, he faced discrimination from his teammates and from fans. During a game against Albion in 1890, "Albion tried to lure Jewett into a violation that would get him thrown off the field. At one point he was charged with 'slugging' and 'the cry went up from the crowd "Kill the n——." The crowd surged on the field, blows were struck, and a riot was in the making when the local police intervened.'"[34] Jewett also faced challenges in his quest to become a physician. In 1893, after graduating from Michigan, "Jewett made the decision to leave for Northwestern and continue his dream. He not only earned his medical degree, he also suited up for the Wildcat football team in 1893 and 1894."[35]

William Tecumseh Sherman Jackson was not only a pioneer in college football during the 19th century but also an accomplished runner. He boasted the country's best half-mile while at Amherst. On May 29, 1890, Jackson established a school record for the 880-yard run in the time of 2 minutes 5.4 seconds.[36] Other standouts in the sport of track and field during the late 1880s and early part of the 20th century included Napoleon Bonaparte Marshall, John Baxter Taylor, and Howard Porter Drew.[37] Marshall, one of the nation's best quarter-milers, finished "third at an 1897 intercollegiate track meet, running the 440-yard event. His best time for the 440 event was 51.2 seconds, which he ran as a sophomore at Harvard."[38] Taylor, an Olympic medalist, won a national title in the quarter-mile and 400-meter title in 1907, representing the University of Pennsylvania. Drew "was the first sprinter to be called 'the world's fastest human.' Porter ran the 100- and 70-meter dashes in Amateur Athletic Union (AAU) record times in 1912 and set the world 200-yard record of 22.8 seconds in 1913."[39]

Few blacks played baseball at predominantly white colleges and universities during the 19th century, but some did. Baseball was established in 1839, and in 1840, Alexander Cartwright is credited with establishing the rules of the game that are familiar today. Cartwright was a founder of the Knickerbocker Base Ball Club in New York City; the club included 30 men of privilege. Cartwright gave the sport the concept of foul territory and the three-out inning. The popularity of the game moved from the North to the South during the Civil War as Union soldiers taught the game to Confederate soldiers in prison camps. Before the shift toward professionalism after 1869, college sports were the place where many made their mark on the game.[40]

William Clarence Matthews was a pioneer in college baseball. Matthews was born and raised in Selma, Alabama. He attended Tuskegee Institute for a time before enrolling at Phillips Andover and then Harvard University. For four years, from 1901 to 1905, Matthews played shortstop despite tensions and boycotts directed at the team. Although Matthews received offers to turn pro, he remained at Harvard "all the while, he had been earning his way taking jobs during the school year, working summers in Pullman cars and hotels, and teaching in a Cambridge night school."[41]

Matthews, like some other players who excelled on the field and in the classroom at predominantly white institutions, went on to have successful careers after his playing days were over. Matthews enjoyed successful careers as a lawyer and a public servant. He served as special assistant to the U.S. district attorney in Boston, Massachusetts. He also worked as legal counsel to Marcus Garvey. "He played a major role in the 1924 presidential campaign. When Calvin Coolidge was elected with the help of a million black votes, Matthews was rewarded with a post in the Justice Department—but his list of 'demands' for the 'recognition of colored Republicans' that he presented to party leaders was ignored."[42]

Basketball was established after football and baseball in America. The father of basketball, James Naismith, did not want the game to interfere with more established sports. The first college basketball game did not take place until 1897. The first professional black teams did not begin until 1923, when the New York Renaissance Big Five was established. Not only did blacks play on segregated teams in college but also in high school, and this lasted for many decades. For example, in 1949 Topeka High School had two separate basketball teams—one for whites and one for blacks. The white basketball team was called the Trojans, and the black basketball team was called the Ramblers. The school also had separate cheerleaders and separate school parties, and blacks were not permitted to use the school swimming pool. The Ramblers played area black teams, and this remained the case until 1950, when some members of the Ramblers were permitted to join the Trojans.[43]

Segregation in amateur basketball was of course not relegated to New York and Kansas. Athletes were segregated across the country prior to the 1950s, including in North Carolina. College basketball teams first took the court in North Carolina in 1906. The state was not known as the college basketball powerhouse that it is today. College basketball teams such as the University of Kentucky and Indiana University were among the best teams during the first half of the 20th century. According to Jim Sumner, North Carolina's place in the history of college basketball changed in the 1940s because of John McLendon.[44] McLendon was a native of Kansas and attended the University of Kansas. Although McLendon could not play basketball at the university because of racial segregation, he could major in physical education. The founder of basketball, Naismith, was one of McLendon's professors.

McLendon began coaching at what is now North Carolina Central University at a time when virtually all areas of social life were separated on the basis of race.[45] He developed an offense that was later modified and used by University of North Carolina at Chapel Hill coach Dean Smith, the "four corners" offense.[46] McClendon is also credited with being one of the first college coaches ever to use the fast-break offense. He later went on to become the first black head coach of any major professional sports team in the country.

McLendon coached in the Central Intercollegiate Athletic Association (CIAA) for much of his career. The league was comprised of HBCUs, where amateur black athletes were given the opportunity to compete with one another. HBCUs played important roles in the lives of black athletes, especially prior to the 1950s.

Many HBCUs were established after the Civil War because of a desire on the part of former slaves for an education. For many generations, there were laws on the books that made literacy illegal for slaves. *Big Box Schools: Race, Education, and the Danger of the Wal-Martization of Public Schools in America*, by one of the coauthors of *Pay to Play*, Lori Latrice Martin, highlights the lengths to which codes in the South restricted black literacy.[47] Martin observed that a South Carolina law called for a fine of 100 pounds for anyone helping a slave learn to read or write, or hiring a slave in a job requiring reading and writing. There were even laws that forbade free blacks from learning to read or write. In Virginia a code on the books in the early 1800s "made it unlawful for blacks, regardless of their status as free, enslaved, black, or mulatto, from assembling in schools for the purpose of teaching reading or writing—day or night. The code also granted the right of officers to inflict corporal punishment on the offender or offenders, at the discretion of any justice of the peace, not exceeding twenty lashes."[48]

After the Civil War, new state constitutions were created throughout the South, and many addressed education. "The 1869 Virginia document allowed for public education for blacks and whites. Although blacks and whites could have access to a free public education, blacks and whites could not attend schools together."[49] Schools were separate and inherently unequal.

Laws also kept blacks and whites separate in other areas of life. The doctrine of separation was segmented with the historic Supreme Court decision, *Plessy v. Ferguson* (1896). Martin outlined the significance of the case to understanding the history of race relations in America. "The case involving Homer Plessy was meant to challenge a system of racial oppression supported by public policies and private practices."[50]

Plessy v. Ferguson (1896) disputed laws on the books requiring separation of the races in railroad cars. Plessy, a man of mixed ancestry, and his supporters argued the laws requiring separation of the races in public transportation was a violation of the Fourteenth Amendment. In a 7–1 decision, the highest court in the land ruled that the law was not a violation of the U.S. Constitution. The decision by the Court was the equivalent of the Supreme Court justices rubber-stamping the false doctrine of white superiority and black inferiority. In the dissent, Justice Harlan summed up the implications of the court's decision when he wrote, "What can more certainly arouse race hate, what more certainly can create and perpetuate a feeling of distrust between the races, than state enactments, which, in fact, proceed on the ground that colored citizens are so inferior and degraded that they cannot be allowed to sit in public coaches occupied by white citizens? That, as all will admit, is the real meaning of such legislation."[51]

The end of the Civil War was marked by an increase in the number of parallel institutions—often created by blacks for blacks due in large part to their exclusion from predominantly white institutions, including colleges and universities. HBCUs filled academic and athletic voids in black communities across the South.

Religious denominations founded some of the earliest black colleges, and other black colleges and universities were founded by individuals or groups or by legislation. The Land Grant Act of 1890 led to the opening of some black colleges. Prior to this act, Congress passed the original Morrill Act, which "provided for the establishment of a Land-Grant institution in each state to educate citizens in the fields of Agriculture, Home Economics, the Mechanic Arts, and other useful professions."[52] Blacks could not attend the institutions established under the first Morrill Act. The law provided for separate institutions for blacks and whites. "Only Mississippi and Kentucky established first Morrill Act, and only Alcorn University was designated Land-Grant."[53]

Failure on the part of states throughout the South to follow the rule of law led to the passage of the second Morrill Act in 1890. The expressed purpose of the second Morrill Act was to support land-grant institutions for blacks. "Tuskegee Institute was created by an Act of the Alabama Legislature; however, 12 years later, the state established and incorporated a Board of Trustees and named the school private. Thus, it is not a Land-Grant College, in spite of the fact that it was granted 25,000 acres of land by the United States Congress in 1899. The triple-mission of the land-grant institutions is the concept of research, instruction, and extension service."[54]

The institutions established after the second Morrill Act included Southern University, Delaware State College, North Carolina A&T University, Fort Valley State College, Langston University, and Tennessee State University. All were founded by their respective state legislatures, with the exception of Fort Valley and Langston, which were founded by a citizen's group and a territorial legislature, respectively.[55]

Other HBCUs established prior to the second Morrill Act included Lincoln University and Alabama A&M University. Lincoln was established in 1866 by a black Civil War infantry, and Alabama A&M was founded by a group of former slaves in 1875. Alcorn State University, South Carolina State University, University of Arkansas, Pine Bluff, Prairie View A&M University, Virginia State College, Kentucky State University, and Florida A&M University were all established before 1890 by state legislatures. A religious group, the Methodist Episcopal Church, established University of Maryland Eastern Shore.[56]

> Some Black colleges were designated "normal" schools whose specific task was training elementary and secondary school teachers. Most of the early Black colleges focused on basic skills, reading and writing, but some of the schools also emphasized religion, vocational, and agricultural courses. Some schools began in one-room structures, perhaps a very small house or barn, accommodating fewer than ten students, ranging from elementary grades through college. In fact, into the new century, it was not unusual that a Black "college" also had a "high school" component.[57]

Some classes were originally held in homes, and in at least one case, classes were first held in an old boxcar. "Atlanta University opened in 1865, conducting its first classes in an abandoned railroad boxcar."[58]

The American Missionary Association provided financial support to former slaves to start Fisk University in Nashville, as well as other black colleges and universities in the South. Fisk opened "in January 1866 in what had been an Army barracks used to house Black cholera victims. Fisk started with 500 students enrolling in the first week but within three months the school had 3,000 students."[59]

For many generations, black colleges and universities were not only some of the few places where blacks could attain a secondary and/or post-secondary education but also among the relatively few places for amateur black athletes to compete. The first black college football game occurred in the early 1890s in North Carolina between Livingston College and Biddle College. Within a few years, black college football games were also played at Virginia Union, Tuskegee University, Morgan State, and Fisk University, to name a few.[60]

Sports represented much more than individual contests. For the black community and for black athletes, victories over white opponents were victories against white racist ideology. Prior to the desegregation of sports after the world wars, blacks developed their own unique patterns of playing sports. Demonstrations of the ability to put on a well-organized match, tournament, and so on, were also viewed as opportunities to undermine stereotypes about the inferiority and ineptitude of blacks.

There were regional differences, however, as to how sports were organized, who participated, and what benefits they earned. In the North, the organizational structure and guiding procedures for competitive play were almost identical to similar white institutions and associations that kept blacks out. The Negro Leagues in baseball and barnstorming basketball teams were examples of the parallel institutions. In the South, greater attention was devoted to the development of high school programs and sports at historically black institutions.

Baseball, basketball, and track and field were sports routinely open to males and females at HBCUs. Sporting events—then and now—were considered social and cultural affairs. Engagement in sports, either as a participant, facilitator, or spectator, often enhanced one's social capital. Athletes at HBCUs could gain access to fraternities and other social positions.

Some of the nation's best athletes could be found at HBCUS throughout the early part of the 20th century. In fact, the best women's track and field teams came from HBCUs, including Florida A&M, Alcorn A&M, Prairie View A&M, Alabama State, Fort Valley State, and Tennessee State. Few programs were as great as the track and field team at Tuskegee Institute. According to *Unlevel Playing Field*, the women's track team won 14 national championships and six national titles for outdoor track and field between 1937 and 1951.

Football was one of the most popular sports at HBCUs, much like at other colleges and universities across the country. The Black College Football Museum chronicles the achievements of black college football players. Coach Eddie Robinson spent over five decades coaching at Grambling

State University in Louisiana and retired with the most wins of any coach in the history of college football, with a record of 408–165–15. When Grambling faced Morgan State in 1976 in Japan, it was the first time a National Collegiate Athletic Association (NCAA) college football game had ever taken place outside of the United States.

Today black college athletes at HBCUs play in one of four conferences: Mid-Eastern Athletic Conference (MEAC), Southwestern Athletic Conference (SWAC), Central Intercollegiate Athletic Association (CIAA), and Southern Intercollegiate Athletic Conference (SIAC). The CIAA is the oldest of the conferences.

According to the official website for the CIAA, it was founded in 1912 as the Colored Intercollegiate Athletic Association and is the oldest of the four African American athletic conferences. The conference holds championships in a number of sports, including football. Champions are also held in the following sports: cross country, volleyball, basketball, tennis, golf, softball, baseball, track and field, and bowling. The CIAA is credited with establishing the current divisional conference football championship game format. The CIAA is perhaps best known for its annual basketball tournament in North Carolina.

In the period preceding the integration of college sports, black athletes participated in a number of sports beyond the gridiron. The establishment of the CIAA occurred around the same time that blacks were moving in large numbers from the South to the North in search of greater economic opportunities and to escape overt manifestations of racism. Wiggins and Miller observed that "[t]he years 1917 to 1921 witnessed a rise in the number of lynchings nationwide as well as bloody riots and massacres in East St. Louis and Chicago; Washington, DC; Elaine, Arkansas; and Tulsa, Oklahoma."[61] Between 1910 and 1940, almost 2 million blacks migrated during what is collectively referred to as the Great Migration. Southern migrants "were quick to reestablish a host of social institutions— their churches, for instance—and to develop new ones, including athletic organizations."[62]

The establishment of high school and college associations for black athletes played important roles in a process referred to as muscular assimilation—the idea that success in athletic competitions, both for the athletes and for the individuals and organizations with decision-making authority, would translate to success in the broader society once the opportunity arose.[63] Black male and black female athletes competed against each other at the high school and college levels. Tuskegee's women's relay team was so successful that between 1937 and 1951, its members "captured fourteen National AAU outdoor championships and six indoor titles."[64]

Many athletes excelled in more than one sport. Members of the women's track team at Tuskegee were also members of the basketball team.[65]

Although some colleges and universities did not field black players until well into the 1960s, efforts to integrate sports, and society more broadly, were underway in the years leading up to Jackie Robinson's appearance on the roster of the professional baseball team the Brooklyn Dodgers.[66] Paul Robeson was born at the end of the 19th century in Princeton, New Jersey. Robeson is well known for success as a singer, activist, lawyer, and athlete. In fact, Paul Robeson played four sports at Rutgers University—track and field, basketball, baseball, and football.[67] Only two other black athletes ever suited up for Rutgers prior to Robeson's arrival at the university in 1915.[68] Robeson's mere presence on the field led to protests. Lucien Victor Alexis Jr. experienced similar manifestations of racism during his time at Harvard University.[69] Alexis was a member of the lacrosse team and was banned from playing in a contest between Harvard and the Naval Academy, drawing protests from Harvard undergraduates and others during the early 1940s.[70]

Efforts to integrate sports and the larger society gained steam in the early part of the 1900s for several reasons.[71] Not only were millions of blacks moving from the South to the North, but blacks were also engaged in a movement which saw people of color demonstrating their rights as citizens and as human beings in a society that worked so hard to maintain its racial hierarchy established and enforced for many generations.[72] The New Negro Movement included black intellectuals and also black athletes in its attempt to define and redefine blackness.[73] Jack Johnson, the first black heavyweight champion, embodied the concept of the New Negro.[74]

For many years blacks were denied basic human and civil rights. After the adoption of the Thirteenth, Fourteenth, and Fifteenth Amendments, influential black leaders, such as Booker T. Washington, cautioned blacks against expecting too much too soon, whereas other black leaders, like W. E. B. Du Bois and, later, Marcus Garvey, called for black unity throughout the African Diaspora and for more radical transformations in the American racialized social system.[75]

Jack Johnson's victories against white boxers, and his unwillingness to conform to the racial norms and etiquette of the day, made him a threat in the eyes of many in the dominant racial group.[76] Blacks coming of age after Reconstruction were earnestly determined to live their lives as free people. No longer were some blacks willing to suffer in silence under an oppressive racial social order, merely hoping and praying that whites would one day find it in their hearts to give them basic human and civil rights. Although blacks prior to this period demonstrated a similar commitment, the expansion of the ideology and the institutionalization of it set the stages for the creation of a massive movement with manifestations in virtually every area of public life. The New Negro Movement, which included not only black intellectuals, but also black athletes to define and redefine blackness. Jack Johnson, the first black heavyweight champion embodied the concept of the New Negro.[77]

Jack Johnson, a native of Galveston, Texas, rose through the ranks of the profession of boxing during the early part of the 20th century to become the world's first black heavyweight champion. His routine violations of the racial etiquette and norms of his day, along with the proficiency and confidence with which he disposed of his white challengers, made him a villain or hero, depending on one's perspective, in the eyes of whites and people of color in the United States and beyond. Johnson was determined to live his life as a free person. Johnson's action—both inside and outside the boxing ring—called into question the racial social hierarchy that characterized much of American history. Additionally, Johnson also challenged the global doctrine of white supremacy and black inferiority.[78]

Despite miscegenation laws—banning sexual contact between whites and nonwhites—Jack Johnson dated white women, frequented white brothels, and married outside his race. Regardless of the laws and the conventional wisdom of the day, Johnson held that he should be able to entertain or marry anyone as long as the woman was not already married. His affinity for white women did not win him favor with many whites—or with many blacks, including black leaders like Booker T. Washington and DuBois. Washington thought Johnson's associations with white women and the flamboyant way he carried himself brought disrespect both to himself and to the race. DuBois disagreed with Johnson's mating and marital choices, but defended his rights to make the decisions for himself.

It was not only Johnson's love of white women, but also his success in the ring and the fact that he served as a poster child for conspicuous consumption that angered less advantaged whites, many of whom believed themselves to be superior to Johnson by virtue of their membership in the dominant racial group. Johnson's rise to fame, as a black boxer, occurred at the same time that the white male body was considered a symbol of supremacy. It occurred as Roosevelt and others expressed concerns about the status of whites in the United States and globally. His ascension to the highest level of his sport came on the heels of the muscular Christianity movement discussed previously.

Johnson experienced the effects of the global color line wherever he traveled. In Australia he was treated not as a person, but rather as a peculiar sideshow attraction. His defeat of Tommie Burns caused whites everywhere to question the future of race relations and at the same time helped non-whites imagine a new global reality. Johnson's defeat of white boxers, such as Jim Jefferies, led to the passage of laws banning the showing of fight films. Whites were concerned about the threat Johnson's victories posed to the racial status quo. The fear was so great that race riots often broke out after Johnson's victories over white fighters.

When efforts to stop Johnson in the ring failed, other measures were employed. Jack Johnson was convicted of violating the Mann Act. The Mann Act, passed in 1912, made it unlawful to transport women across state lines for immoral purposes. The act was referred to as the White Slave Act, aimed at curbing prostitution by white women. Johnson was convicted of violating the act based on a relationship he had with a white woman that predated the passage of the act. The nature of the relationship between Johnson and the white woman also did not fit the spirit of the law. Nonetheless, Johnson was found guilty and sentenced to a year and a day in prison.

Jack Johnson famously escaped to Canada and lived in exile for some seven years, during which time his mother died and he had trouble finding places to earn a living. On his return he was not treated as a hero by most. In fact, boxers such as Joe Louis, the next black heavyweight champion, was compelled by his advisors to fashion his image in such a way as to avoid any comparisons to Johnson. Jack Johnson's story was relatively unknown until the rise of the black power movement and the rise of Muhammad Ali. Ali's own life story and the play *The Great White Hope* increased interest in the story of Jack Jackson.

Jack Johnson—and other rebel sojourners of his time—traveled the world in search of opportunities to seek their fortunes during a time when many American whites refused to see blacks as their equals and maintained efforts to restrict virtually every aspect of black life through both private practices and public policies.[79] Johnson's rejection of the unequal treatment of blacks in the United States served as an inspiration to many blacks and to people of color worldwide, because many of the myths and misconceptions that served as the bedrock for the racial social structure in America were also the foundation for the unequal treatment of people of color on virtually every other continent. Although the United States and Australia were "geographically distinct and demographically different, the two nations shared the same underlying logic of race and the body."[80] Moreover, "the European travels of black sportsmen provided some of the formative moments in which African Americans began to see the transnational reach of the color line."[81] Furthermore, Johnson's acts of resistance also "provided instructive moments about the potential for transnational racial solidarity."[82]

Johnson's success led to legislative changes and to banning black boxers from fighting for a championship for many years. While Johnson was making statements in the boxing ring, with his choice of romantic partners, and in his business ventures, blacks in the military were serving their country in segregated units and eventually embarked on a double campaign— seeking victory against discrimination at home and abroad. Blacks were fighting against a host of injustices.

Race and Amateur Sports during the 1940s and Beyond

Pressure was brought to bear not only on the criminal justice system and the military but in other areas of life too. The modern-day integration of professional baseball had a lasting impact on the integration of both amateur and professional sports for decades to come. Jackie Robinson took the field for the Brooklyn Dodgers on April 15, 1947. The date has been commemorated every year since 2004. On that day, in Robinson's honor, every Major League Baseball player wears the number 42, which Robinson wore when he played. Honoring Jackie Robinson has much to do with Major League Baseball's desire to create a narrative that characterizes the league as one that favored racial equality and is today a post-racial institution.[83] The evidence of the desire to craft the aforementioned narrative was evidenced in the first ceremony in 1972, when Robinson's number was retired.[84] A few months later, Robinson ended his boycott of Major League Baseball at the invitation of the commissioner, Bud Selig, during the World Series.[85]

Prior to the October 1972 invitation, Robinson was involved in a personal boycott of professional baseball because of "the sport's poor record of hiring minorities for managerial and front office positions."[86] Robinson vocalized these concerns during the ceremony but died a few days later after suffering a heart attack, never living to see the day when there was a black manager or a black coach in the league.[87] The next time the league commemorated the integration of modern-day professional baseball was on the 50th anniversary, when Selig and then-President Clinton made comments that placed "Robinson at the top of the racial integration narrative."[88] The commemoration of Robinson's achievement in 2004 did not coincide with a significant anniversary, but did occur at the height of the steroid scandal. This led to claims that the real reason for remembering Robinson at that time was because if the League could "get out in front of the black eye by controlling and constructing its own social and cultural legacy regarding the praiseworthy racial integration of Jackie Robinson, a chapter in the history of Major League Baseball that almost everyone views positively, then the blow could be absorbed more easily. This strategy could be considered to have proven successful."[89]

Regardless of MLB's motivation for commemorating Robinson's accomplishment, there are several clear truths. Robinson was not the first black athlete to play professional baseball. He continued to face discrimination on and off the field after joining the Dodgers, and he was a champion of social justice issues up until the day he died. Robinson believed his personal success meant little if people of color across the country remained relegated to the status of second-class citizens receiving unequal treatment relative to their white counterparts. Nonetheless, Robinson's feat is credited with breaking the color barrier in other sports—even in the broader society—including high school and college sports. The impact on integration for amateur athletes, especially in college sports, was profound.

As was true for the eradication of slavery in the United States, integration occurred in the North before the South.[90] The first college football game featured a contest between Princeton and Rutgers in 1869.[91] Blacks were part of the baseball team at Brown University in the late 1870s; Preston Eagleson was on Indiana University's football team in the last decade of the 19th century.[92] Julian War and Adelbert Matthews were teammates at the University of Wisconsin in 1902, when the squad won the Big Ten championship, and there were others, including Gideon Smith (Michigan Agricultural College); George Flippin (University of Nebraska); and Sherman, Grant, and Ed Harvey (University of Kansas).[93] Although the experiences of black athletes at institutions in the North varied, the athletes had one thing in common: many shared similar experiences about discrimination. The experiences of Jack Trice and Johnny Bright are illustrative of the unequal treatment black student-athletes received.

Jack Trice integrated the Iowa State football team in 1923. In just his second varsity game, against Minnesota, he suffered a broken collar bone when several Gophers gang-tackled him at the end of a play. Trice left the field on a stretcher and soon died of internal bleeding and a ruptured lung.[94]

Johnny Bright, a student-athlete at Drake,

might have been the first black player to win the Heisman Trophy if not for a racist attack on the field. A vicious blow to the face (in the days before face masks) by Wilbanks Smith of Oklahoma A&M fractured Bright's jaw and caused him to miss two games and thus the honors he deserved. A series of photographs of Bright being assaulted on the field won the Pulitzer Prize and heightened awareness of the whole issue of athletic integration.[95]

Southern conferences were relatively slow to integrate—to say the least. Some states went so far as to enact laws banning competitions between black and white athletes. Harvard University, an integrated team, was scheduled to travel to New Orleans to play in a tournament and face an all-white team.

Harvard was the first team, however, with a black student-athlete "to compete in any of the former Confederate states on the home turf of a European-American college in 1947."[96] Nonetheless, opposition to the integration of college sports endured. Louisiana was not alone. "Georgia senator Leon Butts . . . in 1957 said interracial competition should be banned because, when Negroes and whites meet on the athletic fields on a basis of complete equality, it is only natural that this sense of equality carries into the daily living of these people."[97] In the State of Mississippi, the legislature decided to cut off funding to schools completely instead of integrated. "For that reason, Mississippi State skipped the NCAA tournament in 1959, 1961 and 1962."[98] It would be more than a decade before every school in the Southeastern Conference had at least one black student-athlete.[99] Perry Wallace broke the Conference's racial barrier in 1967 when he played for Vanderbilt University.[100] "The South, by resisting integration, became more and more isolated. LSU, for example, did not play a non-Southern opponent, whether at home or on the road, from 1942 until 1970," as part of a "gentlemen's agreement," which kept Southern teams from playing Northern teams with black student-athletes.[101] A turning point in the integration of college sports in the South—well after the landmark *Brown v. Board of Education of Topeka, Kansas*, which opened the doors for black students but did little to increase access for black athletes, and the passage of the Civil Rights Act of 1964, which banned discrimination in areas of public accommodation—occurred in 1970 when the University of Southern California (USC) played Alabama. All of USC's backfield was black. USC defeated Alabama by a score of 42–12.[102]

Sports influences society and society influences sports. Athletic contests have long been an important part of American culture. Sports do not exist in a vacuum. Restrictions placed on blacks—and other racial minority groups—carried over to the world of sports. This chapter showed how the enslavement of people of African ancestry placed limitations on their participation in sports; at the same time sports became a way for people of African ancestry to exert some control over their bodies and their lives, such as in the case of amateur black boxers. The chapter also covered how blacks continued to face unequal treatment in society after the end of the Civil War: their status as second-class citizens was evidenced in exclusionary policies and informal agreements that kept black athletes out of professional associations. The participation of blacks in World War I and World War II was expected to lead to greater acceptance of blacks within the larger society, but blacks fought in segregated units and came home to find racial segregation alive and well. Amateur—and virtually all—professional sports remained segregated until the late 1940s. Even after the integration of many professional American sports, amateur athletics remained segregated for more than two decades. Supreme Court decisions, historic legislative victories, and changing personal attitudes and behaviors were no match for the deeply entrenched racial antagonism that existed in high school and amateur sports, particularly in the South, although evidence of racial discrimination involving black student-athletes endured. The integration of amateur sports lagged behind the integration of professional sports. It could be argued that the integration of professional sports occurred earlier because an economic incentive to integrate sports existed more in the professional arena than in high schools and colleges. As high school and especially college sports became more profitable for institutions of higher learning, surrounding communities, and other stakeholders, greater pressure was brought to bear on these institutions to do what some thought should have occurred centuries earlier—allow black amateur athletes to compete alongside whites and demythologize the idea of white superiority and black inferiority. Black amateur athletes, specifically black student-athletes, competed valiantly against each other at HBCUs. The integration of predominantly white colleges and universities, and athletic conferences, drew students of color, as well as athletes of color, who might otherwise have attended the institutions that contributed to the personal, academic, professional, and athletic development of blacks who were shut out of similar mainstream institutions. The mistreatment of blacks in general, and black amateur athletes in particular, was facilitated by the mischaracterization of the entire black population. The reluctant acceptance of black student-athletes on predominantly white college and university campuses explains ongoing efforts to exploit this group for everyone's benefit. In the next chapter we examine the experiences of black male athletes at predominantly white colleges and universities since the 1970s.

CHAPTER FOUR

Rise of the Black Male Athlete at Predominantly White Colleges and Universities

This chapter chronicles the integration of black male athletes at predominantly white colleges and universities in the post–Civil Rights era. It details the racial representation of student-athletes and coaches at predominantly white institutions (PWIs) in high-revenue-generating NCAA Division I sports (e.g., football and basketball). Because black men are the subjects of continued exploitation in the broader society, we also identify a sample of high-profile cases where black collegiate athletes experienced unequal treatment and were strategically recruited using illegal practices. We highlight the negative impact this has on black student-athletes at PWIs.

Post–Civil Rights Era Racial Integration in Intercollegiate Athletics

Racial integration in K–12 public schools and the supposed scholastic desegregation that it ushered in was a pyrrhic victory for blacks because, in reality, integration never occurred. Critical race theoreticians have argued, chief among them, Dudziak, that the *Brown v. Board of Education of Topeka, Kansas* decision of 1954 represented an "interest convergence" wherein K–12 schools were symbolically desegregated because of a "cold war imperative": countries began questioning whether the United States could be a beacon of hope and a true democracy if it did not allow its black schoolchildren to attend white schools.[1] Desegregation was more rhetorical than real and allowed for segregation to spread further. Similarly, the supposed racial integration that occurred in intercollegiate athletics, according to Davis (1995), also embodied a convergence of interests, namely, the lucrativeness of commercialization and the competitive win-at-all-costs mentality that capitalizes on it.[2]

Therefore, similar to the supposed racial integration of K–12 schoolchildren, the racial integration of black male athletes at PWIs in the post–Civil Rights era has been equally pyrrhic for African American male student-athletes. Hawkins (2010) indicates that "[d]esegregation affected HBCUs' ability to grow and develop athletic infrastructures that nurture and utilize Black athletic talent at the same *commercial* level as their peer PWIs. Therefore, desegregation was pivotal in assisting the structural interdependence between PWIs and Black athleticism" [italics added].[3] Hawkins' 2010 words still hold true. According to current data, the coaches and athletic administrators at PWIs and across the NCAA are mostly white. In 2014, 76.5 percent of NCAA executive/senior/vice presidents were white. Less than 25 percent of people occupying the aforementioned position were black. Nearly 82 percent of NCAA managing directors/directors were white in 2014, and less than 16 percent were black. Of NCAA administrators in 2014, almost 80 percent were white, and 15.8 percent were blacks. There were no black conference commissioners during 2013–2014. Nearly 97 percent of conference commissioners identified their race as white. Head coaches for men's and women's teams, regardless of the sport or the division, were overwhelmingly white and male. Three-quarters of the coaches of Division I men's basketball teams identified their race as white during the 2013–2014 athletic year. Blacks coached less than one-quarter of Division I men's basketball teams during the same year. Nearly 90 percent of Division I football teams had white coaches between 2013 and 2014.

Current research conducted by The Institute for Diversity and Ethics in Sport (TIDES)—specifically the 2014 Racial and Gender Report Card: College Sport—indicates that "the record of the National Collegiate Athletic Association and its member institutions worsened for gender hiring practices, racial hiring practices and the combined grade. It was the worst Racial and Gender Report Card issued among all professional leagues and the colleges in the past year."[4] High-revenue-generating intercollegiate Division I sports, like men's football and men's basketball, compensate their white coaches extremely well. In return for their high salaries, coaches are expected to win games, conference championships, tournaments, and bowl contests. At the time of writing this chapter, the top-10 highest paid coaches were all men and white (see Table 4.1).

Table 4.1   2014 Top-10 Highest Paid NCAA Division I Basketball Coaches, by Race and University

Coach's Name	Total Pay	Race	University
John Calipari	$6,356,756	White	Kentucky
Mike Krzyzewski	$6,043,979	White	Duke
Rick Pitino	$6,004,529	White	Louisville
Bill Self	$4,955,186	White	Kansas
Tom Izzo	$4,006,955	White	Michigan State
Sean Miller	$3,484,500	White	Arizona
Thad Matta	$3,372,000	White	Ohio State
Bob Huggins	$3,265,000	White	West Virginia
Tom Crean	$3,046,250	White	Indiana
Bo Ryan	$2,946,000	White	Wisconsin

Source: http://sports.usatoday.com/ncaa/salaries/mens-basketball/coach

Although the second column—"Total Pay"—indicates the total compensation a college coach receives, it does not accurately indicate the amount of variability in a coach's compensation package. For instance, Rick Pitino is the fourth highest paid basketball coach in the nation, and he receives $1,926,202 in "other pay." Other pay is income listed on Pitino's most recently available, self-reported athletically related outside-income report. Also, Sean Miller is the sixth highest paid coach, but he has $1,260,000 in bonus possibilities. This means the greatest amount that Miller can received if his team meets prescribed on-court performance goals (e.g., NCAA tournament goals, win totals, regular-season and/or conference tournament championships, coaching awards, etc.), academic, and/or player conduct goals is $1.26 million. Mike Krzyzewski doesn't have a maximum bonus. These large differentials in coaches' compensation depend largely on commercialization of college sports. As mentioned earlier in this chapter, commercialization is something that enriches the white coaches and the PWIs that employ them—the NCAA is one "conveyor belt" in the exploitation of black student-athletes. Commenting on the conveyor belt of commercialization and exploitation, Rhoden notes the following:

> Most of the prestigious summer football and basketball camps are operated by white men who invite top high school players to work with and display their talent to invited coaches. At its best, the contemporary Conveyor Belt is a streamlined mechanism for developing players and offering

training and showcases where talented players can display their talents for college scouts.[5]

Meanwhile, the male college players in these highly commercialized sports are black, and the black male athlete is disproportionate to the general population at PWIs. According to research by Martin, "More than half of Division I male basketball players between 1991 and 2010 were black."[6] For example, Harper, Williams, and Blackman (2013) analyzed data from the Atlantic Coast Conference (ACC), Big East Conference, Big Ten Conference, Big 12 Conference, Pac 12 Conference, and the Southeastern Conference (SEC) and the U.S. Department of Education. They examined black men's representation on football and basketball teams versus their representation in the undergraduate student body on each campus. They found that between 2007 and 2010, black men were 2.8 percent of full-time, degree-seeking undergraduate students, but 57.1 percent of football teams and 64.3 percent of basketball teams. Moreover, 96.1 percent of these NCAA Division I colleges and universities graduated black male student-athletes at rates lower than student-athletes overall.

Because college athletes, according to the NCAA, are amateurs, they miss out on being compensated for their athletic abilities and effort. But that's part of the exploitative nature of the NCAA's rules and the ethos of high-revenue-generating athletics at PWIs: "The recruiting process creates a fascinating reversal of fortune: The poor become rich, and those with the least access to higher education receive scholarships to some of the best institutions in America."[7] Indeed, Branch writes that "the real scandal is not that students are getting illegally paid or recruited, it's that two of the noble principles on which the NCAA justifies its existence—'amateurism' and the 'student-athlete'—are cynical hoaxes, legalistic confections propagated by the universities so they can exploit the skills and fame of young athletes."[8] Black athletes, especially those who compete in sports at PWIs, are exploited because their "labor" (playing a sport for a PWI) does not serve their own direct needs, but the long-term needs of the PWI.

In a *New Republic* article entitled "College Sports Aren't Like Slavery. They're Like Jim Crow.," Starkey writes the following that is worth quoting in full:

> The NCAA concocted the term "student-athlete" and wrapped this new phrase in a self-serving mythology that holds that college athletes who profit from their talent are distracted from what should be their first priority: getting a quality education. Many onlookers therefore accept the NCAA's amateurism rules as proper. Paternalism toward "student-athletes," that is, allows this labor-market cartel to remain.[9]

Equally problematic is that the decision-makers within the NCAA are not representative of the players. The majority of the decision-makers are white, whereas the majority of athletes are black. This reality—a mismatch between the athletes and administrators—is a function of many social, political, and economic forces.

Of course, critics will say that athletes receive scholarship money that pays for their higher education. If they don't want to participate, they should take their ball and go home, some critics might argue. Our response is that it is not that simple of a situation. Shouldn't students who are on scholarship for athletics receive a high-quality education in return for their athletic talents? In the next section. we argue that black male athletes at PWIs are academically exploited—that they are used for their talents on the field and court—and do not receive an adequate level of education at some of the most elite colleges and universities in the United States. Although scholarship has continued to document the ways in which black male athletes are academically exploited (e.g., see Hawkins, Martin, and Rhoden), this chapter is important and adds to this literature by contributing information on how the "intercollegiate athletic industrial complex" is connected to documented ways that black male athletes have been recruited to play at PWIs.

Academic Exploitation and Unethical Recruitment Practices of the Black Student-Athlete at PWIs

Hawkins writes that the "intercollegiate athletic industrial complex" at PWIs is similar to the "prison industrial complex" because, much like the modern-day prison industrial complex, the intercollegiate athletic industrial complex represents a new plantation model where servitude is tolerated and black labor exploited. Any reference to the horrific institution of slavery to contemporary times and institutions is often easily dismissed. Some believe it is akin to comparing apples and oranges. However, it is a comparison that other noted scholars have made, too. What are Hawkins and others attempting to evoke in comparing slavery to prisons and college sports to prisons? Hawkins attempts to show how capitalists exploit and profit from the control of black male bodies, especially black labor, which was arguably the lynchpin of the enslavement system in America, and the same social, cultural, economical, and political ideology undergirds and sustains the web of institutions that make up both the prison industrial complex in America and the intercollegiate athletic industrial complex. Hawkins is referring to how PWIs benefit from having eager young men compete for their institution of higher education and receive very little educative value for their time and effort on the field or court. Division I level athletic scholarships are nice and often are very helpful for athletes, especially first-generation college students and those athletes whose families cannot afford the high costs of tuition. Insidiously, though, the intercollegiate athletic industrial complex continues unabated because the supply for athletes is never depleted: there are always more young athletes who can replace those who become injured or whose scholarships are revoked. As Rhoden says in *Forty Million Dollar Slaves: The Rise, Fall, and Redemption of the Black Athlete*, there is a "conveyor belt" that brings kids from inner cities and small towns to big-time programs, where they're cut off from their roots and exploited by team owners, sports agents, and the media.[10]

Meanwhile, intercollegiate athletics is "big business" for PWIs and is highly lucrative. According to the 2011–2012 year, the most recent audited year, the NCAA had revenue of $871.6 million, most of which came from rights agreements with Turner/CBS Sports.[11] According to the NCAA's own website, "Most NCAA revenue (81 percent projected for 2012–2013) comes from media rights, mostly from a $10.8 billion, 14-year agreement with CBS Sports and Turner Broadcasting for rights to the Division I Men's Basketball Championship. Most of the remaining revenue comes from NCAA championships, primarily ticket sales."[12] In many ways, the black athletes who compete for PWIs hope that exposure on televised competitions may someday lead to a professional contract. But the number of college athletes that go on to play in the professional ranks is few.

It is a tragedy that college athletes—especially black ones—are being used and tossed to the side when they fail to serve the interests of the university. Recent examples in NCAA Division I athletics where the best interests of college athletes were not protected can be seen in the termination of the University of Illinois football coach Tim Beckman.[13] According to an external investigation, Beckman mishandled athletes' injuries and attempted to force players off scholarship before they graduated. This is highly problematic, especially when placed in the context of blacks' low graduation rates at PWIs. According to Messer, "the numbers of African American male student-athletes graduating from predominantly white institutions (PWIs) are low, particularly among those in the revenue generating sports of football and basketball."[14] Although the University of Illinois has fired Beckman, the mistreatment of black athletes appears to be an intractable issue the university cannot improve on. Approximately a month before the firing of Beckman, the school released a 226-page report rejecting allegations of racism on the women's basketball team after several former players and their parents alleged bullying and emotional abuse.[15] Despite the findings of the report, Matt Bollant remains the coach at the University of Illinois. One thing is for certain: black athletes at PWIs must endure much more than their white student-athlete counterparts. There is arguably less sympathy for the plight of minority athletes, particularly female athletes and athletes of color; thus these athletes often suffer more hardships than their male and/or white peers.

Recruitment Practices

According to Bennett, Hodge, Graham, and Moore, editors of *Black Males and Intercollegiate Athletics*, "[O]ver the last 50 years, with the eradication of race-based admission policies at predominantly White institutions (PWI) of higher education, African American males have been recruited in great numbers to attend these schools primarily with the purpose of improving athletic teams and producing revenues that support school branding and their other athletic teams."[16]

At the time of writing this book, the University of Louisville men's basketball team has been accused of having engaged in illegal recruitment practices, including paying for escorts to have sex with teenage male basketball recruits and sometimes even the fathers of the recruits. It is unclear whether similar recruitment strategies are used to attract white male players. On the surface, the use of black women, many of whom have been identified as escorts or even as prostitutes, does buy into stereotypes about black bodies, namely, that black males are often driven by insatiable sexual desires that must be controlled and that black female bodies are disposable and less valued than their white female counterparts, as well as that black females are also less virtuous than other females.

Recruiting black high school athletes to play sports at PWIs has led to many other questionable practices, which predate the situation described above in Kentucky. William Rhoden writes about a well-known case at Clemson University in South Carolina. Tates Locke, a former basketball coach at the University, went so far as to create a fictitious black fraternity to give black recruits the mistaken impression that the university was a diverse and welcoming place for black male athletes. Locke showed little concern for the challenges the players would face once they arrived on campus and discovered the lack of diversity and the lack of safe spaces and a feeling of community on full display during the recruitment visits.

In this chapter we chronicled the integration of black male athletes at PWIs in the post–Civil Rights era. We detailed the racial representation of student-athletes and coaches at PWIs in high-revenue-generating NCAA Division I sports (e.g., football and basketball). Because black men are the subjects of continued exploitation in the broader society, we also identified several high-profile cases where black collegiate athletes experienced unequal treatment and were strategically recruited using questionable practices. We also highlighted the negative impact this has on black student-athletes at PWIs, as players and as part of the larger campus community. In the next chapter, we examine efforts to capitalize on the black bodies of male athletes in high-revenue-generating sports and the link between this traditional and resistance to entertaining efforts on the part of athletes in sports where black male athletes are overrepresented to control their images or receive adequate compensation.

CHAPTER FIVE

Commodification of Black Bodies

Capitalizing on the black body is not a new phenomenon in American life, nor is it a new phenomenon in the social institution we call sports. Literally placing price tags on black bodies and otherwise profiting from them for everyone's benefit but their own is as American as apple pie. Even before ink from the fountain pens on the founding documents were dry, many elites were profiting not only on the labor of black bodies, but also on the fear mongering and dehumanization of people of African ancestry, which led to unequal treatment in a host of areas, including the criminal justice system where many continued to live much like slaves. The commodification of black bodies and the commercialization of blackness are evident even in big-time college sports and explain at least part of the unwillingness to see athletes in high-revenue-generating sports beyond conventional narratives where black bodies are viewed as violent, untrustworthy, animalistic, unworthy, and beyond redemption. In this chapter we take a look at historical efforts to exploit the black body in the broader society, specifically in sports. Next, we examine the role of stereotypes in justifying first the sale of black bodies and later in examples of the exploitation of black labor. We focus on dominant caricatures and illustrate how such images are shared in various forms of media. We explore the many ways in which blackness is commercialized and the impact this has on black athletes in big-time college sports. We weigh in on the debate about whether amateur athleticism in America is further evidence of the existence and the persistence of a new Jim Crow or whether such arguments veer far off base.

Creating Race: From Slavery to the Civil War

For far too long the world, was engaged in a trade that included the treatment of human beings as property. Although the Western World did not invent slavery, many Western countries certainly created a different form of slavery where one's status was transferable by virtue of one's birth and racial classification. According to historian Darlene Clark Hine, slavery took many forms in places like West Africa "and was not necessarily a permanent condition. Like people in other parts of the world, West Africans held war captives—including men, women, and children—to be without rights and suitable for enslavement."[1] Hine describe the experiences of slaves within different political and religious systems. Where Islam was dominant, masters during ancient times were responsible for the religious well-being of slaves, and in non-Islamic regions, the offspring of slaves had some rights under the law. For example, the children of slaves could not be sold to other lands. Slaves in the royal courts or armies could even own land. The children and grandchildren of people enslaved by peasant farmers "gained employment and privileges similar to those of free people. Slaves retained a low social status, but in many respects slavery in West African societies functioned as a means of assimilation."[2]

The institution of slavery that emerged in the nation that would become the United States of America had some similarities, but also some important differences from other forms of slavery throughout the course of world history. Hines et al. describe the origins of the slave trade that brought many people from West and Central Africa to the so-called New World, beginning in the 1400s: "When Portuguese ships first arrived off the Guinea Coast, their captains traded chiefly for gold, ivory, and pepper, but they also wanted slaves."[3] Slaves—people of African ancestry—were taken "home as gifts for a Portuguese prince. During the following decades, Portuguese raiders captured hundreds of Africans to work as domestic servants in Portugal and Spain."[4]

The number of slave imports to the Americas grew exponentially for much of the period between 1451 and 1870. Half a million slaves were imported to British North America during that time period. About 4 million slaves went to Brazil, 2.5 million to Spanish America, 2 million to the British Caribbean, and 1.6 to the French Caribbean. "Because Europe provided an insatiable market for sugar, cultivation of this crop in the Americas became extremely profitable. Sugar plantations employing slaver labor spread."[5] Soon, "a new, harsher form of slavery appeared in the Americas. Unlike slavery in Africa, Asia, and Europe, slavery in the Americas was based on race, as only Africans and American Indians were enslaved. Most of the slaves were men or boys were employed as agricultural laborers rather than soldiers or domestic servants. They became chattel—meaning personal property—of their masters and lost their customary rights as human beings."[6]

Slavers provided their human cargo with very basic provisions. Included in the food supplies were beans, flour, cheese, and beef. Lemons, coconuts, and plantains were among the items purchased by the captains en route from various European ports to the Americas. The human cargo was not only often malnourished but also susceptible to various communicable diseases given the unsanitary nature of its members' traveling conditions. Death rates were particularly high prior to 1750, the period that preceded vaccinations and information about hygiene and diet. Without question, poor sanitary conditions continued even after 1750, and slavers went through great measures to prepare their chattel for sale.[7]

A document from the National Humanities Center describes the humiliation of the slave auctions as told by former slaves. One such to tell of his ordeal was Henry Watson, who was sold at auction in Richmond, Virginia, at the age of eight. Watson described how the men and women were sold first and then the children. Watson gave the following account of a slave auction:

> "Gentlemen, here is a likely boy; how much? He is sold for no fault; the owner wants money. His age is forty. Three hundred dollars is all that I am offered for him. Please to examine him; he is warranted sound. Boy, pull off your shirt—roll up your pants—for we want to see if you have been whipped." If they discover any scars they will not buy, saying that the nigger is a bad one. The auctioneer seeing this, cries, "Three hundred dollars, gentlemen, three hundred dollars. Shall I sell him for three hundred dollars? I have just been informed by his master that he is an honest boy and belongs to the same church that he does." This turns the tide frequently, and the bids go up fast; and he is knocked off for a good sum.[8]

Watson painfully recalls his own experience on the auction block. He described how children were often sold after the men and women. He recalled hearing the sounds of voices wanting to know, "How old is that little nigger?" Watson reflected on the deep sadness he felt. After sale, the child and others were placed in private holding cells, "which are for the purpose of keeping slaves in, and they are generally kept by some confidential slave." It was less than 20 feet high, with a room where slaves could exercise. Henry Watson described married men, placed in handcuffs, who were leaving behind their families and were accused of having "the devil in them," shedding many tears.

Henry Watson also recounts the voyage from the auction in Richmond to Tennessee, en route to Natchez, Mississippi, where men were contracted out to pick cotton and where many slaves died because of the elements. Signage let traders know how skilled some of the human cargo was, given that many were blacksmiths and carpenters. Slaves who were in poor health were also identified and sold at a much cheaper price than healthier slaves. Skilled slaves were valued commodities, but literate slaves were not. According to Henry Bibb's narrative:

> If they were found to be very intelligent, this is pronounced the most objectionable of all other qualities connected with the life of a slave. In fact, it undermines the whole fabric of his chattelhood; it prepares for what slaveholders are pleased to pronounce the unpardonable sin when committed by a slave. It lays the foundation for running away and going to Canada. They also see in it a love for freedom, patriotism, insurrection, bloodshed, and exterminating war against American slavery.[9]

Bibb told how his family was sold as a group because traders feared he had a propensity to run away, as evidenced by his intelligence and wounds. Fearing he would not profit from Bibb alone, his owner "asked twenty-five hundred dollars" for Bibb, his wife, and children. Bibb described, as have other former slaves, the process of preparing people for sale. "Everyday at 10 o'clock they were exposed for sale. They had to be in trim for showing to the public for sale. Everyone's head had to be combed and their faces washed, and those who were inclined to look dark and rough were compelled to wash in greasy dish water, to look slick and lively."[10]

William Wells Brown wrote about the business of slavery in 1849, describing his voyage down the Mississippi River to New Orleans, where he and others were to be sold. Brown documented how slaves were kept at night in "negro-pens," ranging from 15 to 20 feet wide, and placed in the yard during the daylight hours.

Brown also described how he was forced by his owner to make the older slaves that were for sale look younger by plucking and/or dying their gray hairs. "I am sure that some of those who purchased slaves of Mr. Walker were dreadfully cheated, especially in the ages of the slaves they brought,"[11] Brown commented. He added,

> Before the slaves were exhibited for sale, they were dressed and driven into the yard. Some were set to dancing, some to jumping, some to singing, and some to playing cards. This was done to make them appear cheerful and happy. My business was to see that they were placed in those situations before the arrival of the purchasers, and I have often set them to dancing when their cheeks were wet with tears. As slaves were in good demand at that time, they were all soon disposed of.[12]

An advertisement for the slave of slaves, published in the late 1850s, highlights how some profited from the exploitation, dehumanization, and commercialization of black bodies. In the advertisement, James Harris, the administrator of Robert Harris's estate, announced that on April 5, 1858, he would "offer at public sale" human beings he described as "slaves for life" in Clay County, Missouri. Harris goes on to describe the slaves.

> One negro man named James, aged about 50 years; one negro woman named Sarah, aged about 40 years, and her child named Nancy Ellen, aged about 1 years; one negro boy named David, aged about eight years, and one negro boy named Jack, aged about six years. Said slaves will be sold to the highest bidder upon a credit of one year bond approved personal security for the purchase money.[13]

Documents from the early 1860s show a list of slaves for sale in Richmond, Virginia. The document, which is signed by Johnson Snyder and Associates, lists the number of people for sale, the condition of the adults, and the height and gender of the children, as well as their respective price tags. In all, on September 20, 1860, there were six men, six women, six boys, and five girls for sale. The adult male slave described as "extra" was priced at $1275 to $1300. Adjusting for inflation, the adult male slave was valued at about $37,000. A woman between the ages of 16 and 22 was valued at $1125–$1175. The most expensive boy for sale was valued at about $1025, and was described as 5 foot 6 inches. A girl 5 feet tall was valued at $875 to $925.

David Horsey, a columnist for the *Los Angeles Times*, wrote a piece on September 9, 2014, in which he lamented the economic exploitation blacks experienced during the enslavement era and the relevance of that exploitation to the contemporary lived experiences of blacks today. Horsey wrote:

> From the arrival of the first slaves in the 17th century until emancipation in the 1860s, most blacks not only had no economic opportunities, [but] the fruits of their labor were stolen from them by their slave masters. After the Civil War, most slaves continued to be locked in servitude as sharecroppers and servants. They were cheated, they were robbed, and they were marginalized, brutalized and lynched. Economic advancement was nearly impossible.[14]

During the Great Migration, many blacks left the South for what they thought were greater opportunities in the North, only to find that "they were blocked from getting better-paying jobs, from putting their children in the best schools and from buying homes, even in poor neighborhoods.

The economic rules and the legal system were rigged against them." Horsey also observed, "The cost of this exploitation is almost incalculable in monetary terms."[15]

The commodification of the black body was clearly evidenced during the enslavement period and continues to be evidenced in contemporary times in what will be described as the modernization of the commodification of black bodies. Arguably, nowhere was the link between the commodification of the black body more evident than at the slave auction where black bodies—male, female, young, and old—were prepared for sale. Black bodies were often lubricated to appear more appealing to prospective buyers and known blemishes were concealed. Black bodies were poked and prodded in consideration for purchase. Similar images are not uncommon even today in sport-related events, for example, at the NFL Scouting Combine and boxing weigh-ins at both the amateur and professional levels.

People of African ancestry were not only exploited and victimized during the enslavement era, but they were also criminalized. Deborah Burris-Kitchen and Paul Burris, authors of *From Slavery to Prisons*, provided an excellent overview of the criminalization of blacks during slavery.[16] It also explained the shift from a reliance on Native American labor to black slave labor. The decimation of Native Americans due to expulsion, extermination, warfare, and disease, and the expansion of plantation farming "expanded the need for African slaves emerged. Enslaving blacks also had to be legitimized by viewing African Americans as less than human. The concept of White supremacy was born before the idea of democracy."[17] The authors acknowledged the hierarchy that existed between indentured servants and slaves and the significant role the Bacon Rebellion played in "setting the landscape for the legitimization of a racial caste system," which was "rigidly bifurcated into white and black, good and evil."[18] Indentured servants worked under contract for a period of years, often under harsh conditions, and at the end of service were granted land to aid in the development of the young country and to provide a means for self-sufficiency. Evidence of the harsh treatment that indentured servants endured is well documented. Going back to the mid-1640s, the story of John Punch is illustrative of the realities and complexities associated with life as an indentured servant. John Punch was a black indentured servant in Virginia, who fled harsh treatment along with two white indentured servants, James Gregory and Victor. Each man did work similar to that of slaves. The three were soon caught, and a judge sentenced each man to receive a whipping. Additionally, James and Victor had their contracts extended for four years. John Punch was sentenced to servitude for life. John's sentence was one of the first documented cases of how the law was used to treat people differently based on race. In the mid-1670s, Nathaniel Bacon was successful in uniting black slaves and white indentured servants to fight against the Native American so-called enemies in a feat that frightened the white ruling class and hastened the transition to racial slavery.

Key to the maintenance of the enslavement system was the codification of "the degraded status of blacks as slaves."[19] Race and economic domination were indistinguishable, and the criminal classification of black people "provided a naturalized hierarchy of rights, privilege, power and domination to the point that no further justification was needed for the criminalization and enslavement of African Americans or the conquest of Native Americans."[20]

Free blacks lacked the protection afforded to white indentured servants, which placed them at risk of being sold into slavery. Property ownership, including the ownership of black people, was about much more than owning real estate. "The identity of whiteness as a legal status (being able to own blacks as property) moved being white from a status of privilege to one of vested interest."[21]

Laws were significant in underpinning the slave economy. "Without slavery, the cotton industry would not have flourished, and given the white colonists their wealth and power, but neither would mining, manufacturing, the construction of railroads, or lumbering. However, Eli Whitney's invention of the cotton gin made slavery that much more important as an institution, making it that much more important to ensure that the status of Blacks remained immoral and inhuman. The continued denial of human rights including rights to political involvement, education, and meaningful work ensured their secondary status."[22] The criminalization and dehumanization of black people was essential to the justification of the unequal treatment they received.

Slave codes played important roles in the criminalization of blackness, as did Negro Courts,[23] where slaves were tried for various infractions, including murder, manslaughter, and burglary. Local justices—often in collaboration with slave owners—decided the fate of free and enslaved blacks during slavery. After the ratification of the constitutional amendment that abolished slavery in the United States except as a form of punishment for a crime, white prosecutors routinely found blacks guilty of crimes they did not commit and returned them back to the plantations where they worked to pay off their debt to society.

Black codes, according to Hollis Lynch of Columbia University, were put into place to restore the social controls taken away by the Emancipation

Proclamation and the Thirteenth Amendment. Rooted in slave codes, "The concept that slaves were property, not persons, and that the law must protect not only the property but all the property owners from the danger of violence."[24]

Although slave codes varied from one place to another, there were many similarities among them. Lynch observed that "in all of them the color line was firmly drawn, and any amount of Negro blood established the race of a person, whether a slave or free, as Negro."[25] The status of a child was determined by the status of the mother. Compliance with the slavery codes was based on the threat of violence and actual physical punishments. "Such punishments as whipping, branding, and imprisonment were commonly used, but death (which meant destruction of property) was rarely called for except in such extreme cases as the rape or murder of a white person."[26] Slave codes were enforced sporadically, but enforcement of the slave codes was often greater "whenever any signs of unrest were detected the appropriate machinery of the state would be alerted and the laws."[27]

Additionally, the codes served the purpose of ensuring a relatively large supply of cheap labor. For example, "there were vagrancy laws that declared a black to be vagrant if unemployed and without permanent residence; a person so defined could be arrested, fined, and bound out for a term of labor if unable to pay the fine. Apprentice laws provided for the hiring out of orphans and other young dependents to whites, which often turned out to be their former owners."[28]

Louisiana's 1724 codes governing what blacks could and couldn't do were based on law established in 1685 for the French Caribbean colonies. For almost 80 years, codes dictated what was acceptable and what was unlawful not only for slaves but also for free blacks. The codes prohibited all religious practices other than "the exercise of the Roman Catholic creed"[29] and demanded that Sundays and holidays be "strictly observed. All negroes found at work on these days are to be confiscated."[30]

Louisiana law banned whites from marrying blacks, regardless of the status of the black person as enslaved or free. "Should there be any issue from this kind of intercourse, it is our will that the person so offending, and the master of the slave, should pay each a fine of three hundred livres."[31] In the event that a child was fathered by the master of the child's mother, "said master shall not only pay the fine, but be deprived of the slave and of the children, who shall be adjudged to the hospital of the locality, and said slaves shall be forever incapable of being set free."[32] Marriage between blacks—free or otherwise—was permitted, "but the consents of the father and the mother of the slave are not necessary; that of the master shall be the only one required."[33]

Also, Louisiana law defined ownership of children born to slaves. Children born to married slaves belonged to the master of the wife if the husband and the wife had different masters. In cases where one parent was free and the other enslaved, the status of the child followed that of the mother. Although Christian slaves were to be "buried in consecrated ground,"[34] slaves could not carry weapons or heavy sticks for face whippings. Slaves were also not permitted to "gather in crowds" if they belonged to different masters. Anyone violating these rules "shall be branded with the mark of the flower de luce, and should there be aggravating circumstances, capital punishment may be applied . . ."[35]

The Louisiana laws pertaining to black people also included language to "forbid negroes to sell any commodities, provisions, or produce of any kind, without the written permission of their masters, or without wearing their known marks or badges, and any person purchasing anything from negroes in violence of this article, shall be sentenced to pay a fine of 1500 livres."[36]

The laws also included sections devoted to the clothing and feeding of slaves, as well as instructions about aged slaves. For example, masters still had to feed disabled slaves. If said slaves were abandoned they would be placed in a nearby hospital and the master would have to pay eight cents a day and have a lien on the master's property.

It was clear the Louisiana did not want slaves to be owners of any kind. "All that they acquire, either by their own industry or by the liberality of others, or by any other means or title whatever, shall be the full property of their masters; and the children of said slaves, their fathers and mothers, their kindred or other relations, either free or slaves, shall have no pretensions or claims thereto."[37]

Slaves in Louisiana could never be parties in civil suits or as complainants in criminal cases, "but their masters shall have the right to act for them in civil matters, and in criminal ones, to demand punishment and reparation for such outrages and excesses as their slaves may have suffered from."[38] Although slaves could not bring cases against their masters—or against anyone else—they could be sentenced to death for "having stuck his master, his mistress, or the husband of his mistress, or their children" if they "produced a bruise, or the shedding of blood in the face."[39]

Theft, when committed by a slave or free black, would result in corporal or even capital punishment. Running away was also criminalized and punishable by having one's ears cut off and branding with the flower de luce. "On a second offence of the same nature, persisted in during one month from the day of his doing denounced, he shall be hamstrung, and be marked with the flower de luce on the other shoulder. On the third offence, he shall suffer death." In other words, the runaway would be maimed and branded with the symbol that today adorns the helmets of the New Orleans Saints professional football team.

Mississippi's black codes were described as the harshest. Under this code, preference for the placement of free blacks and people of mixed black ancestry under the age of 18 who were orphaned or indigent was given to former owners.

The Draconian code of Mississippi also said both male and female apprentices were indentured. Specially, the code read:

> *Be it further enacted*, that the said court shall be fully satisfied that the person or persons to whom said minor shall be apprenticed shall be a suitable person to have the charge and care of said minor and fully to protect the interest of said minor. The said court shall require the said master or mistress to execute bond and security, payable to the state of Mississippi, conditioned that he or she shall furnish said minor with sufficient food and clothing; to treat said minor humanely; furnish medical attention in case of sickness; teach or cause to be taught him or her to read and write, if under fifteen years old; and will conform to any law that may be hereafter passed for the regulation of the duties and relation of master and apprentice:

Moreover, the black codes in Mississippi recognize "model corporeal chastisement" on children and could be apprehended if they escaped from their indenture. Under the vagrancy law,

> *Be it further enacted*, that all freedmen, free Negroes, and mulattoes in this state over the age of eighteen years found on the second Monday in January 1866, or thereafter, with no lawful employment or business, or found unlawfully assembling themselves together either in the day or nighttime, and all white persons so assembling with freedmen, free Negroes, or mulattoes, or usually associating with freedmen, free Negroes, or mulattoes on terms of equality, or living in adultery or fornication with a freedwoman, free Negro, or mulatto, shall be deemed vagrants; and, on conviction thereof, shall be fined in the sum of not exceeding, in the case of a freedman, free Negro, or mulatto, 150, and a white man, $200, and imprisoned at the discretion of the court, the free Negro not exceeding ten days, and the white man not exceeding six months.

The black codes also gave a preference to employers entitling them "to deduct and retain the amount so paid from the wages of such freedman, free Negro, or mulatto than due or to become due; and in case such freedman, free Negro, or mulatto cannot be hired out he or she may be dealt with as a pauper."[40]

Mississippi's black codes also prohibited "any freedman, free Negro, or mulatto to intermarry with any white person; nor for any white person to intermarry with any freedman, free Negro, or mulatto; and any person who shall so intermarry shall be deemed guilty of felony and, on conviction thereof, shall be confined in the state penitentiary for life."

The codes also required every black person to not only have a place to live and employment but also provide evidence, including evidence "authorizing him or her to do irregular and job work, or a written contract . . . which licenses may be revoked for cause, at any time, by the authority granting the same." Moreover, laborers were required to have written contracts for labor arrangements lasting more than one month, and if a laborer quit prior to the end of the contract, he would forfeit wages for that year. Additionally, "Every civil officer shall, and every person may, arrest and carry back to his or her legal employer any freedman, free Negro, or mulatto who shall have quit the service of his or her employer before the expiration of his or her term of service without good cause, and said officer and person shall be entitled to receive for arresting and carrying back every deserting employee aforesaid the sum of $5, and 10 cents per mile from the place of arrest to the place of delivery, and the same shall be paid by the employer, and held as a setoff for so much against the wages of said deserting employee." The codes further provided that anyone aiding a black person in deserting his or her employment, they could face fines ranging from $50–$1500 or up to six months in the county jail.

Under the penal code of Mississippi's black code, blacks who were not in the military were prohibited from possessing "firearms of any kind, or any ammunition, dirk, or [a] Bowie knife" and it granted "every civil and military officer" the right to "arrest any freedman, free Negro, or mulatto found with any such arms or ammunition."

Blacks were further prohibited under the Mississippi black code from "committing riots, routs, affrays, trespasses, malicious mischief, cruel treatment to animals, seditious speeches, insulting gestures, language, or acts, or assaults on any person, disturbance of the peach, exercising the function of a minister of the Gospel without a license from some regularly organized church, vending spirituous or intoxicating liquors, or committing any other misdemeanor." Fines ranged from $10 to $100, and imprisonment was optional but could last for up to 30 days.

The codes applied to slaves, free Negroes, and mulattoes alike. Any black person found in violation of the laws who could not pay the fine and costs within five days of his conviction would "be hired out by the sheriff or other officer, at public outcry, to any white person who will pay said fine and all costs."

Blacks who could not show proof of employment were cited for vagrancy, a law that was applied primarily to blacks. Once criminalized, blacks were forced into the convict leasing system. "Thousands of blacks were arrested on trumped up charges, assessed court costs and fines they could not afford to pay, and were forced to work off the fees before they could be released. "Indebted prisoners were sold to plantation owners, lumber camps, mines, brickyards, railroads and corporations. Many of them did not survive the length of their punishment because of maltreatment and whippings." Convict leasing could best be described as slavery by another name.

The painstaking efforts to criminalize the black body during the enslavement era and in the decades that followed played an important role in maintaining the dominant racial ideology of white supremacy and black inferiority. In order to continue justifying the ill treatment of blacks relative to whites, it was imperative that members of the dominant group continue to see themselves as virtuous and deserving of the many unearned benefits afforded them while remaining blind or generally unconcerned with the ways in which their privileged positions disadvantaged their black counterparts. By criminalizing blackness, by treating blacks as others, they provided a justification for the treatment of blacks as property and later as second-class citizens. The commodification of the black body and of black labor did not end with the abolition of slavery or with the end of the Reconstruction Era. Evidence of the continued criminalization and commodification of blackness is an enduring quality of American life. The Jim Crow Era provides evidence of this enduring American legacy.

The Criminalization of Blackness in the Jim Crow Era

Convict leasing replaced slavery, according to some scholars.[41] "The institution of slavery, as we've come to understand it, actually underwent an evolution of sorts. Instead of having the direct enslavement of blacks with an entire apparatus used to keep slaves in their condition, certain elements of the state apparatus were piecemealed over time to enslave blacks, namely the legal and prison systems."[42] Blacks stopped being slaves to their masters and became slaves to the companies they were leased out to. "To create this system, there not only had to be the involvement of the Southern judicial system and individual Northern and Southern elites, but also the involvement and reinstitution of slavery within a corporate context."[43]

The Thirteenth Amendment abolished slavery and involuntary servitude except in the as punishment for a crime. "Thus, slavery is completely and totally legal if it is part (or the whole) of a punishment for someone who was and is convicted of a crime."[44] Convict leasing was particularly popular in Southern states where there was little interest in caring for prisoners. Although convict leasing predated the Civil War, the end of the War Between the States led to an increase in convict leasing because "corporations had access to an abundance of near-free labor."[45] Labor was scarce, and states took great measures to keep prison labor within the state. To accomplish this, they passed laws like the one in Georgia that assessed a yearly tax of $100 for any county where a recruiter sought labor. The tax increased to $500 within a year. One consequence of convict leasing was "power being taken from the state level and given to those on the local level."[46] Local sheriffs became some of the most power people in their respective counties. They had the power to lease black convicts to farmers, contractors, and corporations. "The economic empowerment awarded to sheriffs created an incentive for them to convict and lock up as many freedmen as possible in order to keep a steady supply of labor. Entire economies eventually formed around the convict lease system, including the development of a speculative trade system in convict contracts."[47]

Noted scholar, Calvin Ledbetter wrote about convict leasing in Arkansas and the eternal question as to "what to do about the state's prison population."[48] The Civil War bankrupted state governments across the South and led to the destruction of many correctional facilities. Additionally, a growth in the prison population also laid the foundation for an increased reliance on convict leasing in Arkansas. Slave owners were in charge of a lot of the punishment of slaves, and the war ended that. With little interest in rebuilding new prisons, or even restoring those that could be saved, Arkansas turned to convict leasing. Charging a fee for the use of convicts by individuals and companies was a source of revenue for the state, local communities, and individual residents. The physical removal of prisoners "kept the convicts hidden from public view in the lease camps and so removed them from the public consciousness."[49] In many cases, convict leasing was very profitable.

Alternatives to convict leasing were proposed but unsuccessful for many years. The reforms included prison farms; the use of inmates for public works projects; and the use of inmates, under state supervision, to manufacture goods for the state and corporations. Soon Arkansas moved from leasing convicts to leasing entire prisons, which was accompanied by an increase in the prison population. "A steady increase in the prison population, from 100 in 1874 to 600 in 1882, underwrote the profits . . . and subsequent lessees enjoyed. By 1900 the prison population had risen to 760, including 15 females, and a black-white ratio of 70–30."[50] The state passed the Arkansas Larceny Act in 1875. The act "made the theft of two dollars or more a felony and provided for imprisonment of from one to five years for each offense."[51]

Contractors routinely subcontracted the labor of inmates, which made tracking inmates difficult. It also made it hard to determine whether "the humanitarian aspects of Act 46 of 1873" were carried out.[52] Convict leasing ended in 1913 after abuses were uncovered and the political tides turned. Nevertheless, "problems remained as to what prisoners in the penitentiary should do and how they should be treated. The abolition of convict leasing 'did not eliminate the persistent evils that characterized it. Prisoners confined to penitentiaries, penal farms, road camps, and county chain gangs still suffered neglect and brutality.' "[53]

The criminalization of blackness continued throughout the first half of the 20th century. It is this period that Burris-Kitchen and Burris claimed "our current views of the Black criminal stem from."[54] White men's fear of newly freed black men made black men "the target of criminalization."[55] Chief among the fears was the belief that black men would rape white women.

Criminalization of Blackness and Lynching

The Equal Justice Institute (2015) recently issued a report on the history of lynching in America. Although there are many differences among the facts of each lynching, many similarities also exist. Equal Justice Institute (EJI) described five common categories: "(1) lynching that resulted from a wildly distorted fear of interracial sex; (2) lynchings in response to cause social transgressions; (3) lynchings based on allegations of serious violent crime; (4) public spectacle lynchings; (5) lynchings that escalated into large-scale violence targeting the entire African American community; and (6) lynchings of sharecroppers, ministers, and community leaders who resisted mistreatment, which was most common between 1915 and 1940."[56]

One-quarter of lynchings in the South during the Jim Crow era were related to sexual violations of white women, often unfounded and imagined. "The definition of black-on-white 'rape' in the South required no allegation of force because white institutions, laws, and most white people rejected the idea that a white woman would willingly consent to sex with an African American man."[57] The EJI report tells the story of Keith Bowen, who in 1889 in Aberdeen, Mississippi, was lynched for simply entering a room where three white women were sitting. A few years later in Reevesville, South Carolina, a black man by the name of General Lee was lynched by a group of whites for knocking on the door of a white woman in 1904. Eight years later, Thomas Miles, a black man, was lynched after he was accused of asking a white woman to join him for a cold drink. The practice

of lynching is arguably most directly linked to the stereotype and unjusti-
fiable fear of the physical prowess of the black male body and the inability
of the black male to control his most basic instincts. These two factors—black
male physical prowess and perceived intellectual inferiority—not only led
to the deaths of many black males, but also, according to scholar Michael
Eric Dyson, kept black males out of participating in mainstream American
sports for most of the nation's history, a topic we revisit in greater detail
later in the book.

Lynchings were often attended by thousands of white residents. The residents sometimes included "elected officials and prominent citizens, gath-
ered to witness pre-planned, heinous killings that featured prolonged
torture, mutilation, dismemberment, and/or burning of the victim."[58] There
was often a very festive atmosphere. "White press justified and promoted
these carnival-like events, with vendors selling food, printers producing
postcards featuring photographs of the lynching and corpse, and the victim's body parts collected as souvenirs."[59]

Arkansas, Louisiana, and Mississippi not only had some of the harshest black and slave codes and were notorious for participating in convict
leasing, but they also ranked highly on the number of blacks lynched each
year per 100,000 residents in Southern States between 1880 and 1940.
Florida had the highest lynching rate, followed by Mississippi, Arkansas,
Louisiana, and Georgia. Of the 3959 lynching identified in the EJI report,
586 occurred in Georgia, 576 in Mississippi, 540 in Louisiana, and 503
in Arkansas. Phillips, Arkansas, topped the list of counties with the most
lynching victims, and four Louisiana parishes were in the top five. In Phillips, Arkansas, 243 blacks were lynched, compared to 54 in Cadoo, Louisiana; 50 in Lafourche, Louisiana; 40 in Tensas, Louisiana; and 35 in
Ouachita, Louisiana.

Efforts to oppose lynching were met with resistance from the highest
levels of society. EJI quoted President Theodore Roosevelt stating that "the
greatest existing cause of lynching is the perpetration, especially by black
men, of the hideous crime of rape."[60] Lynching declined, at least in part, to
national protests, the Great Migration, and the death penalty. "By 1915,
court-ordered executions outpaced lynchings in the former slaves states
for the first time. Two-thirds of those executed in the 1930s were black,
and the trend continued."[61]

Criminalizing the Black Body: The Case of Jack Johnson

In addition to convict leasing and lynchings, several high-profile cases
highlight the criminalization of blackness in general and of black males,
in particular, including black male athletes. The life and legacy of boxer

Jack Johnson is one of the best examples. Johnson rose into prominence in the world of boxing at a time when many blacks were trying to assert their new status as free people while, it must be understood, they still lived under the threat of violence and as second-class citizens. In Chapter 4, we examined how the color line operated in boxing. White boxers refused to fight black boxers, and the U.S. Congress eventually banned interracial fight films. Efforts to prevent interracial fights were not uncommon, but the power of the new medium—moving pictures—reached far more people worldwide than any boxing venue could hold. Johnson's success in the boxing ring and his victories against white opponents—particularly after he become the first black world heavyweight champion—were sources of inspiration for people of color in the United States and throughout the globe. They also served as a source of angst for whites who relied on the false doctrine of white supremacy and black inferiority to justify the unequal treatment of blacks. Johnson refused to live life as a slave. He was determined to live his life as a free man. He was said to have embodied the idea of the New Negro—a person of African ancestry living in the early part of the 20th century who was determined to have access to all the rights and privileges afforded to all U.S. citizens regardless of their color. Long before the Harlem Renaissance—a period known for the black intellectuals and great black writers who challenged the United States and the world about the unequal treatment of people of color, Johnson routinely violated racial norms and racial etiquette of the day. He not only was the embodiment of conspicuous consumption—a term used to describe people who make extravagant purchase not out of necessity, but rather to display their great wealth—with his fancy cars, businesses, and tailor made suits, but he also dated white women at a time when sexual relations between whites and non-whites was not only frowned on, but in many cases against the law. When whites could not beat Jack Jackson in the ring, they used the law to bring him down. Johnson was found guilty of violating the Mann Act, which made it illegal to bring women across state lines for immoral purposes, such as prostitution. The law was worded in such terms as to prohibit a host of consensual sexual activities like the those Johnson engaged in with several white women.

The passage of the legal measure was rooted in racist ideology and based on what some referred to as the hysteria surrounding so-called white slavery in the early part of the 1900s. As more and more women lived in cities, worked outside of the home, and distanced themselves from traditional systems of courtship, efforts to address perceived declines in moral purity and changes in traditional social mores intensified.

Criminalizing the Black Body: The Scottsboro Defendants

The criminalization of the black body persisted throughout the 20th century—both inside and outside of the world of sports—as it persists today. The judicial lynching of the Scottsboro defendants provides yet another example of a high-profile case that shed light on the criminalization of blackness, and of black males specifically. Nine black males (Clarence Norris, Charlie Weems, Ozie Powell, Olen Montgomery, Willie Roberson, Haywood Patterson, Eugene Williams, and Andy and Roy Wright) were accused of raping two white women (Victoria Prince and Ruby Bates)—in the early 1930s on a fast-moving training leaving Alabama and bound for Chattanooga, Tennessee.

The males, ranging in age from 13 to 21 years, were arrested on the testimony of Bates and Price who, like the nine defendants, were hobos. Fearfully that they might have to do more time in jail if the authorities found them riding the trains illegally, the white females made up the story that the nine males raped them. Impoverished, black, male, and accused of sexual violence against white women, the defendants did not have adequate representation in their first trial. The defendants, with the exception of 13-year-old Roy Wright, were swiftly sentenced to death.

The International Labor Defense (ILD) fund, the legal arm of the Communist Party, seized on the opportunity to shed light on the demerits of capitalism, recruit southern blacks to the Communist Party, and expand the anti-lynching campaign of the organization.[62] ILD organized national and international protests and was responsible for providing the nine falsely accused males with one of the nation's top attorneys, criminal lawyer Samuel Leibowitz. Despite Leibowitz's best efforts, and even with Ruby Bates admitting that she lied about the rape, the defendants were found guilty during a second trial, which they were granted after it was shown that they did not have effective counsel during the first trial.[63] Judge James Horton, in a show of great bravery and what amounted to political suicide, overturned the second guilty verdict and called for a new trial. The tragedy ended for the Scottsboro defendants when a compromise was reached that led to the immediate release of four defendants in 1937 and the release of the remaining defendants some 13 years later. Kelley concluded, "Although the ILD did not win the defendants' unconditional release, its campaign to 'Free the Scottsboro Boys' had tremendous legal and political implications during the early 1930s. For example, in one of the ILD's many appeals, a 1935 U.S. Supreme Court ruled that the defendant's constitutional rights were violated because blacks were systematically excluded from the jury rolls."

Criminalizing the Black Body: The Murder of Emmett Till

More than 20 years after the initial arrest of the Scottsboro defendants, another event took place that symbolized the enduring criminalization and dehumanization of the black body. The mid-1950s saw another high-profile case highlighting the criminalization of blackness, and of the black male body in particular, in the killing of 14-year-old Emmett Louis Till. The youngster was born and raised in Chicago. He left the city to stay with relatives for the summer, and his life ended after an encounter with Carol Bryant in a store the town of Money, Mississippi. Young Emmett was accused of whistling at the white woman. Within days he was awakened in his great uncle's home, hauled away, and never seen alive again. Till was brutally tortured and beaten by J. W. Milam and Roy Bryant. Milam and Bryant stood trial for the murder and kidnapping of the 14-year-old boy who'd had so much life ahead of him, but they were found not guilty by a sympathetic, all-white jury determined to maintain the racial status quo. The killers and kidnapers would eventually admit their guilt and share their story with a popular magazine. The criminalization of young black children mobilized many people to join the fight for social justice.

The Criminalization of Blackness and the War on Drugs

The criminalization of the black body endured throughout the second half of the 20th century. Due to legislative changes and landmark Supreme Court decisions, efforts to maintain the racial hierarchy that has characterized much of American life took on different forms, forms that were ever more implicit and covert. For example, public policies and private practices were less likely to include explicit racially charged or racially specific language, but the outcomes of many of the public policies and private practices created or exacerbated persistent racial disparities. The War on Drugs is a much written about example of a series of policies that impacted black and white communities in very different ways. "Waging a war against drugs and targeting minorities and poor people as the enemies in this war is nothing new. The criminalization of people of color is the direct result of the European colonial belief that these drugs affect people of color differently than Whites."[64] Throughout history, science was often used as a justification for differential treatment by race. Scientific racism, or the use of science to justify the doctrine of white superiority and black inferiority, was widely popular during the early part of the 20th century. Burris-Kitchen and Burris further make the claim that the media played an important role in making it appear as though the only way to protect society from "black male rage," which drugs use only made worse, was to isolate and incarcerate as many black males as possible. Politicians and legislation also played important roles.[65]

The War on Drugs, which originated with the Nixon Administration, "was an all-out attempt to completely destroy and incarcerate the entire Black race. Nixon linked crime and drugs to the corrosive nature of rebellion in urban centers."[66] Nixon equated crime with urban areas and urban areas with blacks "and the war on crime meant a bulwark built against the increasingly political and vocal racial other by the predominately white race."[67] Through the Office of Drug and Law Enforcement, the administration essentially went to battle against low-level drug dealers in low-income black neighborhoods, the very same neighborhoods where residents rioted after the killing of Rev. Dr. Martin Luther King Jr. Nixon "played on the fears of White Americans that Blacks were taking over, and that recently introduced social programs were handouts to lazy Blacks who didn't want to get jobs."[68]

The War on Drugs continued through subsequent administrations. Burris-Kitchen and Burris blame Reagan's failed economic strategy on increasing drug use, unemployment, and involvement in the underground economy, especially in black communities in America.[69] The policies created by Reaganomics, according to Burris-Kitchen and Burris, led to the "need to increase law enforcement efforts to control those populations of people left desperate, hungry, and homeless."[70] Maurice St. Pierre's 1991 publication on the impact of Reaganomics on black families, which appeared in *Journal of Black Studies*, described the theory underpinning Reaganomics and included specific examples about the deleterious impact of related policies on blacks in America.

St. Pierre described Reaganomics as a reaction to a legacy of double-digit inflation that was inherited from the Carter Administration. In contrast to the popular call for the stimulation of demand to turn the economic tide, Reaganomics focused on supply-side economics. Reagan called for the stimulation of production. The formula for success for Reagan included lower taxation, increased savings, greater investment, and stronger work motivation designed to stimulate growth and promote price stability. St. Pierre also claimed that the basic idea underlying the policies that emerged as a result of Reagan's economic theory was the idea that there is no such thing as a free lunch.

The Reagan Administration proposed that teen mothers be required to live with their parents in order to receive Aid to Families with Dependent Children (AFDC) and also proposed the elimination of payments to able-bodied AFDC parents whose youngest child was 16 years of age or older.

Reforms to AFDC were to save nearly $200 million. Black families were more likely than white families during this time period to have minor children and to live below the poverty line. Additionally, some school-meal and food stamp subsidies were eliminated, which disproportionately impacted black families relative to white families.

Moreover, St. Pierre also found that efforts to decrease assistance to unemployed Americans also disproportionately impacted blacks relative to whites during the Reagan Administration. The black unemployment rate was about double the unemployment rate for whites. Reagan also increased the amount of discretionary income that families had to contribute to students enrolled in college, and he raised the eligibility ceiling of Basic Education Opportunity Grants and decreased the maximum grant award. Federal aid to needy students was also reduced, and according to St. Pierre the proposals hurt blacks seeking a college degree at predominantly white institutions and at historically black colleges and universities. St. Pierre noted that at some institutions, such as Morgan State University in Baltimore, had to lay off faculty and place a freeze on new hires as enrollment declined. Reagan's policies also increased the maximum allowable rent contribution paid by tenants living in federally subsidized housing from 25 to 30 percent. A moratorium was also placed on funding for new federally funded housing. Blacks were hit harder than other groups as they were had relatively higher levels of participation in the identified programs due to a host a factors. Although the policy changes were intended to save the federal government millions of dollars, they removed many much needed safety nets from some of the most vulnerable populations, who were disadvantaged not because they lacked a work ethnic or motivation, but in large part because of the legacy of racial discrimination that privileged members of the dominant racial group while disadvantaging blacks and other people of color.

The 1984 Crime Control Bill had a particularly profound impact on blacks. The bill included mandatory minimums for crimes involving crack, heroine, and cocaine, with much harsher sentencing for smaller quantities of the drugs used by more economically disadvantaged people and people of color. Blacks were quickly overrepresented among the prison population by the late 1980s, and the amount of money allocated in the federal budget for the war on the nation's own citizens was close to $10 billion, monies that did not go to education, social safety nets, or health care.

Naomi Murakawa, author of *The First Civil Right: How Liberals Built Prison America*, explained the role of racial liberalism in laying the groundwork for the 1984 Crime Control Bill.[71] Murakawa argued that America became a carceral nation during the progressive reform period during World War

II. Progressives surpassed scientific racism as the primary justification for explaining differences on a host of sociological outcomes between whites and nonwhites. Progressive reformers provide an effective justification for incarcerating segments of the population. Ironically, this brand of racial liberalism originated as part of efforts to create discourses that were more tolerant, but also contained a rationalization for the creation of a carceral state. Institutional racism, for example, created segregated environments that bred populations of lawbreakers. Centralizing, modernizing, and increasing the size of the criminal justice system was viewed as the best solution to the ongoing problem of maintaining law and order. Consequently, legislation was introduced as early as the 1950s that took away discretion from judges and law enforcement officials, many of whom potentially held negative attitudes about entire groups of people and also acted on those prejudices, and replaced them with harsher, seemingly rational rules. For example, liberal Democrats were responsible for the passage of The Boggs Act of 1952, which created mandatory minimum sentences for drug offenses.

During the Johnson Administration's Great Society, the process of militarizing local police forces was initiated. The Law Enforcement Assistance Administration provided federal resources to local and state police departments, which were used to purchase such items as gas masks, helicopters, riot gear, and smoke and gas grenades. The underlying assumption was that such racially neutral policies would lead to a more equitable and a more just society and improve relations between the police and communities of color. Murakawa said Reagan Republicans played important roles in helping the United States become a world leader in the incarceration of their own citizens by prosecuting the War on Drugs, and the 1984 Crime Bill is one of the best illustrations of this fact.[72] Murakawa showed how the Reagan Administration virtually did away with parole at the federal level, put in place the detention of accused persons, institutionalized mandatory minimum sentences, and was responsible for treating the trafficking of crack—used more by people of color and people of lower socioeconomic status—more harshly than the trafficking of powder cocaine—used more by whites and people of relatively high levels of socioeconomic status.

The death of Ronald Reagan in 2004 provided an opportunity for historians, politicians, and everyday Americans to reflect on his presidency, and Gerald Shargel characterized it as a tough legacy.[73] The words "radical," "tough," and "ruthless" are used to describe Reagan's economic philosophy and his approach to combating crime. Clearly, Shargel's assessment was similar to that of Murakawa's characterization. Shargel said the Bail

Reform Act of 1984 changed the purpose of bail from assuring that some accused of a crime would return for a required court data to "preventive detention embodying the long-discredited notion that past behavior accurately predicts future conduct."[74] Consequently, America's federal prisons were filled to the seams with people—presumably innocent until proven guilty—"deemed dangerous, or subject to a handful of statutory presumptions that largely result in jailing low-level drug dealers. Lengthy pretrial detentions of a year or more are not uncommon." Shargel described the 1984 Sentencing Reform Act as one of the most significant initiatives of the Reagan Administration, which resulted in long sentences because federal judges were no longer able to "temper justice with mercy."[75] A decade later, President Clinton oversaw the Violent Crime Control and Law Enforcement Act of 1994 that increased the number of officers on the street and seemed to grant law enforcement with more resources to occupy communities of color in the name of ridding the national of illicit drugs.

Criminalizing Blackness from the Streets to the Schoolhouse to the Big House

The War on Drugs did not end with the Clinton Administration, but the effects of the crime bill and other policies are still felt today and continue to contribute to the criminalization of black bodies from schools to prisons. In the book *Big Box Schools: Race, Education, and the Danger of the Wal-Martization of Public Schools in America*, Martin outlines the criminalization of blackness in the school-to-prison pipeline.[76] Martin (2015) points to the overrepresentation of blacks and black youth in the segment of the labor market that is filled with dead-end jobs, no job security, and few opportunities for advancement.[77] Martin describes the linkages between schools, the labor market, and the criminal justice system.[78] She says there is a pipeline between schools and prisons because of networks of privilege that flows between institutions.[79] Correctional facilities and traditional public schools, particularly in urban areas, are considered black spaces. Political discourse and interfaces with the media reinforced negative beliefs about blacks. These prejudices include the misconceptions that blacks undervalue education; that they are born with criminal tendencies; and that they are more inclined to look for a handout than a hand up. Correctional facilities, traditional public schools in inner-city neighborhoods, and social service agencies serve disproportionate numbers of blacks, and other peoples of color. The institutions are set up in such a way that reflects what David Brunsma and his colleagues said reflect "their historical demography, ideology, and associated hegemonies."[80] Bridges to benefits connect members of the dominant racial group in America with one another.

Members of the dominant group work to protect their privilege and reinforce said privileges though their interface with each other through the social institutions identified here.

Martin is in agreement with many scholars cited previously in her claim that the criminalization of blacks and of black youth is not a modern phenomenon, but rather a part of a historical legacy.[81] Martin characterizes the period following World War II "as the period when incarceration was used as a form of controlling the black population—a population many whites, including those in law enforcement feared and stereotyped."[82] Martin cites studies such as the one conducted by Johnson on Philadelphia that showed how blacks reported harassment and brutality at the hands of law enforcement officers who often looked the other way when whites were actually engaged in violations of society's mores.[83] Unequal treatment before the law did not correspond with changes in the crime rate. In other words, it was not an increase in crime that led to harsher or stricter laws, but rather a desire to control certain segments of the population, namely, large segments of the black population.

In more contemporary times, police practices such as Stop and Frisk, a tactic employed by the New York City Police Department throughout the Giuliani and Bloomberg administrations, and civil gang injunctions, a law enforcement strategy used primarily by the Los Angeles Police Department to address gang activity, criminalize black people and other people of color in ways that are similar to strategies used in the past. Martin argues that, like conventional nuisances, "[p]eople of color, particularly black males, are seen in much the same way as public nuisances, as threats to public health and public safety. While the term 'public' seems inclusive, it could best be understood as a colorblind term for white."[84]

For example, Martin compares civil gang injunctions to black codes in that both "criminalize a broad range of mundane activities with the targeted community," such as obstructing public parks, streets, or highways.[85] Martin also found that civil gang injunctions "stigmatize people of color, particularly young males of color, as a problem and extend those characteristics to the neighborhoods in which they live and anyone within the geographic area they come into contact with."[86] Policies employed by law enforcement nationally are often vague, with no single definition of key terms, such as what constitutes a gang or valid membership in a gang. Therefore, it is not what an individual is or is not doing that is criminalized, but his or her very membership in a racial group, or residency in a place that is inhabited primarily by people of color, is criminalized.

The killing of young Trayvon Martin in Sanford, Florida, on February 26, 2012, served as another example of the criminalization of the black body. Neighborhood watch volunteer George Zimmerman killed Trayvon Martin, and many in the media portrayed Martin, the victim in the shooting, as a criminal and a thug. "Diverting public attention away from Zimmerman and issues surrounding his culpability, the Sanford Police, Zimmerman's attorney, and some in the media focused instead on Trayvon Martin's posts on social media, school records, and physical appearance, including wearing a hooded sweatshirt."[87] Leonard summarized Trayvon Martin's treatment best when he wrote, "Black youth are demonized, denied access to a worthwhile educational experience, and funneled from locked down schools to places of incarceration all while the likes of Zimmerman guard gated communities from the intrusion of the unwanted" and as Martin shows, black youth are model children for the unwanted in society, especially young black males.[88]

In "Been There Done That," Martin shows how the Trayvon Martin case not only pointed to the criminalization of black bodies but also to the endurance and durability of white privilege. The loss of Sybrina Fulton's and Tracy Martin's son showed that "the clothing in which a white son left the house would not lead others to look upon him with suspicion. White privilege also meant that it a white child was victim of crime, law enforcement would neither assume he was the aggressor, nor take the word of his killer as true without a thorough investigation."[89] Trayvon Martin was wearing a hooded sweatshirt. Although hooded sweatshirts are worn by people of all walks of life from members of fraternities at predominantly white institutions of higher learning, to the founder of Facebook, when a young black male wears a hooded sweatshirt, he strikes fear in the hearts of some Americans. Martin added, "We could also add to McIntosh's list that if the son of white parents was killed, the parents would have time to grieve his death and not have to do themselves the investigative work commonly done by law enforcement officials. Additionally, if a white child was killed, and the killer's identity was known, the parents could be sure that at the very least the killer would be arrested."[90]

Trayvon Martin's parents were not immediately notified of his death, and the sentiment of many people close to the case was that local law enforcement agents were not treating the death of the young black male as they might treat the death of a young white person. Zimmerman's arrest did not come immediately but some might argue came only after public pressure and protest from Sandford, Florida, and beyond.

Zero tolerance policies—policies that take cause for disciplinary actions related to insubordination, use or possession of firearms, drug use, violence or threats of violence, and so on—and other disciplinary decisions involving, for example, use of a cell phone, use of profanity, and so forth—play important roles in the criminalization of blacks and black youth. Fear of black youth and concerns over violent and drug-related crimes contributed to the rise in zero tolerance policies in majority minority schools.[91] Behavior that used to get students sent to the principal's office now land them in the back of police cars and in front of judges. Skipping school and bringing cell phones or other electronic devices to school were leading to contact with police officers stationed in the nation's mostly inner-city schools. Infractions that in previous generations might lead to a trip to the principal's office today often send the transgressor to juvenile court.

Martin cited governmental reports that exposed racial differences in school discipline, which start as early as preschool. Black students were three times as likely as white students to be expelled or suspended in pre-school. The trend continues in high school. During the 2011–2012 school year, black males had the highest out-of-school suspensions. Under the zero tolerance policies, students who talk back to people in positions of authority are treated much like students who bring drugs or a weapon to school. Sadly, "the criminalization of the classroom has led to the incarceration of students directly and indirectly."[92]

Criminalizing Contemporary Black Athletes: Guns, Stereotypes, and Imagined Threats

Media reports addressing gun ownership by professional athletes focused primarily on black players and showed player photographs that resembled mug shots. The imagery and language used were intentionally inflammatory. "[T]he discursive linking of black athletes to guns further invokes the sport/gang dyad; a trope represents gang culture and urban/gun violence (authentic blackness) as responsible for subverting sports—its values and the possibilities it establishes—and for destroying athletes."[93] Moreover, black professional players and gun ownership is linked with "violent, dangerous, pathological, and otherwise threatening criminals," whereas for white athletes gun ownership is viewed differently: "Players protecting themselves by arming themselves make sense, the discourse also reminds its readers that they too are threatened by a black criminal population, which needs to be controlled, policed, and watched, given the fact that most white athletes (those in NHL and MLB) are not packing heat."[94]

The criminalization of the black body outlined throughout this chapter is rooted in enduring stereotypes or caricatures of blackness that impact the black population as a whole and black athletes in particular. The Jim Crow Museum of Racist Memorabilia at Ferris University identifies several caricatures, including pickaninnies, golliwog, tom, coon, Jezebel, tragic mulatto, sapphire, savage, and brute. The brute caricature pertained to black males and portrayed them as "savage, animalistic, destructive, and criminal—deserving punishment, maybe death."[95] In black brute caricatures, blacks are depicted as predators preying on helpless victims and having an insatiable appetite for white women.

Contemporary examples of black brutes appeared in movies and television programs in the 1980s and the 1990s, where the "brute was nameless and sometimes faceless; he sprang from a hiding place, he robbed, raped, and murdered. He represented the cold brutality of urban life. . . . Actors who played the black brute were usually not on screen very long, just long enough to terrorize innocent victims."[96]

Sports figures, such as Mike Tyson, are often portrayed as black brutes. Tyson was marketed as a savage who was unpredictable and capable of killing someone. "Tyson become the wealthiest and best known athlete on earth. In his mind, he was a 21st century gladiator; to the American public, he was simply a black brute," according to Ferris University. Similarly, the famous Willie Horton ad used in the 1988 presidential campaign, which portrayed Michael Dukakis as soft on crime, included a black man convicted of murder to communicate the idea "that a black brute is worse than a white brute."[97] Likewise, blaming a generic black man for a crime that we later find was committed by a white assailant is another example of the myth of the black brute and its use by ordinary citizens and by law enforcement. When Charles Stuart was seriously shot and his pregnant wife killed in 1989, he told authorities in Boston that a black man had done it. Officers searched predominantly black neighborhoods, looking for the black brute, only to learn that Stuart, who later committed suicide, probably killed his wife to collect insurance money. Susan Smith, a mother in South Carolina, made similar allegations concerning the death of her children; later it was found that no mystery black brute carjacked her and her kids; rather, she herself murdered her 14-month and three-year old sons.[98]

Muwakkil speculated at the end about racial stereotypes in sports, referring to the success of the Williams sisters(Serena and Venus) in tennis and Tiger Woods in golf.[99] Muwakkil described why many people associate certain sports with certain racial groups without knowing the history of these famous sports. The author also noted that in "a culture shaped by assumptions of white supremacy, many white Americans have perniciously associated blacks with bestial behavior" and being "animalistic."[100]

Hodge, Burden, Robinson, and Bennett explore the effect of stereotyping on the psychology of black male student-athletes. Using a critical race perspective, the authors focus on the construction of race, stereotyping, and racism and the association of those constructs on a host of social and demographic factors that impact the academic and athletic experiences of black male student-athletes. Stating that very little attention is devoted to the narratives of black student-athletes, the authors claim that "race becomes more than it is with the stereotypic belief that blacks dominate sports, partly due to their presence and recent successes in basketball and football. It is less salient cognitively for the dominant group, white athletes, who actually do dominate most sports in America."[101] The authors call on faculty and coaches to examine their own racial stereotypes and to provide more support to ensure the academic success of black athletes.

Additionally, everyone in the life of black student-athletes "must do more to help eliminate racist stereotypic beliefs by finding culturally relevant ways to help black students understand the difference the difference between 'acting white' and successfully navigating the educational system."[102] Finally, the authors call for as much attention to be devoted to the academic achievement athletes as their athletic achievements.

The media plays a critical role not only in the criminalization of blackness, but also stereotypes and negative perceptions of black athletes. A 2015 study conducted by Cynthia Frisby, associate professor at University of Missouri in journalism, found that more stories are written about white athletes than black athletes and that black athletes are more likely to be referred to in articles about crime stories and domestic violence. More than half of stories in the media about black athletes are negative compared to less than a third of stories about white athletes. Frisby's research showed the racial bias in the media coverage of black athletes, particularly the stereotyping of black male athletes.

For some time, scholars have contended that sports media is not only male-dominated, but dominated by *white* males. The characterization of the behaviors and actions of black athletes are often described through the lenses of white male writers who often have very limited meaningful interaction with black people, let alone black culture. Arnett reported that less than 8 percent of sports editors of Associated Press are black. "Whites made up 94 percent of sports editors, 89 percent of assistant sport editors, 88 percent of sports columnists, and 87 percent of sports reporters at the time."[103] Arnett's piece includes the term "sportotypes."[104] Sportotypes are "recurring sports figures profiles that may appear harmless on an individual basis, but nonetheless contribute to a message of marginalization of the Black athlete—that show up in sports coverage: Most black athletes are portrayed as the 'model citizen,' the 'diva,' the 'menace to society,' the 'buck,' the 'intellectually suspect' or the 'comic relief character.'"[105] Arnett addresses both racial stereotypes and the unwillingness to see the athletes as humans, rather than as commodities.[106]

Criminalization and the Process of Racial Socialization[107]

We understand the process by which blacks and whites learn what is expected of them to maintain the racial status quo and the myth of white supremacy and black inferiority—or what the author of the book *White Sports/Black Sports* defined as racial socialization.[108] We look to a number of frameworks that might help readers understand what is meant by the terms "blackness" or "whiteness," and might help us understand why members of the dominant group respond to certain behaviors by white and black players in different ways. Following Martin's lead, we look beyond conventional theories about socialization.[109]

As a society, we still see some sports as either black or white. Some maintain the belief that biology equals destiny. Phenotype, bone density, muscle dexterity, and so on, are thought to determine one's athletic destination, with race serving as one of the main filters.[110] One would think that such claims, which have been disproven time and time again, would fade into the deep recesses of our collective consciousness; sadly, they have not. Often cloaked in new raiment, the idea that blacks and whites are predisposed to participation and success in different sports remains with us still.[111] Although there are a host of theories, perspectives, and paradigms in the social sciences, particularly in sociology, arguing for the continuing significance of race in our society,[112] few have found their way into scholarly discussions about sports.[113] Considering that these race-based theories have been used to explain various phenomena, they have been limited in important ways, including the failure to place racism front and center. What is needed is an overarching, unifying framework that will aid in our understanding of not just the continuing significance of race in sports but also the significance of *racism* in sports. The multilevel and multidimensional roles of race and racism in determining athletic participation and destinations can best be understood within this suggested framework.

Understanding why racial groups are drawn to particular sports, and using a critical lens and a keen understanding of the structure and composition of populations, Martin and Horton's work draws from the strengths of critical race theory,[114] the colorism perspective,[115] the population structural change thesis,[116] and critical demography paradigm[117]—namely, the centrality of race—while also addressing thex observed weaknesses. Critical race theory is commonly used in understanding persistent racial inequality in the fields of education and the law by placing the experiences of marginalized groups at the forefront and examining the centrality of race in the function of institutions. Colorism explores how skin complexion matters within and between racial groups, and the population and structural change thesis examines the impact of demographic shifts on social institutions. Critical demography, a paradigm introduced in the late 1999s, rejects the conventional wisdom that data are neutral, apolitical, and speak for themselves. Although critical race theory and colorism place the focus squarely on race and skin complexion, neither places racism at the forefront. Moreover, neither critical race theory nor colorism substantively take into consideration the impact of population size on intergroup relations. Further, to date, neither the population structural change thesis nor the critical demography paradigm has been used to understand the unlevel playing field that characterizes American sports.

Critical Race Theory

Although it has its origins among legal scholars,[118] critical race theory is used to examine the linkages between race and education,[119] the family,[120] immigration,[121] public health,[122] and sports.[123] Critical race theory, like other social theories, theses, and perspectives, has supporters and critics. To fully understand the ongoing debates surrounding critical race theory, it is important to examine more closely its origins, development, and use over time.

Derrick Bell, a former legal professor at Harvard University, is among the scholars credited with institutionalizing the interest in systematically studying the lived reality of race. The purpose of introducing critical race theory—a framework that includes the use of critical theory, the sociological imagination, and moving toward understanding the relationships among race, law, and power—is to draw attention to society as it is and society as it ought be. Bell felt it was necessary to address the gap between the real and the imagined, and to do so in a way that was simultaneously a radical critique *of* the law and a radical emancipation *by* the law. Critical race theory was developed to address the aforementioned tension head on.[124]

Many legal scholars quickly gravitated to critical race theory, due in large part to the key principles outlined. First, critical race theory holds that society is organized around race. Second, people of color receive unequal treatment compared with members of the dominant racial group. The unequal treatment experienced by people of color occurs not only on a personal level but is also, more importantly, institutionalized. Moreover, critical race theory explains how individuals within a given social system participate in the perpetuation of racialized social systems through social practices. Lastly, critical race theory enhances our understanding of racial and ethnic identities as variable, social constructions that change across place and time.[125] Critical race theory has been applied to enhance our understanding of the need for culturally relevant curriculum and culturally competent instructors to narrow racial achievement gaps in education, as well as to understand how race matters in contemporary sports, as evidenced in the overrepresentation of black athletes in sports, such as football, but the underrepresentation of black athletes in decision-making positions, such as in the front office staff.

Critical race theory was intended to assist legal scholars in explaining various phenomena, *and* it was intended to be inclusive and transformative. Critical race theory was to bring to the center, from the margins, scholars of color, whom Derrick Bell argued were often silenced, discredited, or altogether ignored. Bell writes, "We seek to empower and include traditionally excluded views and see all-inclusiveness as the ideal because of our belief and collective wisdom."[126]

As important as the work of Bell and others is and has been, they were not the first to address such concerns about the law or society in general,[127] but their desire to "fight the silence about the intersection of race, racism, and the law"[128] ushered in a wave of scholarly research that moved concepts such as intersectionality,[129] anti-essentialism,[130] normality of race, social construction, and differential racialization[131] toward the forefront of progressive thinking and scholarship. Intersectionality focuses on the simultaneous impact of race, class, and gender, concepts that are often treated as independent of one another. Anti-essentialism is the idea that we must consider the unique experiences of individuals prior to enacting policies that often provide a one-size-fits-all approach to problem solving. Normality of race involves the creation of a racial hierarchy that justifies the unequality of nonwhites, whereas social construction focuses not on biological categories, but on the meanings we attach to the categories, such as the meanings we attach to blackness versus whiteness. Differential racialization means that through the use of personal narratives, among other techniques, critical race theorists also raised awareness about bias, conscious, and unconscious in America's social institutions, including in the criminal justice system.[132]

In the end, critical race theory was to be the driving force behind efforts to bring about a more just society in which people of color would be regarded in the same manner as members of the dominant group and not perpetually regarded as "others," which had historically been the case.

Scholars see merit in applying critical race theory to the sports world because, as Kevin Hylton says, "Racial thinking in sports is perpetuated by four weak theoretical propositions,"[133] elucidated by B. St. Louis:

1. "Sports are based on theoretical principles of equality.
2. "The results of sport competition are unequal.
3. "This inequality of results has a racial bias.
4. "Therefore, given the equality of access and opportunity, the explanation of the unequal results lies in racial physicality."[134]

Despite many examples to the contrary, many fans believe sports competition is a level playing field. Most sports are based on principles of inequality. Sports participation has been limited on the basis of class, race, gender, age, and sexuality. It is not always the better athlete who wins out; far too often it is the athlete who has access to sports participation, including access to the social networks associated with sports participation and the right gender, race, ethnicity, age, or sexual orientation that is even given the chance to win out.

Critical race theory has the power to address the identified weak propositions with its emphasis on race and racism. It also has the power to challenge the notion of color-blindness. Critical race theory has many other positive attributes, including the commitment to social justice and its ability to transcend disciplinary boundaries.[135]

Moreover, critical race theory has the potential to enhance our understanding of the processes involved in the formation of power and ideologies by race.[136] It has the power to inform the process of theorizing in leisure studies and "generate a useful theoretical vocabulary for the practice of progressive racial politics in sport."[137]

Despite the contributions of critical race theory to legal studies, and beyond this, to other subjects, there are identified weaknesses. Scholars call into question whether critical race theory is indeed a theory. Critical race theory "lacks the articulation of a set of precisely stated and logically related propositions that explain a relationship between concepts, to the formation of a structured conceptual scheme that provides a general interpretation or critique of social reality."[138] Critical race theory, at best, say some scholars, is an intellectual movement.

Additionally, the use of narratives or storytelling, although a central feature in the application of critical race theory, is problematic, particularly for social scientists with a quantitative orientation. The narratives, although informative and illustrative of important concepts and themes, fail to meet the robust standards expected by many in the social sciences. One cannot, in good faith, generalize the findings to a known population.

Critical race theory has been used in recent years to understand sports, especially to enhance our understanding about the centrality of race and racism as they relate to sport management, problems of whiteness, perceptions on institutional integrity, mentoring of black female student-athletes, and black male student-athlete success in college sport.

In the 2005, John Singer, a professor at James Madison University, conducted a study to provide students and scholars in the discipline of sports management with an enhanced understanding of how critical race theory could be applied to the field.[139] Recognizing critical race theory for its utility in challenging discourse around civil rights issues with an aim toward empowering people of color, Singer identifies the many research areas within sports that sport management scholars could use critical race theory to investigate and address.[140] The subjects include the underrepresentation of women and people of color in leadership and upper management positions; gender and racial discrimination; marketing of sports to communities of color; representations of people of color in sports media; and the use of stereotypical images in sports organizations. Through the lens of critical race theory, Singer argued that students and scholars in sports management could get ahead of the curve on a host of emerging issues destined to impact their field of study.[141] Among the key challenges Singer identified was the idea that the United States was a colorblind society. Critical race theory helps those in sports management understand the continuing significance of race and racism, which they can then communicate empirically to reluctant athletes, coaches, employees, and fans. Moreover, Singer suggested that critical race theory takes into account the many identities of people involved in sports and sports management. Although race and racism are central, they are not the only social constructions that shape identity formation or impact sports participation, sport engagement, or even sport management, so critical race theory is important in that respect as well.

Additionally, Singer said that an important feature of critical race theory for those in sports management is storytelling. Storytelling and narratives in sports management are critical because they are inclusive as opposed to exclusive; they allow for "other ways of knowing and understanding—particularly stories and narratives of those people of color who have experienced or responded to discrimination and oppression—to be embraced and acknowledged."[142] Lastly, Singer asserted that critical race theory affords students and scholars in sports management the tools required to reflect about their roles as critical scholars and fully understand who benefits from their work and to understand the challenges they may face in dealing with power programs within and external to sports organizations. In short, Singer's work "provided sport management scholars with an explication of the critical race theoretical framework as a starting point for demonstrating the significance of race and ethnicity."[143]

Douglas Hartmann, a professor at University of Minnesota, used critical race theory to examine a controversial issue involving Philadelphia Eagles quarterback Donovan McNabb and Rush Limbaugh during Limbaugh's short-lived career as a sports analyst for *Monday Night Football*.[144] The controversy was about much more than Limbaugh's comments that McNabb was not as good as many people thought and that the praise he received was due in large part to the desire of the media and the NFL to see black coaches and black quarterbacks do well. Specifically, Hartmann used the critical race theory perspective to ask and answer specific questions about whiteness and whiteness in sports.[145] Hartmann questioned "whether the leaders and opinion makers of the sporting establishment realized and repudiated Limbaugh's Whiteness and its associated supremacist functions as might be inferred from the eventual and seemingly decisive resolution of the controversy he provoked."[146] Hartmann raised the issue because reactions to Limbaugh's comments did not come swiftly. Moreover, Limbaugh was well known for making racially insensitive comments about people of color before joining ESPN. Hartmann investigated further what exactly was deemed wrong with what Limbaugh said and what it revealed about the roles of race, racism, whiteness, and white supremacy in modern-day sports. Hartmann concluded that "[t]he most basic purpose of focusing on media responses and public reactions to Rush Limbaugh's racially charged comments has been to illustrate this point— to show how deeply engrained and largely unrealized the discourses and ideologies that perpetuate white cultural power and social privilege are in the American sporting establishment and its attendant media."[147] He concluded that critical race theory was useful in its ability to force scholars to examine the various ways that whiteness "works to perpetuate the normativity of white world views and maintain the privileged position of whites, even without many whites realizing what is going on."[148]

In an article published in 2009, John Singer used critical race theory to examine the perspectives on institutional integrity in college sport for black football players. In the article, which appeared in *Research Quarterly for Exercise and Sport*, Singer defined institutional integrity as a sports program's measureable dedication to academic needs and interests of college students as evidenced in the way related programs function and are structured.[149] Singer considered the need for critically analyzing the role of race in college athletics, especially given the ongoing debates surrounding scholarships.[150] On the one hand, athletic scholarships are said to give athletes, including black athletes at predominantly white institutions, opportunities to earn a college degree that might otherwise be out of reach. However, there is often a gap between what athletic programs say they value and what they do. Singer added that the NCAA and other institutions have a financial interest in maintaining their relationships with the media and corporate America. As a result, it is not beyond the realm of possibility that "the educational interests of the athlete might be trumped by the financial and economic interests of those who run the college sport enterprise."[151] Some solutions include the elimination of athletic scholarships altogether, which is unlikely but does exist to a degree at the Division III, because the commercialization of sports at the Division I level is on the rise, and scholarships serve as bait to lure prospective prospects.

Singer employed the critical race theory framework because it places issues of race and racism as central to our understanding of how sports operate in American society and helps explain how and why black athletes continue to serve as a source of profit for many, both directly and indirectly.[152] Singer found the idea of interest-convergence as particularly important in understanding what some characterize as the exploitation of black male athletes in elite college programs. He described the principle as "a powerful interpretive and explanatory tool that provides great insight into how the integration of African-American male football players into these PWIs have served more in the best interests of the institutions themselves than in the interests of these students."[153] The principle was founded on the idea that people and institutions in positions of power do not always act in the best interest of marginalized groups, but rather act in accordance with "the 'what's in it for me' mentality. As a result, the driving force behind the recruitment of black male athletes into once-segregated programs was based primarily on economic factors, not on a moral desire to provide them with a meaningful educational experience."[154]

To examine the matter further, Singer wanted to know what black football players thought about institutional integrity in college sport and what strategies the players recommended to address issues related to institutional integrity in college.[155] The participants included Division I athletes in a nationally ranked program in the Midwestern region of the United States. Through one-on-one interviews and a focus group interview, Singer found that the black male football players he spoke with felt like slaves. The issues of race and racism were central to their college experiences.[156] They believed black male athletes were entitled to more financial support

than most received. They talked about the limitations placed on their earning capacity all the while that coaches, administrators, businesses, and
media outlets were free to make money off their play. The players also
described the need for spaces where black athletes could safely voice their
concerns, particularly around issues that would bring about institutional
change, all of which are illuminated when the light of critical race theory
is shone on the centrality of race and racism in sports.

Akilah Carter and Alegrian Hart, professors at Texas A&M University
and University of Nevada, Las Vegas, used critical race theory to expand
our understanding of the experiences of black female student-athletes.[157]
One of the features of critical race theory, as mentioned earlier in the chapter, is its attention to multiple jeopardies people might face. In the case of
black female athletes, black females must deal with marginalization based
on both race and gender. Access to mentors who can provide emotional,
psychosocial, and career and professional development to black female
student-athletes may lead to greater success in college and beyond for this
population. "It is shown merit elucidating the Black male collegiate athletic
experience; and the African American female collegiate athletic experience
and identity development," [158] but very little about the benefits of mentoring. Using a quantitative approach, which included the administration of
a survey instrument, Carter and Hart found that mentors were important
and often were biologically related to the black female athletes, and that
experiential knowledge reveals the centrality of athletic needs. The findings challenge dominant ideology and speak to the unique experiences
and needs of athletes with dual-majority group status. Critical race theory
revealed the challenges and hegemonic issues regarding the Black female
athletes' concept of mentor and points toward the need for structured
mentorship programs for student-athletes from historically marginalized
groups, particularly those with membership in more than one marginalized group.[159]

At a PWI in the southwest region of the United States, Albert Bimper,
Louis Harrison, and Langston Clark conducted a study of black male athletes who demonstrated success in sports and in their academic pursuits.[160]
In the article *Diamonds in the Rough*, published in *Journal of Black Psychology* in 2013, they used critical race theory as a framework for understanding self-perceptions and behaviors contributing to their ability to manage
roles as students and as athletes during their college experience.[161] Focusing
on the themes of complex identities, community, and liberation, the authors
examined the following tenets of critical race theory: the idea that race and
racism are deeply rooted in American society; the ideal that America is a

color-blind society, which should be challenged; and experiential knowledge, voice, and counter story are highly valued as a means to inform scholarship related to racial and ethnic minorities.

The purposes of the study by Bimper et al. were to understand how successful blacks student-athletes managed and constructed academic experiences; to explore how the athletes dealt with stereotypes; to explore perceptions of identity; and to examine factors perceived to have fostered academic success. The researchers conducted a qualitative study,[162] which included seven black male student-athletes ranging in age from 19 to 21. The student-athletes were from different majors, ranged in class level from a sophomore to a graduate student, and came from different family types and varying social class backgrounds. The researchers used purposeful sampling. They defined athletic success by looking at the athletes standing at the time of recruitment and they defined academic success using grade point averages of at least 3.0 and academic honors, such as being placed on the athletic director's list for maintaining a grade point average of at least 3.0 for two consecutive semesters.

Michael Regan, Akilah R. Carter-Francique, and Joe R. Feagin, researchers at University of Texas A&M University wrote about critically examined college sports in "Systematic Racism Theory: Critically Examining College Sport Leadership." Systematic racism theory is similar to critical race theory in its placement of race and racism as central to understanding how society works. Systematic racism theory identifies six main tenets, which Regan and his coauthors applied to college sport leadership. Whites' unjust enrichment and black Americans' unjust impoverishment is the first of the tenets. Predominantly white institutions of higher learning, according to the authors, function much like colonizers of portions of Africa with unpaid African labor. In the case of high-revenue-generating sports, not much is done to improve the quality of life for black athletes during or after their college careers; the governing body, the NCAA, is more concerned with revenues from the labor of student-athletes than justly compensating them; and "those who have been most adversely affected by the college athletic experience have been black student-athletes (e.g. racist stereotypes, coaches and athletic departments, unacceptable graduation rates)."[163]

A second tenet of systematic racism theory is racial hierarchy with divergent group interests, which is similar to the idea of interest-convergence in critical race theory. Here, Regan and his colleagues show how white economic elites used force to develop a system of racial oppression that predates the founding of the United States. The system was created and maintained with financial interests and later maintained by industrialists and political elites and by the extension of white privilege to lower-class whites. The unequal treatment blacks received is evidenced in sports, the authors claim. Furthermore, it is perpetuated in the racialized hierarchy of leadership in college sports, where whites occupy the majority of high-level, decision-making positions. For example, "White males currently hold a numerical majority of the athletic director roles (81.8 percent), followed by white females (7 percent), then black males (6.7 percent), and finally black females (0.7 percent)."[164]

The white racial frame is the third tenet. This tenet includes the common belief that whites are both superior and more virtuous than nonwhites and includes a strong anti-black subframe, which incorporates racial narratives, racist stereotypes and prejudices, racial images, racial ideologies, etc.) that were established hundreds of years ago and used to justify white supremacy as well as the oppression of nonwhites. The overrepresentation of whites in positions associated with intelligence, leadership, and interaction, and the marginalization of blacks away from such positions and minimizing their interaction with members of the dominant group, are evidenced of the white racial frame in society more broadly, but also in sports. The authors argued, "When white decision makers consistently concentrate themselves in leadership roles . . . their negative framing toward black Americans can serve as a mechanism to hinder black advancement, while improving the position of whites because them view themselves more positively."[165]

Social reproduction and alienation, extraordinary costs and burdens of racism, and resisting systematic racism are the remaining tenets of systematic racism theory. Social reproduction and alienation explain how economic inequality and privilege are perpetuated in our society. Inequality is embedded in society so that many whites underestimate their racial and social inheritance. Although whites have differentiated access to wealth, power, and privilege, Regan and his coauthors argue, "All whites have gained psychological benefits and other societal advantages (e.g., education, jobs, health care). When considering contemporary white numerical dominance in college sport leadership, it becomes apparent that such control has come about through white social reproduction."[166] The example provided by the authors includes leadership in Division I college football, where there have been almost 400 head football coach vacancies since the early 1980s, but people identifying their race as black filled less than 20 of those positions, representing less than 5 percent.

Extraordinary costs and burdens of racism refer to the significance of understanding the experiences of people of color in an attempt to understand racial oppression. These experiences can help to tell the stories that cannot be told just by looking at numbers, such as in the case of blacks applying for Division I coaching positions. Resisting systematic racism is the final tenet of systematic racism theory and arguably the most important. It is also the only way the authors find to bring about an end to racial oppression. Black demonstrations during the 1968 Mexico City Olympics to protest the oppression of people of color and of black student-athletes is one example of efforts to resist racial oppression in society and in sports. The threatened boycott by football players at University of Missouri in November 2015, in response to former President Tim Wolfe's response to racial incidences on campus, is a more recent high-profile example involving student-athletes in an elite program. Regan and his coauthors say it is critical that we as a society "recognize the institutional racism realities in sport" so that "sport will offer an equal playing field for all those who participate."[167]

Colorism

Still others argue critical race theory does not devote adequate attention to *colorism*, which sociologist, Cedric Herring defined as "the discriminatory treatment of individuals falling within the same 'racial' group on the basis of skin color. It operates both intra-racially and inter-racially."[168] Colorism "is historically contingent on supremacist assumptions. In the United States color preferences are typically measured against putative European (i.e., White) standards."[169]

Critical race theory has been used, almost exclusively, until recently, to understand the black/white dichotomy that has dominated American history since the foundation of the nation. The problem, as identified by scholars, is that although blacks may be disadvantaged relative to whites, blacks may not be equally disadvantaged. A substantial body of literature points to the advantages afforded light-skinned individuals relative to darker-skinned individuals.[170]

Colorism affects socialization practices within racial groups.[171] Moreover, colorism holds that "a person's skin will take on more importance in determining how she is treated by others than her ancestry."[172] Colorism is the result, by some, of a shift in the demographic composition of the nation away from the black-white dichotomy to a more multiracial continuum akin to the color gradient that is prevalent among people of varying skins tones in places throughout Latin and South America, as well as a change in racial ideologies—the web of ideas and beliefs about what it means to have membership in a particular racial group.[173] It is an indication that racism is not dead; rather, discussions surrounding racism are often minimized or diluted or rendered invisible. Harris views colorism as the next stage in the continuum of racialized social systems in America and further argues that colorism and racism are related, yet distinct.[174]

There is much to disagree with in the assertions made by Harris about colorism. First, the implication is that colorism is a relatively new phenomenon. We know that skin tone was used in antebellum America as a mechanism for creating discord and disharmony among enslaved and free black people.[175] Colorism can best be understood, as Cedric Herring conceptualizes it, as a manifestation of racism, not a replacement of it. Moreover, Angela Harris represents scholars who understand colorism to be an intragroup phenomenon. Some even refer to colorism as intragroup discrimination as it is devoid of any relationship to the larger set of processes by which racial groups are systematically oppressed and scapegoated by the dominant group. Herring correctly defines colorism as intra- and interracial. Claims such as those levied by Harris seek to equate tensions *within* racial groups with racism *between* whites and racial minority groups.

Colorism, despite differing views on what it is and is not, is an underutilized perspective in the social sciences. It is particularly underutilized in the analysis of race and sports. John Robst and colleagues conducted one of the few studies linking colorism and sports.[176] The researchers examined the effects of skin tone on wages of free agents in the National Basketball Association. They employed computer software to objectively determine the skin tone of the subjects. The researchers argue this methodological approach represents a departure from other studies on colorism that rely on the judgment of interviewers in determining where a respondent falls on the skin tone spectrum.[177]

The lack of understanding of the relationship between colorism and racism and the potential for bias in classifying subjects based on a sociopolitical construct may point to the need to revisit the perspective by developing more testable propositions with which to examine this form of intragroup and intergroup discrimination, particularly as it relates to the world of sports. Colorism is underutilized in understanding the roles of race and racism in sports, although there is some evidence of it in discussions about within- and between-group differences in endorsements, especially for professional female athletes. Although female athletes often received fewer paid endorsements or receive them at levels lower than their male counterparts, white female athletes may receive more endorsement and at higher levels than black female athletes and among black female athletes, skin-tone matters. Female athletes are often rewarded more for off the field characteristics, including their attractiveness, and historically the prototype of beauty includes Eurocentric as opposed to Afrocentric features. Although Mary Lou Retton, a white female gymnast, and Cheryl

Miller, a tall black basketball player, both won gold medals during the same Olympics, only one appeared on the cover of the coveted Wheaties box, and although Venus and Serena Williams are among the best tennis players to ever play the game, Maria Sharapova, a white professional tennis player, receives the most endorsements of all female tennis players and more than most female professional athletes regardless of their sports. Body shaming that black athletes, especially black female athletes, endure is related to colorism, as is what some consider the whitening of the NBA with international players from Central and Eastern Europe and the presence of high-profile, light-skin black players, such as Steph Curry and Blake Griffin.

Population and Structural Change Thesis

Missing from discussions about race and sports is an adequate treatment of the effects of population and structural change on various outcomes, including on the types of sports blacks and whites are drawn to and the association of specific sports with either blacks or whites. On the one hand, it is apparent that certain racial groups are overrepresented in some sports and underrepresented in others. Beyond exploring events that led to the integration of previously segregated sports, very little scholarly attention has been devoted to understanding the impact of population and structural changes, both inside and outside of the world of sports, on players, spectators, owners, and the like. Population changes might include an increase in the black population in a particular area or region, or the flight of whites from the central city to suburban areas within a metropolitan region. Structural changes might include changes in the economy that increase or decrease employment rates. Structural changes might also include alterations in investments in public education, low- or no-cost sports programs, or even the placement of open spaces and recreational facilities in various communities.

It is difficult to tackle any subject matter involving race without accounting for population and structural changes. The few studies that give these matters due treatment are far too often descriptive in nature and seldom use proven demographic techniques and frameworks for understanding the complex linkages between race and sports. Studies that help us understand the role of population and structural changes are valuable tools that should be widely used in sports studies, particularly if we wish to substantively address issues related to race.

Changes in both the minority population and the social structure, according to Horton and Allen, "interact to exacerbate racial inequality in society."[178] Looking at the effects of place and family structure on black family poverty, Horton and Allen argued that the existence of and the persistence of race as a predictor of black family poverty support the population and structural change thesis. Likewise, the existence and persistence of race as a predictor of a host of sport outcomes provides support for the population and structural change thesis, which has yet to be adequately explored in sports and leisure studies. The significance of this is quite clear.

Beyond the social realities of the sports world, population changes and changes to the social structure matter. As the size and composition of America changes—economically, politically, and culturally, not just in athletics—the effects of race in virtually all areas of society become even more salient, and manifestations of racism become more overt. For example, as predictions that American racial and ethnic minorities will one day become the numerical majority occur at the same time as an economic downturn or a change in the political winds, efforts to reestablish the myth of group superiority become more dominant. This can be seen in many areas of social life, not just in sports.

As the racial and ethnic minority population has increased, efforts to exert more control and authority over matters of criminal justice and education have increased. This is due in part to unfounded fears on the part of some members of the dominant racial group, especially those in the lower and working classes, that their historic position in society is being threatened. Draconian policies that have led to the overrepresentation of people of color in American prisons and in failing schools are just two examples. In the world of sports, population and structural changes have led to the institutionalization of white middle-class standards in the adoption of dress codes,[179] the stacking of players in positions by color,[180] and the existence of glass ceilings and glass walls when it comes to ownership and employment in decision-marking positions.[181] It has also led to the adoption of colorblind language, a topic addressed later in this chapter.[182]

Although the population and structural change thesis can inform research on race and sports, it too has some limitations. The population and structural change thesis does not fully account for variations within racial groups. Again, blacks may not be equally disadvantaged.[183] Skin tone, ethnicity, and social class position are all factors that have been shown to have significant effects on a host of sociological outcomes.[184] Much like critical race theory and the colorism perspective, the population and structural thesis aids in our understanding of race and sports but is limited in the ways outlined.

In her book *White Sports/Black Sports*, Dr. Lori Latrice Martin discusses stacking, or the segregation of players into certain positions based on race.

Professional baseball is a good example of nonwhites playing noncentral positions.[185] In baseball, the pitcher and catcher are considered central positions. Between 2005 and 2011, the percentage of white pitchers went from 69 to 66 percent while the percentage of black pitchers remained the same, at 3 percent. The data showed that one-third of pitchers were Latino in 2011, up from 26 percent in 2005. There was a 1 percent decrease in Asian pitchers; nearly 3 percent of pitchers were Asian in 2005, and only 2 percent were Asian in 2011.

In the case of catchers, between 2005 and 2011, most were white. In 2005, 62 percent of catchers were white compared to 1 percent black, 36 percent Latino, and 1 percent Asian. Six years later, the percentages of white and black players declined. At the same time, the percentages of Latino and Asian catchers increased. Fifty-six percent of catchers were white. There were no black catchers; 40 percent were Latino; and 2 percent were Asian.[186]

There was more diversity in the infielder and outfielder positions during this time period. Fewer than half of infielders and outfielders were white in 2005. By 2011, more than half of players in these positions were white. The percentage of black players was higher among outfielders than infielders. In 2005, 11 percent of infielders in the Major Leagues were black, but by 2011 the number had decreased to 8 percent. About 25 percent of outfielders in both 2001 and 2011 were black. Conversely, the percentages were highest for infielders who were Latino. In 2005, nearly 40 percent of infielders were Latino. About 35 percent of infielders were Latino in 2005. Martin's work also revealed that approximately one-fifth of outfielders in 2005 and 2011 were Latino. Asians made up about 2 percent of infielders and 3 percent of outfielders in 2005 and 2011. Stacking, argued Martin, may be the result of many factors. It may best be understood, as in the case of football, as a result of the social stratification of people by race and ethnicity in the United States. Racial socialization and stacking are connected. For a time, there was a widely held belief there are more costs associated with training for certain positions, such as pitcher, and that given the relative disadvantaged positions of racial and ethnic minority groups, it is not likely they will have the needed resources to train adequately and therefore select other positions on the field. Some young athletes prefer idols that have membership in their racial group, which may help to perpetuate the problem of racial stacking in sports. Baseball has long been considered by many, Martin argues, to be not only America's game but also a white game. The desire to keep the sport white is evident in data for positions in and around the field. In 1990, almost 80 percent of central-office personnel were white; 14 percent were black' and 7 percent were Latino.

None were Asian.* By 2000, 74 percent in this category were white; 14 percent were black; 14 percent were Latino; 2 percent were Asian; and 1 percent were Native American. By 2011, the percentage of people of color was nearly 32 percent, but the overwhelming majority of staffers were members of the dominant racial group in America. Although the Negro leagues offered blacks opportunities to own amateur and professional teams, ownership by blacks in the major leagues has proven to be much harder. In 2005, 31 of the 32 owners were white. There was one Latino owner in that year. In 2012, 96.4 percent of owners were white; less than 2 percent were black; and one majority owner (1.8% of the total) was Latino.[187]

Blacks and other racial and ethnic minorities seem to have problems crashing the glass ceiling where team managers are concerned. For much of the 1990s, nearly 90 percent of managers were white. By 2000, 83 percent were white; 13 percent were black; and 3 percent were Latino. Twelve years later, 83 percent of managers were white, and even fewer managers were black. Two of the 30 managers were black; none were Asian; and 3 were Latino.[188]

Between 1993 and 2012, white coaches, found Martin, made up between 69 and 80 percent of all coaches. The percentage of black coaches ranged between 12 and 18 percent. Latino coaches never constituted more than 21 percent, which was substantially higher than in the 1990s, when the percentage of Latino coaches was mostly in the single digits.[189]

Very few people of color served as the CEO or president in professional baseball between 1999 and 2012, said Martin. In 2004, one black person served in this capacity, but for every other year, 100 percent of the individuals who had the title of CEO or president were white. Likewise, between 1994 and 2012, over 80 percent of general managers or directors of player personnel, senior administrators, team professional administrators, vice presidents, physicians, and head trainers were white.[190]

Critical Demography

The critical demography paradigm addresses some of the shortcomings associated with critical race theory, colorism, and population and the structural change thesis in a manner that has yet to be explored. Established in 1999 by Dr. Hayward Derrick Horton, professor of sociology at University of Albany, State University of New York, the critical demography

---

*Numbers may not equal 100 due to rounding. Also, Hispanics may identify with any race.

paradigm offered a critique of conventional demography.[191] The founder of the critical demography paradigm observed that demographers were very reluctant to use racism as a concept of analysis, particularly demographers conducting research on race. Racism, after all, is a primary component of the social structure and is central to understanding population growth and development.[192]

The main strength of the critical demography paradigm is its ability to show how the social structure differentiates dominant and subordinate populations. To that end, the nature of power is an important part of the paradigm. Unlike in the case of critical race theory and colorism, *race* is not just central; rather, understanding *racism* is essential to any analysis involving minority and majority group relations.[193]

Much of the work conducted by American demographers, argues Horton, is descriptive, but the critical demography paradigm calls for scholarly works that are both explanatory and predictive. Critical demography also calls for analyses that are driven by theory, not data, and analyses that challenge the status quo. In conventional demography, the data speak for themselves, but with critical demography data are placed within an appropriate historical and social context to enhance our understanding of what the data mean and how they matter and enhance our understanding of the society in which we live. Furthermore, critical demography, unlike conventional demography, is reflexive and not assumptive. Critical demography calls on scholars to think critically about the sports or other areas of social life in a way that is based not on assumptions, but on careful introspective and after critically analyzing all of the potential internal and external forces that might be at work.

Scholars who are working in the area of sports and leisure studies should take note of an article in the journal *Perspectives* that includes a discussion among conventional demographers about the Civil Rights Movement.[194] It is observed that this period of social change and upheaval was treated by demographers as a historical event with little, if any, attention devoted to the demographic implications. The role of the Civil Rights Movement in growing the black middle class was not anticipated and studied substantively by conventional demographers, but could arguably have been predicted using a framework akin to the one developed by Horton.

Horton extols the use of the population and structural change thesis to aid in our understanding of the connection between changes in the size and composition of peoples and changes in the social structure and the effects of race on sociological outcomes. In the world of sports and beyond, we have seen that as the composition of players and spectators change, policy changes also. As the number of black players, particularly from economically disadvantaged backgrounds, increased, the number of white fans decreased,[195] and policy changes such as the dress code were established. Under the guise of making players dress more like the professionals that they are, arbitrary rules were instituted by Commissioner David Stern that were directed at the types of clothing common among black players and among urban black youth. Recruitment efforts also changed. Greater efforts to obtain international players in the National Basketball Association, particularly players from Europe, are evidenced by recent draft outcomes,[196] and it may be due, at least in part, to efforts to find the next Great White Hope for professional basketball.

In *White Sports/Black Sports,* Martin also discusses efforts to assimilate athletes, particularly in sports where racial and ethnic minority groups are more numerous and are well documented, and makes the case that the institution of dress codes at the college and the professional levels are great examples.[197] Martin writes about the response to the famed Fab Five at the University of Michigan and the implementation of a dress code in the NBA following a 2004 fight between members of the Detroit Pistons, Indiana Pacers, and fans.

The Fab Five of the 1991 University of Michigan's men's basketball team—Juwan Howard, Jimmy King, Ray Jackson Chris Webber, and Jalen Rose—were described as one the greatest classes ever recruited. They were both loved and hated for wearing baggy shorts, black socks, blasting hip hop music and trash talking. Two decades ago, the Fab Five were viewed as radical revolutionary players who were changing the game in a way that made many people uncomfortable. The starting five were the targets of negative media attention, where they were commonly viewed as thugs.

Martin observes that although many of the team enjoyed successful careers in the NBA, this group of talented young men, several of whom would go on to have stellar professional basketball careers, was vilified. In the ESPN *30 for 30* documentary series about the starting five, Jalen Rose described his experience as follows:

> People do view you based on your appearance and judge you based on that. If we're five black guys at the University of Michigan, and it's like, "You have the nerve to jump up in Christian Laettner's face and talk trash? He's God to us. You have black shoes, black socks, bald heads, long shorts?" Like, that's too much at one time. . . . It wasn't just the media; there were people who really had a sincere hatred because not only did they not like us, but they didn't want their kids to be like us.[198]

Decades later, David Stern, commissioner of the NBA, instituted a dress code in 2005 that some viewed as a move to appease members of the dominant racial group. John Eligon, writing for the *New York Times*, describes the business casual dress code as "the NBA's latest push to look a little less gangsta and a little more genteel." Stern claimed, according to Eligon, that "the reputation of our players was not as good as our players are, and we could do small things to improve that."[199]

Players were suddenly required to wear turtlenecks or shirts with collars at all team or league events and dress jeans, khakis, or slacks. The dress codes also called for players to wear dress shoes or boots with socks.

Many believed that the dress code had less to do with the clothes worn by the players and more to do with the reaction of whites in particular to a number of high-profile scandals, including the 2003 rape charges against Kobe Bryant and the 2004 fight between the Indiana Pacers and Detroit Pistons. Martin also cited the work of scholar David J. Leonard, author of *After Artest*, who noted that shortly after that fight, Stern and others in the league were concerned by the behavior of the 2004 Olympic basketball team, which was made up largely of players from the NBA. Described as "a significant embarrassment for the NBA in the wake of its efforts to conceal blackness from the league," the incident involved a dinner that was held to honor the team. Some members of the team showed up at the restaurant in sweat suits, oversized jeans and shirts, and large platinum chains. The dress code was therefore created in an effort to shape the image of the players in the white imagination.[200]

Martin also described a historical event leading up to the introduction of the dress code, the retirement of the greatest man to ever play the game, Michael Jordan, in 1993—the first of his three retirements. Jordan had such a tremendous impact on the league and the game, including economically, that when he walked away from the game, many fans walked away too. Rick Weinberg, writing in 1993, described the impact of Jordan's 1993 announcement this way: "Sadness and gloom filled the room as a city, a nation, and a league mourns. The impact of the NBA, television, attendance, competition, revenue, merchandise sales (other than MJ's jersey of course) is staggering. The man who generates billions for others is not going to cost them millions. There is no aspect of the league that Jordan's presence doesn't touch."[201] During the 1991–1992 season alone, economists estimate that Jordan generated over $52 million for the league. The loss of Michael Jordan and the search for the next "Great Black Hope" provide an excellent example of how, in the words of Kathleen S. Yep, "Liberal multiculturalism involves racial triangulation and the simultaneous processes of hyper-racialization and de-racialization."[202] Yep, highlights the issue of multiculturalism, or pluralism, which we understand as "a state in which people of all races and ethnicities are distinct but have equal social standing."[203]

The percentage of white players in the NBA, for example, decreased from the 1989–1990 season to the 2012–2013 season while the percentage of black players held relatively steady. The percentage of international players, many of them from European countries, increased during this very same period. During the 2003–2004 season, nearly 76 percent of the NBA was black. Just over 22 percent of players were white, and almost 17 percent were international. By the 2012–2013 season, the percentage of black players remained at about 76 percent while white players fell to 19 percent and foreign players increased to almost 19 percent.[204] Concerns over the loss of white viewers and attendance at NBA games were voiced as early as the 1970s, causing many to hail the arrival of Larry Bird in the early 1980s as the "Great White Hope." His rivalry with Magic Johnson helped to bring back fans that had walked away and even helped to attract new fans. Michael Jordan's superior play drew many white fans and white viewers who abandoned the game when Jordan retired, and the face of the game increasingly resembled a young black male with cornrows and tattoos, as personified in college players like Jaylen Rose at Michigan State and Allan Iverson of the Philadelphia 76ers.

The most important contribution of the critical demography paradigm to the sociology of sports in general, and the sociology of race and sports in particular, is the centrality of racism, not merely race, and the call for the operationalization of this oft-used concept.

A Critical Demography of Athletic Destinations

Martin and Horton pulled together the elements that critical race theory, colorism, population structural change thesis, and critical demography offer studies about racism and sports, and introduced a framework that contributes to the understanding of why people of selected racial groups end up participating in certain sports and how certain sports come to be associated with blacks and other sports with whites. Population and structural changes are important contributing factors that are often neglected. When these changes occur, and particularly when the minority population in a sport and/or in society increases and these increases are accompanied by structural changes (e.g., economic recession, change in political leadership at the federal level), overt manifestations of racism increase. Decline in attendance and viewership, and the institutionalization of policies and procedures targeting historically marginalized groups, are just a few examples.

A critical demography approach to understanding the choices blacks and whites make concerning sports, and the choices that are made *for* blacks and whites concerning sports participation, makes it clear that not only is *race* important, as seen in critical race theory, but *racism* is at the core of all analyses. It can be shown that colorism is not understood as the latest iteration of racism; instead, colorism is itself a manifestation of racism. Population changes matter—whether inside or outside of sports— as do changes in the social structure, such as increases in unemployment, political mistrust, or unrest. Critical demography, with its ability to account for power, is an important paradigm that can and should inform debates about the intersections between racism and sports.

A critical demography of sports participation by race incorporates the following principles:

1. Racism is a central feature of American social systems.
2. Racism is institutional.
3. Institutions, and the groups and individuals that make them up, reproduce these systems through social practices and policies.
4. Members of the dominant group receive unmerited privileges while members of subordinate racial minority groups receive unequal treatment.
5. Racism remains part of the our social system, changing in form, but not function.

Racism is a central feature of sports in America. From the very first time blacks and whites both put on the gloves or picked up a ball, participants were largely separated by race. Blacks were not permitted from racing horses or competing in cycling. Throughout much of American history, blacks could not attend predominantly white colleges, and very few placed for such institutions prior to the mid-1970s. Racism is merely reflected in the behaviors and attitudes of ignorant players, coaches, owners, and fans, but it is institutionalized. Policies have long been in place that privilege some racial groups and disadvantage others. Social practices and policies are reproduced in sports, although, given changes in the society at large, the manifestations of the practices and policies may be harder to detect over time. Acts of racism, even in sports, may become more subtle in the post–Civil Rights Movement era.

Using the critical demography of sports participation by race perspective, we can see how racism was central in determining when, where, and how people of various races participated in and consumed sports. In the case of the U.S. Congress banning the showing of boxer Jack Johnson's fight films in the early part of the 20th century, and in the one of wealthy team owners who set the rules about who was eligible to play based on race, we can see how federal officials were able to exert their will over the society at large, but particularly over the black population, despite opposition, including individual and collective protests, the creation of parallel institutions, and even the use of the courts.

Conclusion

This chapter presented an analysis of the various ways in which blacks in general and black athletes in particular have been criminalized and exploited over time for the benefits of people in positions of power. The chapter also included a discussion about some of the dominant perspectives showing the roles that race and racism have played and continued to play in our society and in the world of sports. Critical race theory is among the most commonly used perspectives for understanding how race and racism matter in the broader society and sports. Colorism, population and structural change thesis, and the critical demography perspective were also shown to provide important insights as to the experiences of such historically marginalized groups as black male and female student-athletes in elite college programs. A unified theoretical perspective was set forth also. In the next chapter, we turn our attention to two contemporary issues: one highlights the principle of interest-convergence and the other, the theoretical perspectives that point to black male student-athletes as laborers fighting against an entire industry controlled by a powerful group who is concerned more about the bottom line than the players in any given line-up.

CHAPTER SIX

Current Controversies: An Analysis of the Northwestern and O'Bannon Cases

Disagreements between laborers, managers, and owners are not new. In this chapter, we explore the history of the labor movement in America from Antebellum America until the present day. We discuss the important roles labor unions played in securing many of the benefits average workers enjoy today. Next, we examine the antiunion sentiment that is sweeping the nation, as evidenced by right-to-work legislation, the replacement of veteran workers with under-qualified temporary workers, and outright policies that discourage union membership. Then, we explore the similarities and differences between sports unions and traditional unions. We detail the work stoppages—both strikes and lockouts—for professional sports teams, and then we explore two significant efforts by former and current college players to level the playing field where amateur athletics are concerned. The 2009 O'Bannon decision and the effort on the part of football players at Northwestern to union are outlined. We begin with a brief history.

A Brief History of the Labor Movement in America

The AFL-CIO identifies a host of significant dates, people, and events in the history of labor in the United States. Labor disputes predate the founding of the nation. As early as 1607, English planters in the newly founded Jamestown colony complained about a lack of laborers. By 1664, laws on the books declared African servants to be perpetual slaves. In 1676, black and white indentured servants and slaves in Virginia organized a rebellion, and in the year that followed the first recorded mistreatment of strikers in New York City was recorded. Striking printers in Philadelphia organized the first successful strike that lead to increased wages for workers. Resistance efforts by slaves characterized much of the period the AFL-CIO describes as the struggle for freedom (1800–1865).

During the Progressive Era, the AFL-CIO highlights a 1909 strike of women workers in sweatshops in New York City against poor working conditions and the sentencing of Industrial Workers of the World sentenced to federal prison for being disloyal to the United States. The Great Depression provided perhaps the best evidence of the ills of capitalism. This period that AFL-CIO refers to as "Repression and Depression," includes the passage of the 1926 Railway Labor Act, which created a framework for resolving labor disputes in the railroad industry and banned discrimination against union members. Although the Great Depression hit all Americans hard, in many ways black workers were already experiencing harsh economic times. President Hoover did little to address the plight of workers, including black workers, and they did not fare much better under Franklin D. Roosevelt. The alphabet soup of organizations Roosevelt established to help the nation's struggling workers did not address racial discrimination.

Economic times eventually improved for the nation as a whole, but blacks continued to lag behind whites:

> The World War II period introduced new industrial opportunities, the Double V Campaign, and the March on Washington Movement, which led to the creation of the Federal Fair Employment Practices Committee. Led by A. Philip Randolph, blacks joined forces and threatened a march on the nation's capital, which prompted Roosevelt to issue Executive Order 8802, banning racial discrimination in government employment, defense industries, and training programs. It also led to the establishment of the Fair Employment Practices Committee.[1]

By 1938, labor unions were successful in getting the passage of the Fair Labor Standards Act, which established the very first minimum wage and the 40-hour workweek that is today the national standard for many. Between 1946 and 1969, the AFL-CIO points to the passage of the Taft-Hartley Act, which placed limitations on the activities of union members.

The 1970s was a period where corporate interests took precedents over workers' rights. In the period AFL-CIO calls "Progress and New

Challenges," the Occupational Safety and Health Act was passed and the Coalition of Black Trade Unionists was formed. Likewise, in the early 1970s the Labor Council for Latin American Advancement and the Coalition of Labor Union Women were founded. The negative attitude toward workers continued into the 1980s as evidenced in the government's role in the PATCO strike. Magdoff and Foster describe Reagan's action as "a major blow to the prestige and power of organized labor." In 1981, President Reagan ended a strike by air traffic controllers.

In more recent years, AFL-CIO points to massive movements by labor unions to protest the Free Trade of the Americas and calling for living wages in communities across the country. In 2007, Congress passed the Employee Free Choice Act, which gave workers, not management, more power in determining whether to organize. Two years later, President Obama addressed pay discrimination when he signed the Lilly Ledbetter Fair Party Act.

Despite the many accomplishments of the labor movement over time, there is continued evidence of persistent antiunion sentiments. For example:

> Union membership peaked in 1979 at an estimated 21 million and was about 16 million in 2003. In 1954, 28 percent of employed workers were union members. In 2003, 15 percent of employed workers were union members. Union membership is important in that union wages are often higher than nonunion wages. Union members tend to enjoy greater benefits, longer job tenure, and lower quit rates. Males, whites, and individuals who are middle-aged, work in the private sector, and have a high school degree or some college are more likely to be union members than others.[2]

Data also reveal that the "level of union membership was greater among white workers than black workers in 2003, 15.6 percent of black workers were union members compared to 11 percent of white workers." According to the Bureau of Labor Statistics, the union membership rate in 2013 was 11 percent. About 15.5 million workers belonged to unions in 2013. Men had higher union membership rates than women. The union membership rate for male workers was nearly 12 percent, compared to about 10 percent for female workers. Black workers were more likely to be union members than white, Asian, or Hispanic workers. Faced with continued discrimination in the labor market, it is not surprising that black workers would seek the protection of labor unions more often than others. Likewise, given the fact that public-sector workers had a union membership rate that was five times greater than the rate for private-sector workers and the fact that blacks are often overrepresented in the public sector versus the private sector, it is not surprising that black union membership is so high. Teachers' unions, state and municipal workers' unions, and trade unions like the Coalition of Black Trade Unionists represent many black workers.[3]

Unfortunately, black workers have historically—and in contemporary times—faced barriers to forming and joining unions causing groups like the AFL-CIO to create a commission to look at how best to address issues of race by member unions. The impetus for the creation of the commission were the days of unrest in Ferguson, Missouri, following the killing of an unarmed black male, Michael Brown, by a white police officer, Darren Wilson. The killing revealed the racial divide that some believed no longer existed, including among members of the AFL-CIO. The unrest also revealed persistent racial disparities in union membership in the Greater St. Louis area. Racial differences in wages, promotions, and union membership may impact how well workers with members in different racial groups bargain collectively, but there is another issue facing unions and workers today, and that is what appears to be a very pervasive and growing antiunion sentiment throughout the country.

Antiunion Sentiment

Antiunion sentiments are evident not only in the decline of union membership in some cases but also in the public policy aimed at diminishing the collective power of workers, such as right-to-work legislation, which has a long and storied history in this country.

In more contemporary times, people like Governor Scott Walker of Wisconsin were banking on their antiunion sentiments to propel them to higher office. In an article appearing in *Newsweek* on April 8, 2015, by Nina Burleigh, attacks on organized labor by Republican politicians are outlined.[4] In Illinois, Governor Bruce Rauner called on municipalities within his state to create areas where workers in unionized jobs could opt out of paying dues to the union. Burleigh describes Rauner as "part of a clique of Midwestern Republican governors challenging unions in a region where behemoths like the United Auto Workers and massive public employee unions covering teachers and other state employees have dominated."[5] Burleigh adds that in 2011, Walker "diminished the power of the state's public employee unions in 2011 by pushing through a law that cut their benefits and limited their collective bargaining power."[6]

Walker's move to harm workers through an assault on their collective bargaining power famously led to a recall effort, which seemed to make him more popular among Republicans nationally and motivated other elective officials who share his views in the Great Lakes area. Soon the governor of Michigan, Rick Snyder, made his state a right-to-work state, as did Mitch Daniels, then governor of Indiana. In March 2015, Walker joined the ranks and signed a law that made Wisconsin the nation's 25th right-to-work state.[7]

Walker, Rauner, and Snyder are not only misleading people by using the term "right-to-work," but they are also attempting to convince workers in general—and the American public more specifically—that unions are inherently evil, and any attempts to collect dues to finance the work of fighting against capitalist elites is anti-American. The governors and other proponents of right-to-work legislation use the term "forced unionism." The use of the word "forced" implies that workers are being denied a particular freedom to do or not do something, and framing the issue in that manner appears to violate some of the most basic principles that Americans hold so dear, namely, fairness, freedom, choice, and liberty. The governors express little interest in helping workers to understand that even when they are not actively engaged in union activities, they are nonetheless beneficiaries of the victories. These victories are far more likely to occur through collective bargaining than through individual workers seeking redress from persons holding the means of production and from the elected officials, who are often beholden to those persons because of both personal and political ties. The idea that workers who do not pay dues should not reap the benefits of the labor of someone who has taken the bulk of the risks is also an American value. However, the ability of governors and corporate elites to use their bully pulpits and the threat of retribution against union members is a position that is difficult to counteract. In short, Rauner's strategy is "setting fires in small towns" around antiunion sentiment and "surely inflame the union."[8]

Burleigh adds that there are questions about the legality of the right-to-work zones.[9] The level of authority sought by Rauner and others is typically reserved for states, not for towns.

Roland Zullo, research scientist at the Institute for Labor and Industrial Relations at University of Michigan, lays out the arguments for and against the right-to-work movement.[10] Supporters of the right-to-work legislation make the case that such laws attract business and promote growth. Zullo finds a lack of consensus among scholars and other analysts to support claims that right-to-work policies lead to increased investments into communities.[11] The economic problems in Michigan, according to Zullo, are the result of the problems plaguing the automobile industry, for which right-to-work laws do not provide a remedy.[12]

Another key argument for supporters of right-to-work laws is the ideal that no one should be forced to give money against his or her will. The term "right-to-work" in the appropriate context means "the right to work in a unionized setting, and reap the benefits of collective representation, without having to contribute toward the cost of obtaining those benefits."[13] The unearned benefits might include wages that are substantially higher than nonunionized workers. Beyond the economic benefits, there are also provisions of due process. "Nearly all union contracts feature an informal form of the due process: a grievance procedure that ends in final and binding arbitration through which unions resolve disputes over contracts and employer discipline."[14] Nonunionized workers who are employed at the pleasure or at the will of the employer can be terminated without case, and workers have little, if any, recourse.

Antiunion sentiments can also be found within some of the nation's largest corporations. Walmart is one example. Walmart has over 11,000 stores in 27 countries and employs over 2 million people. If Walmart were a country, it would be the twenty-sixth largest economy in the world.[15] A quarter of every dollar spent on groceries in America is spent at a Walmart. About 90 percent of Americans live less than 20 miles from a Walmart. The company has taken direct and indirect measures to prevent their workers from organizing.[16]

History of Unions in Sports

Sports do not operate in a vacuum. Sports are very much a reflection of the larger society. The treatment of American laborers, of black laborers, is both similar to and different from the treatment of amateur and professional athletes who are treated as a special class of workers. The possibility of college athletes—or even undergraduate college students—unionizing seems like a foreign concept to many Americans, but sports unions and sport-related labor negotiations are not recent inventions. In the late 19th century, a group of baseball players joined forces to fight for better wages and became known as the Brotherhood of Professional Base Ball Players. The union was short-lived, and it would be many decades before another professional sports union was formed. Major League Baseball players established a union in 1953. The players "wanted security—higher wages, a pension plan, pay when they were unable to perform due to injury sustained on the job, and compensation for extra work such as exhibition games."[17]

Unions for professional athletes have a lot in common with traditional unions, which may be contrary to popular opinion. Most scholars (and laypersons) may point to the fact that athletes tend to use their collective bargaining power to fight the reserve clause to obtain free market outcomes, whereas traditional workers are viewed as attempting to circumvent the market for higher wages.

There are other similarities and differences between players unions and traditional unions. The researchers describe the Clayton Act of 1914, which granted exemptions from antitrust laws to professional baseball. Unions were generally permitted to negotiate wages, which reduce competition between laborers as long as they do so singly in the context of collective bargaining negotiation. Traditional unions sought to limit subcontracting. Free agency, which did away with the practice that gave teams exclusive rights in negotiating with a player once his contract expired, became a feature in all of the four major sports between 1976 and 1996, which resulted in the relatively high salaries we associate with elite players in professional sports. In addition to free agency, lockouts and strikes were important features in the history of labor relations in professional sports.

Lockouts are a tool used by management and owners to enforce the terms of labor contracts or to try to force workers to accept change, whereas strikes are used by employees and players to bring attention to demands outlined in the midst of labor disputes and/or negotiations. According to a timeline put together by the cable news network CNN, the players' union for professional football players voted to strike in 1968, and the owners responded by locking the players out during training camp, representing the first such sports labor action. The owners and the players' association eventually reached an agreement on pensions. This was the first collective bargaining agreement for the league. Two years later, there was another lockout during training camp, which prompted players to go on strike, resulting in a nearly $20 million deal.

In 1974, there was a 41-day strike that ended without an agreement. There were two strikes in the 1980s about revenue sharing and free agency. CNN reports no work stoppages in the 1990s, which the National Football League made up for during the 2000s, especially during 2011. The collective bargaining agreement was extended and included a mechanism for sharing nearly $9 billion in revenue. Owners received $1 billion off the top, and the players shared three-fifths of the revenue stream. After a little more than two years, the owners of the professional football teams voted to end the agreement after the 2010–2011 season. By 2011, the players and owners of the National Football League were involved in federal mediation. Negotiations quickly broke down, which resulted in players not only walking out but also decertifying the union. The purpose of the decertification was to allow the players to file an antitrust lawsuit against the league. Another lockout began on March 12, 2011, and the ruling was in favor of the players. Despite an appeal by the owners, the 136-day lockout eventually ends, and the players and owners agree to a 10-year collective bargaining agreement.

The 1990s was a particularly active period in the history of labor disputes for the National Basketball Association (NBA). NBA owners locked players out for a period of 80 days because of a dispute over salaries between July 1 and September 18, 1995. The players were dissatisfied with their representation. An agreement was eventually reached, and it involved a six-year deal, involving some $5 billion. Three years later, there was a lockout over collective bargaining that lasted for almost 200 days. In July 2011, a 161-day lockout ended when the owners and players reached a decade-long collective bargaining agreement. During the labor dispute, the owners claimed that the players' union engaged in an unfair labor practice, and entered into federal mediation. Like the NFL players, the NBA players also disbanded in order to file a class-action antitrust suit. More than 300 games were cancelled in 2011.

Professional hockey players went on strike once between the early 1990s and 2015 and were locked out three times. National Hockey League (NHL) players went on strike in April 1992 and were locked out for more than 100 days during the 1994–1995 season. As a collective bargaining agreement was to expire in 2004, NHL owners locked out the players, and the entire 2004–2005 season was cancelled. The lockout eventually ended with a deal that included salary caps and a limit on spending. By the time the collective agreement bargaining agreement was to expire in 2012, there was a lockout. A Memorandum of Understanding was reached in the early part of 2013, ending the lockout.

The league that started the unionization of professional sports, Major League Baseball (MLB), experienced five strikes and three lookouts between the early 1970s and 2015. Pensions and arbitration led to a strike in 1972 that lasted about two weeks. Lockouts also occurred in 1973 and 1976 around issues of free agency and reentry drafts. Reentry drafts occur annually and allow teams to select players who are not currently under contract with a team. . During the 1980s, there was a strike about free agency and a strike in 1985 about just how much owners should contribute to player pensions. By 1990, there was a lockout around the issue of revenue sharing, salary cap, and salary arbitration.

Revenue sharing refers to the distribution of losses and profit among players and owners. In 2014, according to Sporting News.com, NFL teams shared about 60 percent of total revenues the leagues generates.[18] Each franchise keeps its suite, club seating, and sponsorship revenues from naming rights and other properties. The MLB, the NBA, and the NHL all share national television revenues. A salary cap is an arrangement that places limits on the amount of money a team can spend on the salary of players. The limit is a per-player or a team limit for a given team, or both. Teams that go over the limit may be fined, lose draft picks, or lose contracts. According to SB Nation.com, Major League Baseball is the only league that does not have a salary cap.[19] In 2014, the Los Angeles Dodgers spent more than any other team in the MLB on players, spending more than $235 million on players, which was five times more than the Houston Astros. The salary cap for Jacksonville Jaguars, an NFL team, was over $168 million compared to the salary cap for the Cleveland Browns, an NFL team with a salary cap of about $162 million. According to the Salary Arbitration in Sports Conference, only the NHL and MLB use salary arbitration to determine players' salaries. The process is guided by a set of rules and involves experienced agents and practitioners. *USA Today* published an article on February 16, 2016, about MLB salary arbitration. More than 150 players filed for salary arbitration. When players and teams are unable to agree on a salary, they participate in arbitration hearings.

Five years later, salary caps were an issue again and resulted in a lockout. A 232-day strike resulted from a dispute over the salary cap. The playoff and World Series schedules were missed during the 1994–1995 season. Players threatened to strike again in 2002, but a settlement was reached. "The deal marks the first time in the last 30 years that a collective bargaining agreement between players and owners was reached without a work stoppage."[20] A new agreement was reached in 2011 that included testing for performance-enhancing drugs, increasing the number of teams in the playoffs, and the eventual movement of the Astros from the National to the American League.

Small Victories: From O'Bannon to Northwestern

The year 2009 was a significant year in the history of amateurism in America, especially as it relates to collective action and controlling one's own destiny. In 2009, Ed O'Bannon, a former standout in basketball at UCLA took historic action. O'Bannon did not set out to fundamentally change college sports. According to an article in *Washington Times*, published on February 19, 2014, O'Bannon was innocently visiting a friend at the friend's home. Someone in the house was playing a video game, when O'Bannon noticed that one of the players in the game looked very familiar. The player had a bald head, was left-handed, played forward, and was wearing a UCLA uniform. The image was obviously O'Bannon's own likeness. There was O'Bannon leading his team to the national championship in 1995, the first one in more than two decades. O'Bannon described his reactions to seeing his likeness in the game in the article "Ex-UCLA star selling cars, taking on NCAA over pay," and the emotions ranged from surprised to flattered, to embarrassed, to feeling cheated. O'Bannon quickly came to the realization that the NCAA and Electronic Arts were making money off his image and that he and other current and former athletes depicted in the game were getting nothing.

O'Bannon sells cars at a Toyota dealership in a suburb of Las Vegas. After leading UCLA to the national championship and a 32–1 season, he was drafted ninth by the New Jersey Nets. He played three seasons for the Nets and for the Dallas Mavericks. He also played for seven years on teams in Europe and South America. Married to a school counselor and now the father of three children, he not only sells cars but also coaches his son's high school baseball team.

Like the majority of former student-athletes, including those who played in elite programs and in high-revenue-generating sports, O'Bannon was doing something other than playing the game he loved. According to statistics generated by the NCAA, more than 460,000 athletes compete in college sports, but very few go on to play professionally or in the Olympics. Data are calculated to show the figures for NCAA athletes, based on the number of available draft slots in the NFL, NBA, Women's National Basketball Association (WNBA), MLB, NHL, and Major League Soccer (MLS) drafts only, and are referred to as percent NCAA to Major Pro. Percent NCAA to Total Pro includes other professional opportunities for NCAA athletes, including Canadian Football League, Arena Football, NBA D-League, and international opportunities. The results for 2015 showed that although 71, 291 athletes played football, less than 16,000 were eligible for the draft, and there were only 256 draft lots. The percentage of NCAA athletes to Major Pro was 1.6 percent, and the percentage of NCAA athletes to Total Pro was 3.7 percent. In the case of men's basketball, there were over 18,000 NCAA athletes, and about 4000 of those athletes were draft eligible to fill 60 draft slots. Less than 50 NCAA athletes were drafted in 2015. The percentage of NCAA to Major Pro for men's basketball was 1.2 percent, and the percentage of NCAA to Total Pro was 11.6 percent. The NCAA report points out that the likelihood of earning a college degree is far greater and touts its graduation success rates for Division I (84%), in Division II (72%) and in Division III (87%).

A Gallup-Purdue Index Report examined the outcomes of former NCAA student-athletes and also identified many benefits related to participation in college-level sports. In the report, "Understanding Life Outcomes of Former NCAA Student-Athletes," the findings from a survey of four-year college graduates are presented.[21] Gallup interviewed 1670 former NCAA student-athletes about their lives and compared the findings with about 23,000 non-student-athletes who graduated from the same institutions. The NCAA was interested in knowing how former student-athletes and non-student-athletes compared on a number of measures of well-being, and the NCAA wanted to know if there were differences on the measures of well-being for former student-athletes who played football and men's basketball relative to other sports. Gallup focused on three categories: Great Lives: Well-Being; Great Jobs: Workplace Engagement; and Great Experience: Alumni Attachment. The results showed that more than 80 percent of former student-athletes were employed either full-time or part-time at their desired level compared to 78 percent of non-student-athlete graduates. The report also showed that the rates of unemployment were similar for student-athletes and non-student-athletes (3%). Gallup also found that former student-athletes and non-student-athletes reported similar rates when asked about their financial well-being. Thirty-eight percent of former student-athletes said they were thriving financially compared to 37 percent of non-student-athletes. The percentage of former football and men's basketball players who said they were thriving financially was 38 percent compared to 39 percent of former student-athletes in other sports. The report did not provide comparisons based on the race of the players.[22]

Not everyone is celebrating the NCAA's record on graduation rates and life after college sports, precisely because of the differences in the experiences of student-athletes of color. The Center for Study of Race and Equity and Education at Penn State examined the experiences of black male student-athletes and racial inequities in NCAA Division I college sports in a report authored by researchers Shaun Harper, Collin D. Williams Jr., and Horatio Blackman.[23] Harper and his colleagues offered a four-year analysis of black men's representation on football and basketball teams relative to their representation in the undergraduate student body on one of the 76 institution members in the six athletic conferences of the NCAA (the ACC, Big East, Big 12, Pac 12, and SEC). The scholars also compared black male student-athletes across four cohorts to student-athletes overall, undergraduate students overall, and black undergraduate men overall at each institution. Among the most compelling findings, the results showed that across the four cohorts (2007–2010), half of black male student-athletes graduated within six years, compared to nearly 67 percent of student-athletes overall, nearly 73 percent of undergraduate students overall, and 55.5 percent of black undergraduate men overall. More than 965 of NCAA Division I colleges and universities graduated black male student-athletes at rates lower than student-athletes overall. More than 97 percent of institutions graduated black male student-athletes at rates lower than undergraduate students overall.

Graduation rates vary by institution and conference. Harper, Williams, and Blackman found that the graduation rate for black male student-athletes were well below 40 percent at some institutions. The graduation rates for black male student-athletes across the four cohorts were 37 percent at University of Minnesota; 36 percent at Mississippi State University, Arizona University and Indiana University; 34 percent at Florida State University and University of Florida; and 31 percent at University of Arkansas, University of Arizona, and University of South Florida. Iowa State University had the lowest black male student-athlete graduate rate at 30 percent.[24]

The comparisons within the conferences revealed even more startling findings. In the Atlantic Conference, which includes such teams as Duke University and University of Virginia, black male student-athlete graduation was lower than all student-athlete graduation at each institution. The percentage difference was very small at University of Miami (1%), and relatively large at places like Virginia Polytechnic Institution & State University (19%), University of Virginia (20%), Clemson University (22%), and Florida State University (23%).

A coauthor of this book, sociologist and author of *White Sports/Black Sports* Lori Latrice Martin, wrote about dreams of many black male student-athletes, who hope to improve their lot in life, and that of their family, through their athletic abilities.[25] Some of these young men are successful at attaining their dreams, and others fall very short and hard from athletic grace. Martin observed that we could look at the news reports, biographies, and autobiographies of some of the nation's most talented athletes to understand the details players' desires to make it big and improve the socioeconomic position of themselves and their families. The media is filled with accounts of how a particular neighborhood sports legend did or did not realize their athletic goals. One example is that of a former top college basketball player, Mark Lyons of the University of Arizona. Lyons, born and raised in the Hamilton Hill section of Schenectady, New York, is a phenomenal athlete. He attended one of the nation's top prep schools and was also a standout at Xavier University in Ohio, before joining the squad in Arizona.[26] The news reports highlighted all of the obstacles Lyons faced growing up in a crime-ridden section of New York's capital region. Lyons's father died in a crash, reportedly running from police, when Lyons was just 15 months old. When Lyons was 10 years old his aunt was brutally killed by a boyfriend in Lyons's home. Lyons expressed a desire to "go pro" and make enough money to get his mother and the family out of their Hamilton Hill neighborhood.

Lyons's story is not unique, particularly among young black males with aspirations of playing sports professionally. The film *Hoop Dreams* follows two talented players in the Chicago area in the 1990s. Basketball prodigies Arthur Agee and William Gates grew up in economically disadvantaged neighborhoods where drugs, poverty, and violence were all too common.[27] Arthur Agree was obsessed with Isaiah Thomas and had hoped to use basketball to help his family—who were struggling to keep their lights on and food on the table—achieve a better life. Agee and Gates had to travel hours to and from their under-resourced neighborhood to an affluent school to receive the type of professional coaching and develop the social capital required to make it to the next level. Conversely, the high schools that most black youth attended were not only under-resourced, but athletic competitions were seen as places of potential violence. A win or a loss could result in a violent episode. The lack of academic rigor at these schools also meant that the student-athletes were ill-prepared for success in high school or college. In fact, when Agee and Gates got to the elite school, they were reading several grade levels lower than they should have been.

Martin also described the life of Bronx legend Allen Christopher Jones in her book, *White Sports/Black Sports*, as another good example of the fixation on stories of talented young black males seeking to use sports as a vehicle to leave under-resourced and sometimes violent and drug-ridden neighborhoods.[28] Jones recently published a memoir in which he highlights how basketball helped him leave a neighborhood that was rapidly changing. *The Rat That Got Away*, however, is much more than a memoir.[29] Sure, within its pages one can read about a youngster's transition from boyhood to manhood. One can also read about a sojourn from the hallways of Paterson Houses in the Bronx to legendary outdoor basketball courts, to the floors of financial institutions in Europe. Equally significant are the author's reflections about a host of issues of interest to scholars and laypersons alike. These issues include neighborhood change; the influence of various agents of socialization such as family, peers, and religion; the impact of social movements on local communities; variations in the quality of education by race and place; culture shock; the challenges facing student-athletes; delinquency; and even identity formation.

As Allen Jones begins his tale, we find the Paterson Houses as a place friendly to families. It began as a multiracial, multiethnic, mixed socioeconomic community with dual-headed households employed in an array of occupations. As time passes, the Paterson Houses becomes a very different place. The change from a stable to a distressed community is attributed to a number of factors, including white flight, the exodus of middle-class blacks, drug use, and drug abuse.

Martin added that as Jones comes of age during some of the most tumul-
tuous times in modern American history, the 1960s and 1970s. Jones and
his peers lived through the Civil Rights Movement, the black power movement, the antiwar movement, neighborhood blight, and drug epidemics.
He, like many others, did not come out unscathed.[30]

As the nation struggled, Allen struggled. His struggles were both internal and external, both personal and communal. Although raised in the
Catholic faith, Jones would soon stray from the church's teachings. Fortu-
nately, basketball was Allen's saving grace. It opened doors of opportunity,
and Allen eventually walked through to become a professional player and
a success in the financial industry. The former church boy exchanged his
devotion to the church for "street credibility," which ultimately led to petty
theft, a heroin addiction, and a stay in one of New York City's most notorious penal institutions.

Although his nation, his neighborhood, and Jones himself experienced
a lot of changes, his one constant was his love for basketball. Jones was a
gifted athlete, and like many young people today he had dreams of becoming a professional athlete. Unlike many of them, however, basketball was
not his immediate ticket out of a distressed community; rather, basketball
in some ways kept him connected to it. Allen gained street credibility for
his athletic abilities, his association with criminal elements in the community, and his own reputation for engaging in illegal activities ranging
from drug use and abuse to robberies.

Having gained a great deal of respect from many people in his neighborhood, Martin says, a great commodity in the Paterson Houses and other
distressed communities, Allen Jones was treated with the utmost respect
by individuals—the hustlers and dealers—who were contributing to the
decline of the quality of life in the community. At the same time, the star
treatment he received left him ill prepared for the "real world," for the world
outside the Paterson Houses.[31]

Because of the special treatment that Allen Jones received as an elite basketball player, he bought into the notion that as long as he excelled in
athletics, little else would be expected of him. This clearly conflicted with
the expectations that his parents had for him and the expectations he'd
once had for himself. This attitude cost Allen tremendously. He was under
the mistaken belief, like far too many student-athletes, that he would just
get a pass through life; that teachers and professors would promote him
regardless of his academic performance. Needless to say, Allen Jones did
not receive the quality education that facilitates admission into one of the
colleges connecting to the professional athletics pipeline. This was partly
Allen's fault, as well as a failure on the part of the educational system. Allen,

like some other student-athletes, forgot that he was a student first and an athlete second.

Once Jones realized the importance of excelling on and off the court, his eyes widened and his universe expanded. This was evidenced by the culture shock he experienced. Allen Jones did not need to go to Europe to experience culture shock; like many students of color on predominantly white college campuses today, he experienced culture shock without ever leaving the United States.

Jones's basketball talent enabled him to attend a junior college hundreds of miles from where he grew up. He was surprised by the disparities in wealth he witnessed and how badly prepared he was for academic success. The difference in the levels of wealth between the faculty and students at the college and the people living in and around Paterson Houses was very apparent. Moreover, Allen Jones was shocked at the audacity shown by some white students in their drug use, as compared to the secrecy, paranoia, and covert use he had witnessed in the more distressed community where he had grown up. Allen was becoming acutely aware of the benefits associated with what some scholars call "white privilege."

Allen Jones, like many young people living in distressed communities that are often also racially and ethnically homogeneous, faced the challenge of trying to maintain credibility with those involved in illicit activities while at the same time reaching for higher goals. Jones's book offers some insight into the struggle that young people face and some explanation as to why some succumb to the pressures while others do not.

For one, it is evident that the amount of pressure placed on young people in distressed communities may vary by gender. Young males may be more likely to give in to such pressures than young females, which is not to say that young females are immune. Strong family values and the presence of positive adult role models are important too, as is the accumulation of not only monetary but also social capital. Much of Allen's ultimate success came from the strong foundation laid by his parents and from the social capital and social networks he developed and nurtured, owing in large part to his status as an elite athlete.

The Rat That Got Away serves, in many ways, as a model for helping a subset of young people who all too often find themselves in the same situation as Allen, torn between the glitter and glamour of illicit activities and legitimate pathways to wealth, status, and power.[32]

Unlike in the case of Allen Jones, not everyone gets away or wants to get away. A 1990 story in the New York Times about Joe Hammond of Harlem provides an example of one who didn't get away.[33] Hammond—known in the neighborhood as the Destroyer when he played as a young man—was, at the age of 40, peddling greeting cards to get enough money to eat. It was a far cry from the days when he sold drugs and had hundreds of thousands of dollars stashed in his apartment. Jones never played high school or college basketball. Martin writes that Hammond was recruited by the Los Angeles Lakers and the American Basketball Association's New York Nets. A high school dropout, Hammond shined in the city's summer leagues and was offered a $50,000 contract. However, the $50,000 contract paled in comparison to the money Hammond was making "dealing drugs and shooting dice," according to the article.[34]

Hammond also owned a nightclub, expensive cars, and real estate. The appeal of playing alongside Laker greats like Wilt Chamberlain was not enough to pull him away from the magnetic appeal of the streets. Hammond's success as a street hustler was short-lived. It landed him in prison and cost him his worldly possessions.

In the book *White Sports/Black Sports*, Martin tells of a game where Hammond played against basketball great Julius Erving, also known as Dr. J. Hammond scored 50 points to Erving's 39. Hammond claimed that he wanted the Lakers to pay him what they were paying players like Erving, but the Lakers refused. In the article, Hammond states, "I told the Lakers that I deserved what those guys were making because I was better than most of them, but they refused to pay me. Then I asked them for a no-cut, guaranteed contract, and they refused me again. They couldn't understand how this poor boy from the slums could be playing hardball with them. And of course, I couldn't tell them."[35]

How might Hammond's life have been different had he accepted the offer from the Lakers? How might his life have been different if the Lakers acquiesced and paid him what top players in the league were earning at the time? We can never know, but we do know that he did not get away.

The idea that sports are a ticket to a better life for anyone, but especially black males in disadvantaged neighborhoods, is a narrative that is all too common in our society. The persistence of this narrative is fodder for scholars and laypersons who believe that we are living in a post-racial society. It is instrumental in perpetuating the myth that all of the material spoils that we associate with success in American society are accessible to all people, if they would only work hard and live up to their full potential. The narrative, which can be heard virtually everywhere we look, is an important tool in the racial socialization of black and white athletes, such that black athletes come to see sports as one of few legitimate avenues for advancement in a society with a history of undervaluing and vilifying blacks in general, and black males in particular.

The long history of overemphasizing the physicality of the black male in sports and beyond helps to explain how black athletes are affected by messages communicated through the process of racial socialization in sports. The association of the black male with physicality leads young black males to see their bodies as superior when it comes to physical abilities, which encourages some young people to believe it is their destiny to play certain sports and play them better than others. Martin cites the work of Jay Coakley, a sport sociologist, and agrees with his assessment that sport-related stereotypes in the face of limited mainstream economic opportunities and heavily sponsored opportunities to develop skills in certain sports, results in increased motivation to play selected sports, such as football and baseball in the case of black male athletes.[36] Over time, black male athletes come to believe that it is their calling to excel in those sports, especially relative to whites. Segregation in American neighborhoods and schools only exacerbate things, so that there is a tendency for black males to be identified in a way that undermines their success in claiming identities that don't fit expectations based on racial ideology and sport.

Martin also addresses the overrepresentation of black male athletes, like Ed O'Bannon, in selected sports.[37] The overrepresentation of blacks in a relatively small number of sports supports the claim that blacks perceive limited options for upward social mobility apart from sports, and especially the sports that are most accessible to minority youth in under-resourced neighborhoods, even when the numbers don't support that idea. Martin says, one need only look to data provided by the Institute for Diversity and Ethics in Sports to see how concentrated black athletes are, for example, in basketball.[38] During the 1995–1996 NBA season, 80 percent of the players were black and 20 percent were white. By the 1999–2000 season, 78 percent of players were black and 22 percent were white. For the 2011–2012 season, 78 percent of players were black and 18 percent were white. The overrepresentation of black players is evident over time, as is the underrepresentation of blacks among owners and front office staff. The figures aren't much different in the Women's National Basketball Association (WNBA). In 1999, 64 percent of players were black and 32 percent were white. By 2005, 63 percent were black and 34 percent white. By 2012, about 75 percent of players in the WNBA were black compared to only 16 percent white.

Martin found similar patterns were observed for the National Football League (NFL).[39] In 1996, 1999, and 2012 about 67 percent were black and about 31 percent white. The percentage of black players in Major League Baseball (MLB) has declined over time.[40] In 1996, 17 percent of players were black and 62 percent were white. By 1999, black players made up only 13 percent of players and the number of white players decreased by 2 percent. In 2005, less than 10 percent of MLB players were black and 60 percent were white, and these numbers were matched by the 2012 season. In Major League Soccer (MLS), the percentage of black players has increased between 1999 and 2012, while the percentage of white players has decreased. In 1999, 16 percent of MLS players were black, compared to 65 percent white. For the latest year that data is available, about a quarter of MLS players were black and less than half, or 49 percent, were white.

Looking only at Division I, Martin also highlights data that show an increase in the percentage of black college basketball players and decreases, although relatively small, in football and baseball. During the 2009–2010 academic year, 61 percent of basketball players were black and 30 percent were white. For the 2004–2005 academic year and the 1999–2000 academic year, there were a higher percentage of white players than black players. In the earliest year, 35 percent of Division I basketball players were black and 55 percent were white. Five years later, the percentage of black players dropped to 32 percent and the percentage of white players increased to 58 percent. For women, the trends are similar. Between 2004 and 2010, the percentage of black athletes surpassed that of white athletes. By 2010, 51 percent of the women's players were black and 40 percent were white. Five years earlier, 45 percent of players were white and 44 percent were black. In 2000, 54 percent were white and 36 percent were black.

At the Division I level, black football players represented half of all players in 2000, 45 percent in 2005, and 46 percent in 2010. Blacks were clearly underrepresented among Division I baseball players. In 2000 and in 2005, 7 percent of players were black and about 84 percent were white. By 2010, 83 percent of players were white and only 6 percent were black.

Few scholars have written about the association of sports participation with the potential for upward mobility so eloquently as Dr. Harry Edwards. Edwards is the founder of the sociology of sport and a professor of sociology at Berkley. Writing in the late 1960s, Dr. Edwards set forth the argument that "to no small degree, blacks' highly visible accomplishments as athletes in four or five sports have served to veil the more unsavory realities of their sports involvement and to obscure the fact that virtually all other American sports remain largely segregated and lily white."[41] This enduring finding about race and sports shows that American sports are "more a treadmill than the fabled escalator providing escape from the deprivations afflicting the black community. And because of its interdependence with other institutional structures and social processes in America, sport constitutes not only a treadmill for the overwhelming majority of aspiring black athletes, but also a cruel and wickedly subtle trap, ensnaring the whole of black culture and society."[42] Edwards added that the idea that sports provides an avenue toward upward social mobility for blacks "amounts not to mere naïveté, but to inhuman mockery."[43]

Edwards adds that the "singular visibility of black athlete role models" is directly responsible for the fact that "high numbers of black youth are channeled into athletic career aspirations."[44] Consequently, high numbers of black youth are not focusing their attention on other careers such as in science, technology, engineering, and math, nor are black youth being encouraged to pursue such careers by institutions of racial socialization such as the media and schools.

Edwards revealed how unlikely it was for black youth in high school to gain the ultimate prize—a college scholarship. Only a select few elite athletes make it to the college level and the number of whites receiving athletic scholarships far outweighed the number of black athletes receiving athletic scholarships. In the mid-1970s, "whites were still receiving slightly more than 94 percent of all collegiate athletic support."[45] Stacking and poor graduation rates are some of the problems facing black college athletes. A group of black athletes at California State University at Los Angeles even filed a lawsuit against the operation of the athletic program at the university Edwards goes on to show that black participation in sports at the collegiate level were limited to a few sports and that this was the case at the professional level, too. While many high-profile professional athletes are black, most black professional athletes in Edwards' era earned less than whites with similar skill sets. Additionally, black athletes in Edwards' era are in positions where the likelihood of injury is greater than the positions where whites are commonly found. Edwards also showed that up until the late 1970s an athlete did not typically reap the "post-career pension benefits" and "seldom gets the secondary benefits of a sports career; for example advertising contracts, coaching, managing, sports media, or front-office jobs after retirement from active participation."[46] As of the late 1970s, black athletes were also less likely to gain entry into the Hall of Fame when compared with white professional players with similar athletic abilities.

Unfortunately, much of what Edwards observed in the late 1970s is still occurring today, argues Martin in *White Sports/Black Sports*. The Institute on Diversity and Ethics found in 2012 that "the percentage of white male student-athletes, in all of Division I athletics, stands at 61.2 percent, a decrease of 1.7 percent from 2011. Of all Division I male athletes, 22 percent are African American, which was a 0.8 percent increase from 2011."[47]

Almost 70 percent of male student-athletes at the Division I, II, and III levels combined were white. The percentage of white female student-athletes at the Division I, II, and III levels combined was over 76. Black males accounted for 16 percent of athletes in the combined levels and black females accounted for less than 9 percent of athletes in the combined levels.

Moreover, whites held most of the coaching positions at each of the divisional levels in 2012. Over 86 percent of coaches in Division I were white, 88 percent in Division II, and nearly 92 percent in Division III. Blacks "held 8.3 percent, 5.2 percent, and 4.2 percent of the men's head coating positions in Divisions I, II, and III, respectively" and similar patterns were found where women's head coaching positions were concerned.[48] The representation of blacks among athletic directors, college associates, and assistant athletic directors is more dismal.

Despite the relatively low likelihood of black youth making it to the pros and escaping disadvantaged neighborhoods, black youth are inundated with images of exemplary talented black athletes who, we are told, come from similar backgrounds. At the same time, very few counter-narratives are offered. As a result, not only are ideas about black dominance in sports and little else reinforced, but high numbers of black youth come to see athletics as one of the few legitimate avenues toward upward social mobility. Continued problems such as crime and under-resourced schools serve the purpose of reinforcing the belief that blacks have limited occupational choices. The fact that most aspiring athletes will not have a rags-to-riches experience means they will have to face an already unfavorable labor market, for which far too many are ill-prepared and that already prefers white males with a criminal record to black males with no criminal record.

One of the ways to combat the systematic issues, including systematic racism, that is part of American sports, according to scholars like Joe Feagin, a sociologist at Texas A & M and founder of systematic racism theory, is to resist; to engage in activism. Ed O'Bannon's decision to fight back against the NCAA and Electronic Arts, makers of the video game bearing his likeness and that of other student-athletes, is within the tradition of athletic activism. O'Bannon filed a lawsuit on behalf of former athletes "whose names, images, and likenesses appeared in television broadcasts and in video games to the financial benefit of their universities as well as the NCAA."[49] The suit challenged rules established by the NCAA, which prohibited players from getting paid for the use of their names, likenesses, and images. The policies "required athletes to relinquish 'in perpetuity' the right to license for commercial purposes the use of their names, images and likenesses as associated with their participation in college athletics."[50] O'Bannon and other former athletes made the argument that the aforementioned policies violate the Sherman Antitrust Act.

The court agreed that O'Bannon met the burden of proof as to the suppression of the athlete's rights to license their own names, images, and likenesses, although the court did believe it made sense to limit the level of compensation a player could receive so that it would not negatively impact the overall academic environment. "The court agreed that some limits on athletes' compensation could be justified by the wedge that money would drive between athletes and other students."[51] In short, the court ruled in such a way as to force the NCAA to make some serious changes and "modify its amateurism policy."[52]

The injunction first prevents the NCAA from enforcing any rules that would "prohibit its member schools and conferences from offering their Football Bowl Subdivision (FBS) football and Division I (men's) basketball recruits a limited share of the revenues generated from the use of their names, images, and likenesses, in addition to a full grant-in-aid."[53]

Another significant effort to change big-time college sports as we know them concerns efforts on the part of a Division I football team to unionize. Football players at Northwestern University attempted to unionize with some success, but their success was short-lived. Players of the Division I NCAA program formed the College Athletes Players Association (CAPA) and petitioned Region 13 National Labor Relations Board for recognition as a union. Region 13 agreed that the CAPA qualified as a labor union because it met the following essential two conditions: "(1) its football players who receive grant-in-aid scholarships are found to be 'employees' within the meaning of the Act; and (2) the petitioned-for-unit was found to be an appropriate unit within the meaning of the Act."[54] At issue was the claim by CAPA that as employees they were entitled to "choose whether or not to be represented for the purposes of collective-bargaining."[55] Northwestern University says the players are not employees; rather, "its players are temporary employees who are not eligible for collective bargaining."[56]

The decision describes the university as a private and nonprofit teaching institution. It also notes that the university is part of the Big Ten Conference in 19 varsity sports, 8 for men and 11 for women. In all, roughly 500 people participate in at least one of the sports each year for the university. The document goes on to describe the football team.

The football team is part of the NCAA's Football Bowl Subdivision (FBS) and is led by a coach and other key staffers, including a Director of Player Personnel and a Director of Player Development. The staff also includes nearly 10 assistant coaches, employed full-time, and several graduate assistants. Full-time strength coaches, administrative staff, and videographers are among the other staff members. The football coach, according to the findings, reports to the athletic director and the university president. In all, more than 100 people are on the football team, and the majority of them receive football scholarships that cover the cost of tuition, fees, books, and room and board. On average, grant-in-aid for the players is about $60,000 each academic year.

The decision also included the finding that freshman and sophomore players must live on campus. "Under current NCAA regulations, the Employer is prohibited from offering its players additional compensation for playing football at its institution with one exception. The Employer is permitted to provide its players with additional funds out of a 'Student Assistance Fund' to cover certain expenses such as health insurance, dress clothes required to be worn by the team while traveling to games, the cost of traveling home for a family member's funeral, and fees for graduate school admittance tests and tutoring."[57]

Until recently, players were not permitted to receive renewable scholarships, but that changed in 2012–2013. The document from the National Labor Relations Board also outlines the content of the National Letter of Intent and four-year scholarship every recruit signs. Recruits are informed that their scholarships may be reduced or cancelled if any of the following occurs:

1. Renders himself ineligible from intercollegiate competition
2. Engages in serious misconduct warranting substantial disciplinary action
3. Engages in conduct resulting in criminal charges
4. Abuses team rules as determined by the coach or athletic administration
5. Voluntarily withdraws from the sport at any time for any reason
6. Accepts compensation for participating in an athletic contest in his sport
7. Agrees to be represented by an agent[58]

The document also describes the grievance and appeal process for any football player in jeopardy of losing their scholarship, which has only happened in two cases over the past five years, once for the violation of an alcohol and drug policy, and another time when a player shot a BB gun in a dorm.

In deciding whether the players were employees of Northwestern, the Board considered the special rules that apply to football players that other students at the university do not have to follow. Again, freshmen and sophomore players must live on campus. Upper classmen may live off campus, but the coach must approve their leases first. Players also need permission to get outside employment. Additionally, players have to tell their coaches about the vehicles they drive and abide by "a social media policy, which restricts what they can post on the social media sites, including Twitter, Facebook, and Instagram. In fact, the players are prohibited from denying a coach's 'friend' request and the former's postings are monitored."[59] Players may not give media interviews unless the Athletic Department arranges the interviews. Football players are also not allowed to curse in public "and if a player 'embarrasses' the team, he can be suspended for one game. A second offense of this nature can result in a suspension up to one year."[60] Among the other rules football players have to follow that other students do not are drug testing and adherence to antigambling policies. Additionally, there is a dress code the players have to follow. They must wear a suit to a home game and team issued travel sweats to away games. They must remain within six-hours from campus on game days and may be required to attend a study hall if they are late for practice. "Irrespective of their GPA, all freshmen players must attend six hours of study hall each week."[61]

In reaching the initial decision to consider the players as employees, the Board outlined the time commitment to the sport of football. Training camp, which is at the beginning of August, is described as one of the most time intensive periods of the season. The players receive schedules from the coach that they must follow. The schedules outline a host of items, including practice and meal times. Each player's day is planned from the time he wakes up until about 10:30 p.m.; then all of the players are expected to be in bed. Each player devotes "50 to 60 hours per week on football-related activities."[62]

The demands on the players continue after training camp. The Labor Relations Board described the regular season, which consists of 12 games. It is estimated that players spend 40–50 hours on football-related activities during the season.

> During each Monday of the practice week, injured players must report to the athletic training room to receive medical treatment starting at about 6:15 a.m. Afterward, the football coaches require the players to attend mandatory meetings so that they can begin to install the game plan for their upcoming opponent. However, the only physical activity the coaches expect the players to engage in during this day is weightlifting since they are still recovering from their previous game. The next several days of the week (Tuesday through Thursday), injured players must report to the athletic training room before practice to continue to receive medical treatment. The coaches require all the players to attend mandatory practices and participate in various football related activities in pads and helmets from about 7:50 a.m. until 11:50 a.m. In addition, the players must attend various team and position meetings during this time period. Upon completion of these

practices and meetings, the scholarship players attend a mandatory "train-ing table" at the N Club where they receive food to assist them in their recovery. Attendance is taken at these meals and food is only provided to scholarship players and those walk-ons who choose to pay for it out of their own pocket.[63]

It is not uncommon for the players to meet in the absence of the coach-ing staff for additional drills, say the findings. The document also describes the travel schedule for away games and home games. Additionally, the doc-ument describes the transition to Spring football, which happens in mid-February, where about 20 to 25 hours are required of their time until about mid-April.

At the end of the academic year, the players will return to their respective homes for a couple of weeks (which are discretionary weeks) before being required to report back to campus for Summer workouts, which are once again conducted by the strength and conditioning coaches. The team leaders will also use this time to teach the team's offense and defense to incoming freshmen. In fact, the players participate in 7-on-7 drills from 7:00 p.m. to 10:00 p.m., two times per week and watch film as part of their preparation for the upcoming season. In total, both the upperclassmen and incoming freshmen devote 20 to 25 hours per week on summer workouts before the start of training camp.[64]

The document declaring the players employees of Northwestern Uni-versity also includes a description of the recruitment and academic life of scholarship players. The Board finds it clear that the players are recruited because of their athletic abilities, not because of their academic abilities. It is "only after the employer's football program becomes interested in a high school player based on the potential benefit he might add to the employ-er's football program does the potential candidate get vetted through the employer's recruiting and admissions process."[65]

The document goes on to describe how the coach observes a recruit's athletic ability by attending one of his high school games and later visits with the recruit in his home. The purpose of the home visits is to explain the expectations. Coaches may make a total of six home visits. During the recruitment process, a decision about whether to admit a student is made by the Admissions Office, and the coach is not to have contact with the Admissions Office during the process. Instead, the coach instead works with the Deputy Director of Athletics for Student-Athlete Welfare, who works with the Admissions Office. "If the recruit is pre-approved for admission, he completes the formal admissions application with the understanding that he will be admitted as long as his academic record is maintained. However, some recruits are not deemed admissible such that the coaches will have to cease recruiting that individual."[66]

The regional board also acknowledged the following about the recruitment process and academic life,

> Further, to be eligible to play on the football team, the players must be (1) enrolled as full-time students; (2) making adequate progress toward obtaining their degree; and (3) maintain a minimum GPA. For players entering their second year of school, they must pass 36 quarter hours and have a 1.8 GPA. For players entering their third year of school, they must have 40% of their degree applicable units completed and a 1.9 GPA. For players entering their fourth year of school, they must have 60% of their degree applicable units completed and a 2.0 GPA. For players entering their fifth year of school, they must have 80% of their degree applicable units completed and a 2.0 GPA. For this reason, players normally take three to four courses during the Fall, Winter, and Spring Quarters. The players spend about 20 hours per week attending classes each week. The players also have to spend time completing their homework and preparing for exams. Significantly, the players do not receive any academic credit for their playing football and none of their coaches are members of the academic faculty.[67]

Players offered testimony about the limitations placed on their career aspirations. They related conversations with coaches whereby players were discouraged from pursuing certain majors, especially if the courses conflicted with football activities. If a scholarship player had to choose between class and practice, the players said they had to choose practice. Furthermore, "This continued in the Spring with scholarship players being told by their coaches and academic/athletic advisors that they could not take any classes that started before 11:00 a.m. as they would conflict with practice. Even during the Summer session, players were generally only permitted to enroll in classes that were 6 weeks long since the classes that were 8 weeks long would conflict with the start of training camp."[68] Northwestern University told a different story, where academics were highly valued, and efforts to help players thrive academically and as part of the larger university community through service.

Finally, the Board outlined the revenues and expenses associated with the football program at Northwestern. Ticket sale, broadcasting contracts, and merchandise are among the many ways the football team generates revenue. Between 2003 and 2012, the football team generated $235 million in total revenues and $159 million in expenses. In one academic year, between 2012 and 2013, the football program generated over $30 million in revenue and about $22 million in expenses. "The profit realized from the football team's annual revenue is used to subsidize the Employer's non-revenue-generating sports (i.e. all the other varsity sports with the exception of men's basketball). This, in turn, assists the Employer in ensuring that it offers a proportionate number of men's and women's varsity sports in compliance with Title IX of the Education Amendments of 1972."[69] One of the key issues treating athletes in high-revenue-generating sports as employees or in compensating them beyond room and board, tuition, scholarships, and so on, is the impact on programs that directly and indirectly benefit from these elite programs. Thus, some people are comfortable with the exploitation or unequal treatment experienced by some groups if they themselves continue to benefit in some way.

The potential impact on women's sports and non-revenue-generating sports is a serious point of contention for many athletes and non-athletes. Buzuvis described the tension, making the following points:[70] "The NCAA is right: In a world where male athletes in revenue generating sports are paid, Title IX would require payment of female athletes using some measure of equality.[71] Second, that NCAA's critics are right: athletes are being exploited by the present system. But, the reformers needn't fear the NCAA's use of title IX as a shield. Used properly, Title IX presents the reformers with a sword" and forces the NCAA and colleges and universities to "address concerns about the exploitation of uncompensated labor, gender equity, and cost containment."[72]

By August 2015, the National Labor Relations Board dismissed the petition filed by the football players essentially reversing the decision by the regional director in March 2014. The National Labor Relations Board, made up of five members, said they did not have jurisdiction over schools run by the state, and 85 percent of the schools in the NCAA's Division I FBS fall into that category.

The players may have inspired the recent actions of athletes at the University of Missouri. Football players threatened to boycott all football activities until the embattled president of the university resigned or was fired. The campus gained national attention as students and staff protested the administration's inadequate responses to a series of racially motivated incidences at the university. Although students and staffs were engaged in acts of protests, including civil disobedience and a hunger strike, it was not until the football team threw in their support that the president resigned. The new millennium may be remembered for the resurrection of the activist athlete, but only time will tell.

Conclusion

The history of the labor movement in America is filled with many examples of American workers winning small victories only to find themselves at the mercy of capitalists more interested in profit than in the economic well-being of their workforces. We showed how labor unions were able to secure some benefits for workers. We discussed the politics surrounding right-to-work legislation and showed how proponents of it attempted to co-op social justice language to mask their effort of weakening labor unions. We described the antiunion sentiment that exists throughout many areas, including in education where alternative teaching credentialing programs are taking over classrooms that were once guided by veteran teachers. We then showed how sports unions and traditional unions have more in common than most people think and that players' groups have been engaged in many strikes and lockouts. We addressed the significance of the 2009 O'Bannon decision and the effort on the part of football players at Northwestern to unionize. Increasingly, college athletes are not only recognizing their economic value in the marketplace, but they are also recognizing their right to be treated as total persons and not be used for everyone else's benefit but their own.

CHAPTER SEVEN

Pay to Play: The Case for Compensation

Whether student-athletes in elite programs are worthy of compensation beyond room and board, scholarships, books, and other in-kind compensation is a hotly contested subject, even without the injection of race, which alone constitutes a subject that divides friends, families, neighbors, and even nations. In the preceding chapters, we examined this history of race and sports, with a special emphasis on the criminalization and commercialization of blackness and of black bodies. The authors of *Pay to Play* highlighted two recent events—the O'Bannon case and the effort by Northwestern football players to unionize—in an effort to show just how hotly contested these issues are and how they can also be understood through a critical race lens. To further determine the pulse of the public on the issue of whether to pay college athletes in general, and also to determine the extent to which race is an important factor, the authors of this book conducted a study in two phases. The first phase involved reaching out broadly to current student-athletes, former student-athletes, and non-athletes across the nation. We used nonprobability sampling to create a questionnaire using Google documents and shared the link with people in our network via email. We also shared the link on social media sites. About 150 people, at least 18 years of age, responded to the invitation to share their thoughts. The link to the questionnaire was available during the early part of 2015. The respondents were asked to comment on a range of topics (see Table 7.1 for a sample of questions and Appendix A for the complete list of questions). The respondents were not asked specifically to reflect on the role of race because we wanted to see whether race emerged as an important factor.

Table 7.1   Selected Questions from Survey Instrument to Assess Attitudes of Current Student-Athletes, Former Student-Athletes, and Non-Athletes

Do you think big-time college athletes should unionize? Why or why not?

Do you agree or disagree with the following statement: "Top-tier college athletes already do get paid, in the form of lucrative scholarships?" Why or why not?

Do you agree or disagree with the following statement? "Top-tier college athletes benefit from critical training and exposure that enhances their draft prospects." Why or why not?

Who do you think profits the most from college athletics, and why? Cite examples.

Do you agree or disagree with the following statement? "Turning student-athletes into salaried professionals would fundamentally change sports." Why or why not?

Do you agree or disagree with the following statement? "Turning student-athletes into salaried professionals undermines the academic mission of colleges and universities." Why or why not?

Do you agree or disagree with the following statement? "Yes, it's unfair that certain football and basketball players produce enormous riches for their schools and don't get to reap the spoils. But paying them would be a logistical nightmare; indeed, it would prove impossible to devise a truly 'fair' revenue-distribution scheme. There are better ways to make college sports more equitable." Why or why not?

To what extent do you think your college or university is committed to your success as a student-athlete? Explain.

Should big-time college athletes have the right to endorse products, get paid for speaking engagements and be compensated for the use of their likenesses on licensed products? Why or why not?

Should big-time college athletes be allowed to negotiate an actual contract with a professional sports league and have an agent?

In your opinion, which term most accurately describes big-time college athletes: student-athletes or full-time athletes? Why?

Next, we also extended an invitation to students enrolled in two courses about society and sport during the spring semester of 2016 to respond to a subset of questions. The students were asked specifically about the role of race. The students were enrolled in one of two courses in an institution located in the Deep South. The institution is a Research 1 program. Student-athletes participate in Division I sports, with many sports teams nationally ranked (see Table 7.2 for a list of questions). We begin with the findings from the first phase of research.

Pam, a 22-year-old white female runs cross-country and track and field. She participated in cross-country for seven years, four of which were at the college level. She is on a team in the mid-west in a Division I program. She wants to become an early childhood educator. For Pam, amateur athletes are willing to play without pay. She agreed that big-time college athletes should be considered amateur athletes, but not in every case. Pam said that big-time college athletes are amateurs "for the most part. Not all big-time college athletes are on full-ride scholarships, so a large portion of their time is devoted to playing for their team despite not necessarily getting all of school paid for." Pam seems to view scholarships as a form of payment. She distinguishes between student-athletes who receive scholarships and those who do not. Student-athletes receiving scholarships could be considered as something other than amateurs; however, athletes in big-time college programs who are not receiving financial support represent the ideal type of amateur athlete.

According to Pam, there are key distinctions between professional and amateur athletes. "Professional players are all paid larger sums to a certain degree, and some big-time college athletes may not be on any [scholarship] or very little scholarship altogether. They also have the job of attending classes and a certain number of credit hours while in season."

Pam is against athletes unionizing. We asked whether big-time college athletes should unionize. She disagreed, saying, "No, because oftentimes the big-time college athletes are well taken care of on a full ride. Their only job is to be a good student and work hard at their sport. I don't think they need to get paid in addition to having school paid for."

Drawing from Pam's experience, she believes that top-tier college athletes already get paid in the form of lucrative scholarships. She also agrees that athletes at top-tier college programs benefit from the training they receive and the exposure they get, which ultimately enhance their prospects for a draft.

Some programs, like football and baseball, are among the most profitable, says Pam. Turning student-athletics into salaried professions would change sports, according to Pam. "I think that sports would become even more politically driven for the worse, and there would be a large decrease for students considering 'walking on' to different sports teams." Pam added, "Any college athlete should first and foremost consider themselves *student*-athletes." Paying athletes would be a difficult task, and Pam believes that "scholarship distributions should already largely take care of this dilemma."

Pam's university already provides most student-athletes with a host of support services. Pam says, "I believe my university is very committed to my success as a student-athlete because of the academic advisors, tutors, and facilities that are readily available. Our coaches emphasize academic success, which helps support each and every athlete as well."

Like many athletes across the country Pam puts in a lot of hours training for her sport. According to Pam, she practices "20 plus hours a week Monday through Saturday. Twice a day on Mondays and Wednesdays." Pam typically travels from Friday until Saturday evening and practices on her own on Sundays.

Mary is an 18-year-old white female. She is in her first year playing volleyball, although she has been playing volleyball for more than a decade. Mary agrees with Pam that amateur athletes do not get paid, so by definition athletes in big-time programs are not amateurs because they do not get paid, and that is the greatest difference between amateur and professional players. Mary does believe that athletes in big-time college programs share "an extraordinary skill set in their chosen sport" with professional players.

A member of a Division I rowing team, Rachel, age 18, does not think athletes should receive payment beyond the scholarships received because "people would only do it for the money," and the focus on education would be lost. Rachel says her institution stresses the importance of both sport and education but places greater emphasis on "academics because that will be valuable the rest of your life." Although Rachel does not receive an athletic scholarship for her participation, she does devote a great deal of time to her sport. On average, Rachel spends about 30 to 40 hours training, which includes "weight sessions 2 times a week, practice 4 to 5 times a week, 2 games a week, 1 or 2 film sessions, and rehab with athletic trainers."

Mark—a white male—is a 20-year-old football player in an elite program in the south. Mark does not liken his membership on the football team to that of a professional. "Professionals are paid for what they do. It's their job, not a hobby." Amateurs, on the other hand, do what they do "for fun." For Mark, athletes are compensated because they "get a free meal plan and education as well as housing on campus and tutors for classes. That takes care of all major expenses." Student-athletes also benefit because "you won't go professional without college exposure."

It is acceptable for Mark, and others, that student-athletes in elite programs have their basic needs met for participating in what is equated to a hobby, despite the claim by Mark that his institution "makes enough money from seven home football games to finance all other sports programs at the school." Mark concedes that colleges are the greatest beneficiaries of the revenue generated, but does feel that athletes should be permitted to endorse projects, although he thinks unionization is unnecessary and that students' focus should be "to learn."

Sam, an 18-year-old Asian male, defines an individual with little experience playing a specific sport as an amateur and sees some similarities and differences between amateurs and professionals, particularly when comparing student-athletes in elite programs with professionals. Both have tremendous responsibilities and play at great physical risk. Sam finds that earning an education is a reward in and of itself and does not believe that athletes in elite college programs should receive monetary compensation. College play provides athletes with the type of "education" they need on the field to be successful on the professional level, according to Sam.

John is a 19-year-old swimmer at a Division I school in the South. John is against players unionizing because, he says, "There are many benefits now and more in the future to come for these athletes." He adds that some big-time college athletes are already getting paid. John writes, "I already witness the extra money that flows throughout top-tier college athletes. They are very close to already getting paid just by the university itself, or boosters." Nevertheless, John acknowledges that "the university profits the most with the additional revenue and exposure it gains." He also worries, as do some other people, that paying athletes will fundamentally change college sports. "It would make universities a business and force them to become more athletically concentrated since that is where the money will be." Moreover, John fears that "athletes will have even less of a sense of duty to pursue any academic goals they might have." John has a solution: "I feel like if there is someone who has that ability to play professionally should not have to go to school at all. Universities would only lose 20 kids max a year, and yes, college football would not be as productive, but the athletes would be the ones making the profit instead of the university, which is more important."

The perspective from former athletes was somewhat similar to that of current college athletes. Most respondents defined amateur athletes as people who competed but did not get paid to do so; others clearly pointed to the exploitation of athletes in elite programs. Matt, a 24-year-old black male said, big-time college athletes should be considered amateurs because "[d]uring my time as an athlete, we not only represented ourselves and our families, but the brand of our schools. Even as walk-ons, we were held to very high standards. We were expected to look, act, and speak a certain type of way. We were trained under 'voluntary' workouts. I believe an amateur to be kids or adults who play the game recreationally. However, when you put in [an] excess of 50 hours a week, in a multi-*billion* dollar industry, or you put on a show in front of what was 92,000+to now 110,000 people on Saturday night, and you see your teammate's faces on tickets, on the covers of the Gameday Programs being sold for the profit of the respective universities, [it] pulls my thought away from that amateur balderdash . . . because that's exactly what it is."

Matt described many similarities between big-time college players and professional athletes. Both put in "long hours, you play in front of huge crowds, both groups play in a multibillion dollar industry, huge media exposure, we provide a reason for media to employ more folks, you live under a microscope, you are no longer 'Trent Detz of Leesville,' you are 'UK Football Player, Trent Detz,' you are expected to do community service, required to make certain appearances, fans will not allow you to be alone." On the other hand, Matt notes, "As a college athlete, your brand *is* the college. As a pro, you have your own brand. College players never get the choice on where they want to go. Pros have a free agency period. The most important thing: college athletes don't get paid for their services and professional athletes do."

Matt expressed support for unionization. He argues that players should have the right to unionize because this way they would be able to at least have a voice in their exploitation. "As long as players aren't unionized, they are de facto slaves, who at the whim of a coach or program could be dismissed. Even after *literally* dedicating their life to the said program. The program is a machine and all the athletes are the cogs. If you get worn out, they take you out and they throw you away and replace you. That's the system. Do I blame the schools? No. Because it's *just* a business to the schools, but the players are not *expected* to see it that way. It's supposed to *just* be a game to us and whenever I hear that, I think that's absolute BS."

Scholarships are important, but they are simply not enough, according to Matt. He observes, "Scholarship is essential, absolutely. However, there is way more to school than just class when you are an athlete. If you have your face on billboards and you can't afford to eat on the weekend, what good is your scholarship? If you want to go on a date with your girlfriend and you spent all your money for the month on bills at the beginning of the month, can you go for free somewhere? No, 'It's a violation of NCAA rules. The cost of college for the athlete is so much more than books, room and board. The average student will not understand.'"

Speaking for big-time college athletes who feel disenfranchised, Matt makes the following passionate statement: "If you take away my opportunity for employment, snatch away my personal life, place me under the microscope, plaster my face on a schedule to be passed out all over the city of my respective university, have me run my head into this 265-pound linebacker who is all-American 40 to 50+times a game, make me work out 'voluntarily,' the least you can do is give me exposure I need to help me get to the next level. My coaches and university has made millions off of the labor I do, don't I deserve to be exposed?"

For Matt, not only do the players face great risks, but the athletic directors, the conferences, and the NCAA are the greatest beneficiaries. "The athletic directors get paid to make sure the program is running smoothly, the conferences get a piece of every payoff for participating schools and the NCAA makes *most* of its money off of March Madness." Why the roles of administrators are more highly valued than that of the players is unconscionable. Matt asks, "What is the difference between paying the people on the field versus the one's on the sidelines? Coaches get paid *millions* and the people busting their asses on the field can't afford to go out on the weekends? What image is the university trying to portray? That their athletes don't matter?"

College programs must address the following question, according to Matt: "How do you plan on making college sports more equitable without NCAA violation?" Matt concedes that the university he played for—a premier football conference in the south—offered him many opportunities, but it also led much suffering. Matt recalls, "I had teammates who came from poor backgrounds and had to send money out of their check home and were not able to work anymore to pay those bills that were still home while they were away chasing their dreams, I had teammates that would go and come to my house to eat because there were no other places they could afford to go, which could be interpreted as a violation, but I was doing what I had to do to help."

Lee, a 50-year-old black male represents a very different perspective from that of Matt. Lee thinks the major difference between college athletes in big-time programs and professional athletes is not only the fact that one is paid and the other is not, but the educational requirements and "the focus required to do well in class and carry the obligation of sports, one could argue that their attention is divided unlink a professional that lives their profession daily. The university provides students with much needed services, according to Lee, including the development of "physical strength, maturity and going from directed structure at the University to bring on your own as a professional." The focus should not be on playing college athletes; rather, "I think the focus should be on a fund for injuries and a long-term commitment to pay for college education. Instead, for four years you get six years to complete." Lee makes the aforementioned claim believing full well that universities and TV ad sponsors are among the greatest beneficiaries. Universities "receive revenues from licensed merchandise in which the sales are highly connected to sport success. They also make revenue from TV relationships in the form of dedicated revenue sharing." Paying athletes would fundamentally change the game. Lee says, "The experience of being a college athlete trumps paying for pay. The struggles are shared by all teammates. To disrupt this would break many bonds that exist as teammates. It's what they reflect on 20 years later. What needs to be done is to have injury coverage and extended time to complete."

Jim is a 47-year-old Hispanic male who played soccer for the same Division I team in the South as our earlier participant, Matt. Jim describes the conference he played in as "a large corporation" and adds that "the 'employees' are not even given slave wages. The NCAA is an even greater corporation guilty of the same." Although Jim is not sure whether players should unionize, he does agree that "they should have better representation" than is currently available. Jim lists the greatest beneficiaries of big-time college programs as coaches, conferences, NCAA, sports companies, and universities. He implies that the salaries coaches receive are well deserved in his statement that "coaching at the college level is almost as critical as pro coaching." Jim also thinks athletes in elite college sports programs should receive "a stipend at least. Maybe guarantee them an amount upon graduation that they can draw against while in school." The stipends could include money athletes receive from endorsements. Jim says, "In these days of branding via the Internet, everyone is using social media to display an identity. Many benefit from this, and athletes should not be punished because they are amateurs." Jim contends this would address the hardships that some athletes face today and avoid the experiences some athletes faced in the past. Jim recalls, "In the eighties, I know of ball players that had to live in horrid conditions at times."

John—a 30-year-old white male—does not think athletes should be paid or treated as employees; rather, "the money that is made from sporting events should be pumped back into the school and future students in order to raise education levels across the country. College is too much of a corporate structure already, and being an athlete solely does not improve society. If we are to go back to the Roman days and we are happy with the idea of that, then go ahead, pay your college athletes, and don't find a way to make sure more of society is educated. Though, I believe strongly that all education should be free to the individual and paid for by the people for the people. In that instance, I bet you'd see a lot less [sic] athletes. Are universities for making athletes or to educate the people of its country to make a well-informed and a functioning member of our society?" John—like many other people in this country—finds benefiting from the labor of big-time college athletes to be perfectly acceptable. Not only would John like to see money from athletics going to the masses, but he also thinks that paying college athletes would fundamentally change college sports because athletes would no longer have an incentive for earning a degree.

Lee is a 41-year-old black male and believes big-time athletes and professional athletes have quite a lot in common. "The hours needed to participate in college sports equal a full-time job." Lee also things student-athletes should have the right to use a collective bargaining agreement. "Scholarships are not lucrative," adds Lee. College coaches are among the greatest beneficiaries, and college athletes should be given a greater voice. Lee also disagrees with commonly held beliefs that big-time college athletes live high on the hog. In fact, Lee sees little economic differences between student and non-student-athletes. Lee says of athletes in big-time programs, "They were poor students like most of us."

Mary—a 21-year-old white female former athlete—does not equate scholarships to compensation for the work athletes perform, but does not think that big-time college athletes should be able to endorse products, get paid for speaking engagements, or be compensated for the use of their likenesses on licensed products until after turning pro because paying big-time college athletes would drastically change the game, and higher education. "If athletes in college start getting paid, priorities will be different. Students will attend school to get paid, not to compete and to learn. It will also attract people who are not passionate about sports and will then change the game." Mary adds, "Paying athletes would be extremely difficult, since most sports do not bring in much revenue."

Brian is a 24-year-old Asian male and thinks something must change. "I agree with that top-tier athletes can get more money, but not lucrative scholarships. Top-tier athletes just means they can improve more their sports skills in college and more opportunities to get into professional league." Colleges are among the greatest beneficiaries, according to Brian. Not only do colleges benefit monetarily, Brian says, but big-time college sports also help colleges "attract more students to enroll in the school."

"Big-time" college athletes, according to Pam, a 30-year-old white female former college athlete, "are excellent at their sport and have the opportunity to hone their skills further, against excellent competition to potentially go on and play professionally." Most importantly, "they are kids who are there to get an education. If their talents help them get that education, or not, that is all they are there for. Plus, the variety of different collegiate levels would be hard to categorize for unionizing." Pam, like others, is not arguing that unionizing is not an option, nor does she disagree that it is important, but wonders how it would work. Moreover, Pam is of the belief that student-athletes are already well compensated. She remarks, "They get their education paid for, their room and board paid for, their food paid for, and a lot of clothing! They do not need extra cash for anything." Paying athletes will undermine the academic mission of colleges and universities, Pam claims. "Most universities' academic mission isn't to make money and fund their school via athletics programs. You could pay a very athletic person to play sports for your school . . . but they may not be the brightest . . . and pull down your academics! Totally discredits the school. I don't know how anyone could disagree with that." Pam also states, "I don't think it is 'unfair' that certain players don't get to 'reap the spoils.' I think those certain players *do* get to reap the spoils. They get their fame, and their skills honed, as well as getting the opportunity for their name to get out there and play professionally. Most students attend school to get a job after school. So do athletes. They may not do it in the classroom, but the gym. In the end, if they get a 'job' playing their sport professionally—they have reaped the spoils." (And also yes, paying them would be a logistical nightmare.)

"They provided student-athletes with a special study area and study help. They helped with scheduling to make travelling for sport easier and not miss so many classes. That's about it though." At the same time, Pam says, "Anyone should have the right to get paid for speaking engagements and be compensated for use of their likeness. But there would have to be very specific contracts with their scholarship and the company paying." Pam also cautions against lumping all Division I sports programs together and reminds us that at her institution "high-revenue sports weren't that high revenue."

Rachel is a white female in her early forties, and she does not believe athletes should be considered employees. As a former player Rachel has unique insights and says, "Athletics is a great catalyst for many things, but their degree is foremost. Union advocates for employee rights; athletes are not employees. They are students." Although some believe athletes are least likely to benefit, Rachel contends, "The college, the athlete, the community as a whole benefits. No one entity." She is in full agreement that paying big-time college athletes would undermine the mission of higher education. "School first, athletics next. Leave the salaries for the professionals. This would also create gaps on the playing fields . . . schools with more money *could* get the better players regardless of academic rigor. Players *could* decide based on salary and academic program solely rather than a comprehensive exploration of the schools." Rachel adds, "I don't begrudge schools for making money," but apparently begrudges college athletes from doing the same. She plainly states, "I don't agree the players should be paid." At the same time, she thinks, "Sports can be made more equitable." Rachel is clearly concerned about the potential impact of paying big-time college athletes on women's sports.

We also asked a series of questions of respondents who were neither current nor former college athletes. The overwhelming majority of this population said big-time college athletes should not unionize. Former and current athletes also did not support unionization, but some called for an overhaul of college athletics, without providing many specifics. Following are some of the responses to the question about whether big-time college athletes should unionize, from people who were not former or current athletes:

"No—each school should take care of their athletes. If they unionize that could start a domino effect where if one player starts a walk out it will turn players who want to play from being able to."

"It's good to be united, but I think a union is too much. It's a privilege to play."

"No, I personally don't believe in unions."

"They go to college for free and do not need any more rights that exceed the rights of a regular student."

People whose response was like the one that follows were in the numerical minority:

"Yes, college athletes should unionize to make sure they are adequately represented and taken care of. There is strength in numbers."

When asked who profits the most from big-time college sports, this population reported that the institutions and the NCAA are the largest beneficiaries. Most also agreed that paying athletes would undermine sports and change the academic mission of colleges and universities.

"It would blur the lines between professional and college. There's a spirit about college sports that shouldn't be monetized. That's why coaches shouldn't be making millions, TV deals should bring in less money (even if that means not being able to watch games on TV), and other rules should be changed by the NCAA. The focus should be brought back to the education, and athletes should have the opportunity to skip college and go straight to professional if they would like. College athletics should be for amateurs and those who want to learn. And people should accept that not everyone wants to learn."

"Yes! I have said it before. It should not be the point of a university to bring in athletes and then pay them huge sums. It's a university! It would certainly undermine the academic mission. Imagine the message. Come to college to improve your critical thinking skills and get a degree that helps you get a job. It will cost you a lot of money, you'll probably have to go into debt; however, if you are an athlete, you can come, get paid a lot of money, have personal tutors, perform poorly in your classes and graduate."

"I agree because it would create an atmosphere where students would compete for increased monetary compensation and would be able to leverage universities for even more money."

And a small minority belief was captured in the following statement:

"No. I don't think it would change the game. But money should probably go toward more educational purposes!!!!!!"

Respondents were more open to big-time college athletes being compensated for their likeness and the use of their image, although there were some naysayers.

"Yes. They are the ones working on the court and sacrificing their bodies. Their athletics career only lasts a select amount of time, and they should benefit from it, especially when their *coach* can benefit from endorsing products. If they bring in the attention/money, they should be able to use it, just like any other student could go on speaking engagements."

"Only if it does not interfere with their goals as a student or athlete. Pick a set schedule for them to do so."

"Yes they should be compensated if they endorse products and if their likeness is used. As far as speaking engagements, that should be done from the heart 'cause you never know your words could turn a child's life around. That should be payment enough."

"Yes, college athletes are individuals, not property of any institution."

"Absolutely! It is a matter of identity and property rights. The fact that they are not compensated is completely exploitative."

"Yes. Again, these students become college 'superstars' that influence a host of people. Their stardom is similar to that of professional athletes in many ways."

"Absolutely. If they want to do that, they should be allowed to. Their likeness and speaking talents should be owned by them, and they should be allowed to profit from them."

"No. They are not professional. The organizations can make negotiations with the school. Too many students would be taken advantage of and lose focus on being a student."

"No, because it would further the weight of their personal lives in the public world."

"They should receive some regulated benefit for their likeness being used on licensed products, but as far as endorsing products and getting paid for speaking at events, I do not agree. When you commit to playing a sport for a college university, you do dedicate a lot of time to that sport. As far as endorsing products goes, I think that aspect should be left to the professional athletes and not college student-athletes."

"Yes. This should be implemented because this is their name and they have to make themselves appealing to those who may be looking to hire them as a professional athlete."

"I actually do believe that this should be okay because it is the person them self [sic] that is being asked to endorse a product or speak to an audience. If it is the person alone, separate from the team, I think that it should be okay to receive pay. However, this could cause complications when some loopholes are found in the system."

"No. It isn't fair to other students to be compared to classmates who are big-time celebrities."

"Yes if it is a sponsorship for the individual."

"No, I think American society places too much importance on sweaty people running around with a bag filled with air."

"No. They're still students. Just doesn't seem natural."

"No. College athletes should not get paid because they are supposed to be at school for school and not just sports."

Overall, respondents were not enthusiastic about players unionizing. Many feared changing the way we reward college athletes in big-time programs would fundamentally change institutions of higher learning both in terms of pursuing their educational missions and where college sports are concerned. Respondents were more open to college athletes controlling their images, but were rather weary of said athletes retaining agents. Although most respondents acknowledged that college athletes are among the least likely people to benefit from the revenue generated by big-time college sports, many thought the current pay structure for elite college athletes was acceptable. When we did not explicitly ask whether race informed opinions about paying college athletes, the issue of race never came up directly. This is not surprising, as Americans have become accustomed to discussing racial disparities in nonracial terms in the so-called post-racial era. It is sad, although not surprising, that athletes and non-athletes alike support a system that exploits and marginalizes workers for everyone's benefit but their own.

When we asked respondents about race directly, the responses varied. Some respondents clearly identified race and racism as playing key roles in the controversy surrounding whether to pay student-athletes in high-revenue-generating sports.

Nearly 50 students enrolled in a course about sports and society volunteered to participate in the study. The students were enrolled in one of two courses. One course focused specifically on race and sports, and the other

Table 7.2   Pay to Play: Race-Specific Questionnaire

1. Should student-athletes playing in high-revenue-generating sports receive compensation beyond room and board, books, and free tuition?
2. What role, if any, does race play in the current controversy about whether to pay college athletes? Explain.
3. What is your age?
4. Are you a student-athlete?
5. What is your gender?
6. What is your race/ethnicity?

Table 7.3   Pay to Play: Descriptive Findings for Race-Specific Questionnaire

Should student-athletes playing in high-revenue-generating sports receive compensation beyond room and board, books, and free tuition?	Yes: 37.78% No: 62.22%
What is your age?	18–24 (97.83%) 25–34 (2.17%)
Are you a student-athlete?	Yes: 15.22% No: 84.78%
What is your gender?	Female: 63.04% Male: 36.96 %
What is your race/ethnicity?	American Indian: 2.17% Asian/Pacific Islander: 4.35% Black or African American: 26.09% White/Caucasian: 63.04% Multiple ethnicity/Other: 4.35% Hispanic: 0%

course was more of a survey course of the sociology of sport. The same professor taught both courses. The professor is a sociologist by training and specializes in research on race in general, and race and sports specifically.

Samantha, a white non-athlete enrolled in the survey course on sports and society, exemplified respondents who don't think college athletes in high-revenue-generating sports should receive any more compensation then they already receive. Samantha saw the issue as more of a class than a race issue. Samantha said, "I do not believe race plays a role in the current controversy. If anything I believe that socioeconomic status plays the bigger role, especially for those student-athletes coming from lower-income families. I do feel that a free education that most people pay for along with all the other perks they receive is plenty compensation, and I do not think they should be paid until they are hired as professional athletes." Samantha appears to be using class as a proxy for race. She sees college athletes in elite programs as privileged and as getting a free ride that students from hard-working families do not enjoy. She does not even concede that the athletes have to give anything or that they even have to work to keep and maintain their athletic and academic standing.

Jennifer, also a white, non-athlete, traditional college student, goes further than Samantha to say that it is not about race or class, but about ethnics. Jennifer is not talking about treating college athletes in a way that is in keeping with an institutions mission; rather, she thinks it is unethical for student-athletes to receive benefits that non-student-athletes like herself do not enjoy. Jennifer responded, "Ultimately, I don't think it is a question of race; I think it is a question of ethics. Non-student-athletes are shelling out a lot of money to go to college, while student-athletes receive room and board, books, and free tuition, and I'm sure they receive stipends as well."

John, a black male student-athlete enrolled in the survey course on sports and society, disagreed with Samantha and Jennifer. John said race does play a role. When asked to elaborate further, John said, "I think a lot [is] because most of the people who run NCAA is [sic] white." He clearly sees the underrepresentation of blacks in leadership positions within the institutions governing college athletics as problematic.

Derrick, who is also a black male student-athlete enrolled in the same course as John, believed student-athletes should receive compensation beyond scholarships, room and board, and books. Derrick also believes that race places an important role in the controversy. Derrick commented, "I think if football players were majority white, the NCAA would pay the players because the United States is racists [sic]." Derrick sees the issue of race as foundational to the nation and to the world of sports. Rachel, a white female in Derrick's class, had a similar response. Rachel said, "I think race has as big a role as any on the current controversy about paying college athletes. Race is always going to be a factor and contribute to decisions such as this."

Dione, a black female in the race-specific course, was in agreement with Derrick and Rachel. She said, "Majority athletes are African American players. Therefore they try to hold them back by not allowing them to be paid for their entertainment." The interest of the dominant group is valued more than the fair market value of the product produced by the athletes, according to Dione.

Like Samantha and Jennifer, Danielle, a white female, does not think that race plays a role in the controversy surrounding paying college athletes in high-revenue-generating sports. She also doesn't think such athletes should be paid. She does acknowledge the existence of racism in professional sports, but not in collegiate sports. Danielle remarked, "I would like to hope that race doesn't hold any importance in college sports, unlike professional sports." Historically, college sports have sought to distinguish themselves from professional sports, and from Danielle's comments we can see that some people continue to believe that to be the case.

Mary, a white female, agrees that race places a role in controversy surrounding compensating elite athletes, but she does not think student-athletes should receive additional financial support. Mary stated, "I believe that race plays a major role in this controversy. One of the major ways in which the sports administration gets athletes to come play for them is by compensation beyond normal means. For athletes of color (or any athletes in general) who do not have the funds to attend a certain college, yet are star athletes, they will be paid to play, which greatly influences where they will go as well. Depending on the school offering the most money seems to be where a student-athlete would most likely play."

Barbara Ann, a black female in the survey course on sports and society, is not a student-athlete. She did not agree that race was an important factor, but she did think that athletes in elite college programs should receive additional compensation. Barbara Ann responded by saying, "No, I do not believe race has anything to do with the pay of college athletes because white athletes are not getting paid as well." The fact that black athletes are overrepresented was apparently not relevant for the respondent as she clearly felt that all student-athletes were equally disadvantaged.

Although the responses from the students enrolled in the sports courses were varied, they reveal just how complex the controversy regarding race and sports is in modern times. There are those who believe we are living in a post-racial society where race does not matter, at least not in this particular aspect of sports; and then there are those who see race as foundational and central to understanding the issue about compensating student-athletes in high-revenue-generating sports; and finally there are those who minimize the role of race by focusing on class or using class as a proxy for race. The confusion about how and under what conditions we can consider race contributes to our national paralysis from moving forward on issues about race and racism in general and issues about race and racism in sports, in particular, such as whether to pay student-athletes in high-revenue-generating sports. Because many in our society refuse to see racism, even when it is "hidden" in plain sight, our ability to account for race and to push back against the unequal treatment of historically marginalized groups remains stagnate. In the next chapter, we call for transformations in how we think about college sports in a way that truly levels the playing field.

CHAPTER EIGHT

Rules for Transforming Amateur Athletics

Many people, from those in the White House to those in Congress, to the press, have opinions about whether to pay college athletes. In a sit-down interview with *The Huffington Post*, President Obama called on universities to show more responsibility for student-athletes. He favored guaranteed scholarships. He acknowledged the high revenue generated from the talent of student-athletes. According to the article, several big-time conferences have already passed reforms like the one President Obama suggested. The conferences include the Big Ten, the Big 12, the SEC, and the ACC. However, the reforms are somewhat limited. For example, in some cases student-athletes can lose their scholarship if they get injured while playing.

The president also weighed in on the idea of college athletes as amateurs. Efforts to maintain amateurism in college athletes have led to rules set and enforced by the NCAA that are overly punitive, in the president's estimation. Lamenting on the amount of revenue the athletes generate, the president remarked during a 2015 interview with *The Huffington Post*, "What does frustrate me is where I see coaches getting paid millions of dollars, athletic directors getting paid millions, the NCAA making huge amounts of money, and then some kid gets a tattoo or gets a free use of a car and suddenly they're banished. That's not fair."

Like many of our respondents, the president, an avid basketball fan, did not call for the unionization of athletes, nor did he say athletes should be paid. From his comments, it can be inferred that the president thinks determining who gets paid what would be challenging. President Obama

stated in the 2015 interview with *The Huffington Post*, "In terms of compensation, I think the challenge would just then start being, do we really
want to just create a situation where there are bidding wars? How much
does an Anthony Davis (a professional basketball player] get paid as
opposed to somebody else? And that I do think would ruin the sense of
college sports." It might ruin the "sense of college sports," but it does not
address the relatively disadvantaged position that far too many athletes in
big-time college programs experience.

The president also highlighted the finding that "for the vast majority of
players, college isn't a stopover on the way to a lucrative pro career." Colleges and universities are not "just a farm system for the NBA or NFL," which
"means that universities have more responsibilities than right now they're
showing."

Steve Siebold, a former professional tennis player, national coach, and
a contributor to *The Huffington Post*, agrees with the president that coaches
are compensated well and makes the case that players should receive pay
too.[1] He cites the $38 million, seven-year contract Jim Harbaugh received to
coach football at the University of Michigan. Siebold holds up Harbaugh's
case to show that "[c]ollege sports are a business and in business you pay
your top performers. It is that simple."[2] He adds that everyone makes money
when a school has a successful program—except the athletes. He does not
begrudge Harbaugh or any other coach making millions of dollars coaching college sports, but he makes the argument that, like coaches, college
athletes in high-revenue-generating sports should demand their share of
the billion-dollar pie and work collectively "to protect their rights and their
interests. They need to unionize," argues Siebold.[3]

A group of professors representing a number of academic disciplines
agrees with Siebold and created the College Athletes Rights & Empowerment Faculty Coalition (CARE-FC).[4] The stated mission of CARE-FC "is
to support college athletes in their quest to fundamentally change the existing college sport industry by recognizing they are employees who deserve
protections afforded such status."[5] CARE-FC is committed to work with
college athletes playing football and basketball "who seek relief from the
fraudulent business practices used by college sport organizations, which
rob them of basic civil rights to be compensated for their labor, work in a
safe environment, be protected when injuries beset them as a result of the
work they do, and be treated with human dignity."[6]

CARE-FC wants to work closely with college players associations and
other concerned faculty to impact public policy makers by increasing their
understanding "about the realities of exploitative practices of the current

college sport industry" and the impact on racial minorities.[7] Furthermore, CARE-FC is committed to working for "justice and fairness for athletes whose labor generates revenue for their institutions, the NCAA, conferences, and the corporations that invest in college sports."[8]

There are a number of things we must come to understand if we are to transform big college sports in such a way that predominantly black male bodies are not exploited for virtually everyone else's benefit but their own. To do so, we draw from work on racial realism and that on educational and penal realism. We show there are several truths that must be acknowledged if we are to journey onward.

First, we must acknowledge that efforts to resist the rights of college players to unionize and negotiate in their own interest reflect the fact that sports as well as colleges and universities are social institutions. Like all other social institutions, they were created not only to meet the basic needs of a given society but also to protect the economic and political dominance of elites and control their public image. Thus, the exploitation of largely black bodies in big-time college sports should not come as a surprise to anyone; rather, sports and colleges and universities were constructed to meet the demands of the dominant group in society, and the dominant group today demands that talented black athletes give their blood, sweat, and tears to bring millions of dollars annually to an institution that would—in far too many cases—find their mere presence loathsome.

Second, another important principle acknowledges that so long as people of color represent the majority of athletes in high-revenue-generating sports, colleges and universities—and any other entity benefiting from the labor of student-athletes—will never represent, serve, or address the interests of college athletes in high-revenue-generating sports. This is a demonstration of the interest-convergence principle outlined by Derrick Bell and other adherents to critical perspectives about sports and society.

Third, the economic imperatives of the U.S. economy, as well as the local economies that depend on big-time college sports for their very survival, are the central driving force in decisions to continue the marginalization and exploitation of big-time college athletes. Because the founders of the United States intended to make sure that only members of the dominant group would have access to wealth, status, and power, even sports participation was limited to certain groups. Over time, sports were open to people of color, but they do not serve, address, or meet the needs of everyone in the field.

Fourth, everyone included in big-time college athletics, whether well intentioned or not, both contribute to and benefit from the exploitation of athletes in big-time college sports. Desire to serve in activist roles has limits, through convergence with personal economic interests. Big-time college athletes may want to raise awareness about their concerns regarding the gap between what many people believe their lives are like relative to how they actually live, but they understand that doing so may jeopardize their playing time at the collegiate level and thus reduce their prospects of going to the next level in their sport. Weighing the costs and the benefits, many athletes choose to suffer in silence.

Fifth, because personal and private interests allow for the sacrifice of athletes in big-time college sports, elite college athletes will continue to be offered up in service of the historically and contemporarily overrepresented. It cannot be overstated just how much and how many people benefit from local college sports. Not only do small, medium, and large cities owe their very survival to the presence of colleges and universities, but this is even more so the case when it comes to big-time college sports. A recent example of this involves the unexpected relocation of a big-time college game, involving the LSU Tigers and the South Carolina Gamecocks, from one medium-sized city to another because of a natural disaster,. The news coverage in the city given just days to host the conference game was filled with reports from business owners discussing just how much they make during home games compared to away games or in the off season. Comments about the number of additional employees that are needed to meet the demands of people who may not go to the game, but wish to enjoy the festivities with other loyal fans. Additionally, the number of law enforcement officials required to cover a game where tens of thousands of people will attend often results in many, many hours and overtime pay. From national chains to mom-and-pop stores, to local barber shops and beauty salons, big-time college sporting events are a generator of community economic development for just about everyone except the athletes taking the field, some of whom suffer gruesome, life-altering, even life-ending, injuries, from which they may never recover. Prayers and lamentations about the athletes' courage, and placing them on pedestals to be hailed as inspirations to all, pale in comparison to the price they paid.

The sixth principle is that equality is a ruse aimed at distracting the populous. Some people are resistant to the idea of paying athletes in big-time college sports because they think the right thing to do is to treat all athletes equally. However, the evidence is clear that all athletes do not contribute equally. Individuals in relatively low-revenue-generating sports have ridden the coattails and benefited from the exploitation of athletes in high-revenue-generating sports for so long that the unequal treatment of the athletes—most, black males—became normative. It became acceptable—a marker of white privilege, if you will—to continually benefit from the labor of another simply because you could and to portray those individuals as less deserving of just compensation than the dominant society. The dominant group has historically justified paying historically disadvantaged groups less than what they deserve, and their unwillingness to adequate compensate athletes in big-time college sports is no different. Thus, seventh, we hold that equity is the only potential course of action that could counterbalance the racist underpinnings of big-time college sports. The time has long since passed for athletes in big-time college sports to get what is right for them and to retreat from the idea that everyone in college athletics should get the same thing.

As a society, we should always work to do what is right, not what is easy. Few people apparently ascribe to this idea when it comes to paying college athletes in big-time programs. Because many find the task far too daunting to figure out, or because this is the way we have always been doing things, many are resistant to change. As the authors of *Pay to Play*, we offer the following plan for changing the course of college sports; we understand that it shall be met with resistance, but in the tradition of what is known as adaptive leadership, we accept the task of mobilizing people to tackle tough challenges and thrive.

Colleges and universities may elect to offer academic scholarships for students who play on relatively low-profile college teams. These contests are not covered by multibillion-dollar deals with media conglomerates, for example. Student fees, state and federal aid, and donations pay for the scholarships from alumni and local businesses. Elite programs model professional teams and essentially function as semiprofessional and/or developmental teams. Players still wear a college logo but are not students. They participate in a draft that is akin to the draft for professional players. Players are not required to spend a set number of years at this level and may be "called up" at any time to join the professional team(s) associated with the program. This would allow for the maintenance of traditional college sports but reduce the extent to which players in high-revenue-generating sports are exploited for their labor. For example, football players in the semiprofessional league who play wearing a Rutgers University logo could be associated with one or more professional teams, such as the New York Jets or New York Giants. The professional teams would enter into agreements with the colleges and universities that would include financial support to take the place of funds that used to go directly to the colleges and universities.

There are a number of barriers to overcome. What we are proposing calls for colleges and universities to give up some control over their traditional sources of revenue, and it calls on owners of professional teams to enter into essentially a profit-sharing arrangement with colleges and universities. Most importantly, our plan is calling on colleges and universities and professional sports teams and associations to do the right thing and pay to play.

Appendix

Questions for current college athletes in elite (big-time) sports programs

What sport(s) do you play?

_____

_____

How long have you played the sport?

_____

_____

How long have you played the sport(s) at the college level?

_____

_____

List your current college or university.

_____

_____

List all colleges or universities you attended previously and the sports you played, including the NCAA division.

_____

_____

Describe your academic and professional goals.

_____

_____

Define the term "amateur athlete."

_____

_____

Are big-time college athletes amateur athletes? Why or why not?

_____

_____

What are the major differences and similarities between big-time college athletes and professional players?

_____

_____

Do you think big-time college athletes should unionize? Why or why not?

_____

_____

Do you agree or disagree with the following statement? "Top-tier college athletes already do get paid in the form of lucrative scholarships," Why or why not?

_____

_____

Do you agree or disagree with the following statement? "Top-tier college athletes benefit from critical training and exposure that enhances their draft prospects" Why or why not?

_____

_____

Who do you think profits the most from college athletics, and why? Cite examples.

_____

_____

Do you agree or disagree with the following statement? "Turning student-athletes into salaried professionals would fundamentally change sports," Why or why not?

_____

_____

Do you agree or disagree with the following statement? "Turning student-athletes into salaried professionals undermines the academic mission of colleges and universities." Why or why not?

_____

_____

Do you agree or disagree with the following statement? "Yes, it's unfair that certain football and basketball players produce enormous riches for their schools and don't get to reap the spoils. But paying them would be a logistical nightmare; indeed, it would prove impossible to devise a truly 'fair' revenue-distribution scheme. There are better ways to make college sports more equitable." Why or why not?

_____

_____

To what extent do you think your college or university is committed to your success as a student-athlete? Explain.

_____

_____

Should big-time college athletes have the right to endorse products, get paid for speaking engagements, and be compensated for the use of their likenesses on licensed products? Why or why not?

_____

_____

Should big-time college athletes be allowed to negotiate an actual contract with a professional sports league and have an agent?

_____

_____

In your opinion, which term most accurately describes big-time college athletes: student-athletes or full-time athletes? Why?

_____

_____

Describe an average week for you during your athletic season.

_____

_____

How many hours per week do you devote to your academic studies?

_____

_____

How many hours per week do you devote to your role as an athlete?

_____

_____

How much do you receive in athletic scholarships and grants?

_____

_____

How much do you receive from all other sources? Please explain.

_____

_____

Are you aware of athletes in high-revenue-generating sports experiencing economic hardships? If so, please elaborate.

_____

_____

What is your race? (check all that apply)
a. Asian
b. Black
c. Native American
d. White
e. Other (Describe)

What is your ethnicity?
a. Hispanic
b. Non-Hispanic

What is your age?

_____

_____

Describe your mother's educational attainment. What is the highest degree she earned?

_____

_____

Describe your father's educational attainment. What is the highest degree he earned?

_____

_____

Which of the following social class positions best describes your family's income level during your senior year in high school?

a. poor

b. working class

c. middle class

d. upper class

During your senior year, did you live in a housing unit that was owned or rented?

_____

_____

Did you attend public or private school?

_____

_____

Which of the following describes the community where you lived during your senior year in high school?

a. urban

b. rural

c. suburban

d. other (please explain)

What is your gender?

_____

_____

Do you have siblings? If so, how many?

_____

_____

Do your siblings currently play sports at the college-level? Where? Which sports?

_____

_____

Questions for former athletes

What sport(s) did you play?

_____

_____

How long did you play the sport(s) at the college-level?

_____

_____

List all the college or university you attended.

_____

_____

What is your current occupation?

_____

_____

Did you or are you playing a professionally?

_____

_____

How long did you play professionally? Describe your experience.

_____

_____

Define the term amateur athlete?

_____

_____

Should big-time college athletes really be considered amateurs? Why or why not?

_____

_____

What are the major differences and similarities between big-time college athletes and professional players?

_____

_____

Do you think college athletes should unionize? Why or why not?

_____

_____

Do you agree or disagree with the following statement? "Top-tier college athletes already do get paid, in the form of lucrative scholarships." Why or why not?

_____

_____

Do you agree or disagree with the following statement? "Those with professional aspirations benefit from critical training and exposure that enhances their draft prospects." Why or why not?

_____

_____

Who do you think profits the most from college athletics, and why?

_____

_____

Do you agree or disagree with the following statement? "Turning student-athletes into salaried professions would fundamentally change sports, undermine the academic mission of colleges and universities, and lead to further correction." Why or why not?

_____

_____

Do you agree or disagree with the following statement? "Yes, it's unfair that certain football and basketball players produce enormous riches for their schools and don't get to reap the spoils. But paying them would be a logistical nightmare; indeed it would prove impossible to devise a truly 'fair' revenue-distribution scheme. There are better ways to make college sports more equitable." Why or why not?

_____

_____

To what extent was the college or university you graduated from committed to your success as a student-athlete? Explain.

_____

_____

Should big-time college athletes have the right to endorse products, get paid for speaking engagements, and be compensated for the use of their likenesses on licensed products? Why or why not?

_____

_____

Should big-time college athletes be allowed to negotiate an actual contract with a professional sports league and have an agent?

_____

_____

In your opinion, which term most accurately describes big-time college athletes: student-athletes or full-time athletes?

_____

_____

As a college athlete, were you aware of athletes in high-revenue-generating sports experiencing economic hardships? If so, elaborate.

_____

_____

What is your race? (Check all that apply)
a. Asian
b. Black
c. Native American
d. White
e. Other

What is your ethnicity?
a. Hispanic
b. Non-Hispanic

What is your age?

_____

_____

Describe your mother's educational attainment. What is the highest degree she earned?

_____

_____

Describe your father's educational attainment. What is the highest degree he earned?

_____

_____

Which of the following social class positions best describes your family's income during your senior year in high school?

a. poor

b. working class

c. middle class

d. upper class

Did you attend public or private high school during your senior year in high school?

_____

_____

What is your gender?

_____

_____

Which of the following best describes your employment status?

a. employed, full-time

b. employed, part-time

c. unemployed

d. student

e. other (please explain)

What is your annual salary?

_____

_____

What is your total household income?

_____

_____

What is your marital status?

a. married

b. never married

c. divorced

d. widowed

What is your age?

_____

_____

Questions for non-athletes

Define the term "amateur athlete."

_____

_____

Should big-time college athletes really be considered amateurs? Why or why not?

_____

_____

What are the major differences and similarities between big-time college athletes and professional players?

_____

_____

Do you think college athletes should unionize? Why or why not?

_____

_____

Do you agree or disagree with the following statement? "Top-tier college athletes already do get paid, in the form of lucrative scholarships." Why or why not?

_____

_____

Do you agree or disagree with the following statement? "Those with professional aspirations benefit from critical training and exposure that enhances their draft prospects." Why or why not?

_____

_____

Who do you think profits the most from college athletics, and why?

_____

_____

Do you agree or disagree with the following statement? "Turning student-athletes into salaried professions would fundamentally change sports, undermine the academic mission of colleges and universities, and lead to further correction." Why or why not?

_____

_____

Do you agree or disagree with the following statement: "Yes, it's unfair that certain football and basketball players produce enormous riches for their schools and don't get to reap the spoils. But paying them would be a logistical nightmare; indeed, it would prove impossible to devise a truly 'fair' revenue-distribution scheme. There are better ways to make college sports more equitable." Why or why not?

_____

_____

To what extent is your college or university committed to your success as a student-athlete? Explain.

_____

_____

Should big-time college athletes have the right to endorse products, get paid for speaking engagements, and be compensated for the use of their likenesses on licensed products? Why or why not?

_____

_____

Should big-time college athletes be allowed to negotiate an actual contract with a professional sports league and have an agent?

_____

_____

In your opinion, which term most accurately describes big-time college athletes: student-athletes or full-time athletes?

_____

_____

As a college athlete, were you aware of athletes in high-revenue-generating sports experiencing economic hardships? If so, elaborate.

_____

_____

What is your race? (check all that apply)

a. Asian

b. Black

c. Native American

d. White

e. Other

What is your ethnicity?

a. Hispanic

b. Non-Hispanic

What is your age?

_____

_____

Describe your mother's educational attainment. What is the highest degree she earned?

_____

_____

Describe your father's educational attainment. What is the highest degree he earned?

_____

_____

Which of the following social class positions best describes your family's income during your senior year in high school?

a. poor

b. working class

c. middle class

d. upper class

Did you attend public or private high school during your senior year of high school?

_____

_____

What is your gender?

_____

_____

Which of the following best describes your employment status?

a. employed, full-time

b. employed, part-time

c. unemployed

d. student

e. other (please explain)

What is your marital status?

a. married

b. never married

c. divorced

d. widowed

What is your age?

_____

_____

Notes

Chapter 1: Amateur Athletes and the American Way

1. Richard Lapchick with John Fox, Angelica Guiao, and Maclin Simpson (2015) "The 2014 Racial and Gender Report Card: College Sport. The Institute for Diversity and Ethics in Sports," March 3, http://nebula.wsimg.com/308fbfef97c4 7edb705ff195306a2d50?AccessKeyId`=DAC3A56D8FB782449D2A&dispositi on=0&alloworigin=1.

2. Ibid.

3. Ibid.

4. Ibid.

5. Ibid.

6. Ibid., 6.

7. Ibid., 7.

8. Ibid.

9. "2010–2011. Fiesta Bowl Festival of College Football Economic Impact Study," https://fiestabowl.org/news-room/festival-of-college-football-creates-354 -million-for-arizona-economy/.

10. "NCAA Tournament Can Mean Billions for a School" (2015) *NBC News*, March 10, http://www.nbcnews.com/business/consumer/ncaa-tournament-run -can-mean-billions-school-n320876.

11. Ibid.

12. Ibid.

13. Ibid.

14. Ibid.

15. Chris Isidore (2015) "Wildly Profitable College Football about to Get More Profitable," *CNN Money*, January 13, http://money.cnn.com/2015/01/12/news /companies/college-football-profits.

16. Ibid.

Chapter 2: Creation of the Amateur Athlete in America

1. W. E. Winn (1960) "Tom Brown's Schooldays and the Development of Muscular Christianity," *Church History*, 29(1): 64–73.
2. Ibid.
3. Ibid.
4. Ibid.
5. Ibid.
6. Ibid., 66.
7. Ibid.
8. Ibid., 69.
9. Ibid.
10. Ibid.
11. Ibid.
12. Ibid., 70.
13. Ibid.
14. David K. Wiggins and Patrick B. Miller (2003) *Unlevel Playing Field* (Chicago, IL: University of Chicago Press), 41.
15. Ibid., 41–42.
16. N. Gernham (2001) "Both Praying and Playing: Muscular Christianity and the YMCA in North-East County Durham," *Journal of Social History*, 35(2): 397–407.
17. Ibid., 398.
18. Ibid.
19. Ibid.
20. Ibid., 401.
21. Ibid.
22. David P. Setran (2005) "Following the Broad-Shouldered Jesus: The College YMCA and the Culture of Muscular Christianity in American Campus Life, 1810–1914," *American Educational History Journal* 2005, 32(1): 59–66.
23. Ibid., 60.
24. Ibid.
25. Ibid.
26. Ibid.
27. Ibid.
28. Ibid.
29. Ibid.
30. Ibid., 61.
31. Ibid.
32. Leroy G. Dorsey (2013) "Managing Women's Equality: Theodore Roosevelt, the Frontier Myth, and the Modern Woman," *Rhetoric & Public Affairs*, 16(3): 425.
33. Ibid., 428.
34. Ibid., 431.

35. Ibid., 434.

36. Setran, "Following the Broad-Shouldered Jesus," 62.

37. Ibid.

38. Ibid.

39. Ibid., 63.

40. Ibid., 64.

41. Michael Perelman (n.d.) "Muscular Christianity and Football," Chico: California State University, http://www.csuchico.edu/~mperelman/foot.pdf, 2.

42. Ibid.

43. Ibid.

44. Ibid., 4.

45. Ibid.

46. "Eugenics Movement Reaches Its Height 1923," People and Discoveries, WGBH, http://www.pbs.org/wgbh/aso/databank/entries/dh23eu.html.

47. "Origins of Eugenics: From Sir Francis Galton to Virginia's Racial Integrity Act of 1924," Historical Collections at the Claude Moore Health Sciences Library, http://exhibits.hsl.virginia.edu/eugenics/2-origins/.

48. Ibid.

49. Ibid.

50. "Compensating N.C. Eugenics Victims" (2014) *The Charlotte Observer,* August 15.

51. Thomas Leonard (2005) "Retrospectives: Eugenics and Economics in the Progressive Era," *Journal of Economic Perspectives*, 19(4): 207–24.

52. Ibid.

53. Ibid.

54. Ibid.

55. Lutz Kaelber (2012) "Eugenics Sterilizations in Comparative Perspectives," Social Science History Association.

56. Ibid.

57. Jonathan Martin (2013) "The Recurring Cancer of Eugenics," Opinion Northwest, *The Seattle Times*, July 15, http://blogs.seattletimes.com/opinionnw/2013/07/15/the-recurring-cancer-of-eugenics/.

58. Ibid.

59. Jon Entine (2014) "Let's (Cautiously) Celebrate the New Eugenics," *The Huffington Post*, December 13, http://www.huffingtonpost.com/jon-entine/lets-cautiously-celebrate_b_6070462.html.

60. Ibid.

61. Ibid.

62. Jon Entine (2012) "Gattaca Alert? Or Should We Welcome the New Age of Eugenics?" *Forbes*, November 26, http://www.forbes.com/sites/jonentine/2012/11/26/gattaca-alert-or-should-we-welcome-the-new-age-of-eugenics/#78b7374c2292.

63. Juliet Macur (2008) "Born to Run? Little Ones Get Test for Sports Gene," *New York Times*, November 29, http://www.nytimes.com/2008/11/30/sports/30genetics.html.

64. Ibid.

65. Ibid.

66. See Darlene Clark Hine (2010) *African American Odyssey* (Upper Saddle River, NJ: Pearson).

67. K. S. Moore (2005) "What's Class Got to Do with It? Community Development and Racial Identity," *Journal of Urban Affairs*, 27(4): 437–51.

68. Ibid.

69. K. R. Lacy (2004) "Black Spaces, Black Places: Strategic Assimilation and Identity Construction in Middle-Class Suburbia," *Ethnic & Racial Studies*, 27(6): 908–30.

70. Ibid.

71. Wiggins and Miller, *Unlevel Playing Field*, 3.

72. Ibid.

73. Ibid., 4.

74. Ibid.

75. Ibid.

76. Ibid., 87.

77. Ibid., 444.

78. Stephen Finley (2010) "Masculinity," in Charles Lippy and Peter Williams (eds.), *Encyclopedia of Religion in America* (Thousand Oaks, CA: CQ Press), 1322–33.

79. Ibid., 1323.

80. Ibid., 1324.

81. Ibid., 1326.

82. Ibid., 1329.

83. Ibid., 1330.

84. Ibid.

85. Ibid., 1333.

Chapter 3: Racial Segregation and Amateur Athletics

1. John W. Blassingame (1979) *The Slave Community* (New York: Oxford University Press).

2. Errol D. Alexander (2015) *The Rattling of the Chains*, Xlibris Corporation, Bloomington, Indiana.

3. Ibid.

4. Ibid.

5. "The Culture of the Corn Shuck" (n.d.) Colonial Williamsburg, Education, http://www.history.org/history/teaching/enewsletter/volume2/september03/primsource.cfm.

6. Lisa K. Winkler (2009) "The Kentucky Derby's Forgotten Jockeys," April 23, http://www.smithsonianmag.com/history/the-kentucky-derbys-forgotten -jockeys-128781428/?no-ist.

7. Ibid.

8. Ibid.

9. Randy Sparks (1992) "Gentleman's Sport: Horse Racing in Antebellum Charleston," *The South Carolina Historical Magazine,* 93(1): 15–30.

10. Ibid.

11. Ibid,

12. Ibid.

13. Ibid., 16.

14. Ibid., 25.

15. Ibid., 25–26.

16. Ibid., 15–30.

17. Winkler, "The Kentucky Derby's Forgotten Jockeys."

18. Ibid.

19. Christopher Bates (2015) *The Early Republic and Antebellum America* (New York: Routledge).

20. Ibid.

21. Paul Magriel (1951) "Tom Molineaux," *Phylon,* 12(4): 329–36.

22. L. L. Martin (2015) *White Sports/Black Sports* (Santa Barbara, CA: Praeger).

23. Ibid.

24. Evan Albright (2007) "Blazing the Trail," *Amherst Magazine,* Winter, https:// www.amherst.edu/aboutamherst/magazine/issues/2007_winter/blazing.

25. Ibid.

26. Ibid.

27. Evan Albright (2005) "William Henry Lewis," *Harvard Magazine,* November–December, http://harvardmagazine.com/2005/11/william-henry-lewis -html.

28. Ibid.

29. Ibid.

30. Albright, "Blazing the Trail."

31. Jason Woullard (2013) "George Jewett: College Football's Original Renaissance Man," *The Shadow League,* October 4, http://www.theshadowleague .com/articles/george-jewett-college-football-s-original-renaissance-man.

32. Rachel Reed and Greg Kinney (n.d.) "Celebrating George Jewett: A Look at the Achievements of Michigan's First African American Football Letterman," Bentley Historical Society, University of Michigan, http://bentley.umich.edu /features/celebrating-george-jewett/.

33. Ibid.

34. Ibid.

35. Woullard, "George Jewett: College Football's Original Renaissance Man."

36. "The Athletes Who Paved the Way" (1997) *The Morning Call*, June 5, http://articles.mcall.com/1997-06-05/features/3143223_1_african-american -african-american-all-american-african-american-football.

37. Dennis Tuttle (2005) "Famous Early African American Track Stars," *Footsteps*, 7(3), May/June, 10.

38. Ibid.

39. Ibid.

40. Martin, *White Sports/Black Sports.*

41. K. Lindholm (1998) "William Clarence Matthews," *Harvard Magazine*, September–October, https://harvardmagazine.com/1998/09/vita.html.

42. Ibid.

43. Ibid.

44. J. Sumner (2011) "College Basketball Pioneers in North Carolina," *Tar Heel Junior Historian*, 51(1).

45. Ibid.

46. Ibid.

47. L. L. Martin (2015) *Big Box Schools: Race, Education, and the Danger of the Wal-Martization of Public Schools in America* (Lanham, MD: Lexington Books).

48. Ibid., 15.

49. Ibid., 17.

50. Ibid., 18.

51. Ibid., 19.

52. "1890 Land Grant History" (n.d.) *Prairie View A&M University*, http:// www.pvamu.edu/library/about-the-library/history-of-the-library-at-prairie-view /1890-land-grant-history/.

53. Ibid.

54. Ibid.

55. Ibid.

56. Ibid.

57. "Why Black Colleges?" (2009) *The Black College Football Museum*, http:// www.theblackcollegefootballmuseum.org/why.html.

58. Ibid.

59. Ibid.

60. E. B. Henderson (1939) "The Negro in Sports," *The Associated Press*, Washington, DC.

61. D. Wiggins and P. Miller (2003) *The Unlevel Playing Field: A Documentary History of the African American Experience in Sport* (Chicago, IL: University of Chicago Press), 85.

62. Ibid.

63. Ibid.

64. Ibid., 116.

65. Ibid.

66. Martin, *White Sports/Black Sports.*

67. Wiggins and Miller, *The Unlevel Playing Field.*

68. Ibid.

69. Ibid.

70. Ibid.

71. Martin, *White Sports/Black Sports.*

72. D. C. Hine (2010) *African American Odyssey* (New York: Pearson).

73. Ibid.

74. Wiggins and Miller, *The Unlevel Playing Field.*

75. Hine, *African American Odyssey.*

76. Martin, *White Sports/Black Sports.*

77. Wiggins and Miller, *The Unlevel Playing Field.*

78. T. Runstedtler (2012) *Jack Johnson Rebel Sojourner* (Berkeley, CA: University of California Press).

79. Ibid.

80. Ibid., 32.

81. Ibid., 110.

82. Ibid., 226.

83. D. Naze (2014) "Jackie Robinson Day: The Contemporary Legacy," in L .L. Martin (ed.), *Out of Bounds: Racism and the Black Athlete* (Santa Barbara, CA: Praeger), 135–58.

84. Ibid.

85. Ibid.

86. Ibid., 138–39.

87. Ibid.

88. Ibid., 138–40.

89. Ibid., 138–42.

90. Richard Lapchick (2008) "Breaking the College Color Barrier: Studies in Courage," *ESPN.com: Black History 2008*, February 20, http://sports.espn.go.com /espn/blackhistory2008/columns/story?id=3254974.

91. R. Pennington (n.d.) "Racial Integration of College Football," http:// richardpennington.com/index.php/publications/entry/racial-integraton-of-college -football-in-texasracial-integraton-of-college.

92. Ibid.

93. Ibid.

94. Ibid.

94. Ibid.

95. Ibid.

96. B. Pennington (2012) "In 1956, a Racial Law Repelled Harvard's Team," *New York Times*, March 14, http://www.nytimes.com/2012/03/15/sports/ncaa basketball/in-1956-a-racial-law-soured-harvard-on-a-trip-to-new-orleans.html? _r=0.

97. "Integration on the Court: College Basketball in the South" (2012) Sports in Black and White, October 21, http://www.sportsinblackandwhite.com/2012 /10/21/integration-on-the-court-college-basketball-in-the-south/.

98. Lapchick, "Breaking the College Color Barrier."

99. Ibid.

100. "Integration on the Court: College Basketball in the South."

101. Pennington, "In 1956, a Racial Law Repelled Harvard's Team."

102. Lapchick, "Breaking the College Color Barrier."

Chapter 4: Rise of the Black Male Athlete at Predominantly White Colleges and Universities

1. M. L. Dudziak (1988) "Desegregation as a Cold War Imperative," *Stanford Law Review*, 41(1): 61–120.

2. Timothy Davis (1995) "The Myth of the Superspade: The Persistence of Racism in College Athletics," *Fordham Urban Law Journal*, 22(3): 615–98, http://ir .lawnet.fordham.edu/cgi/viewcontent.cgi?article=1664&context=ulj.

3. Billy Joe Hawkins (2010) *The New Plantation: Black Athletes, College Sports, and Predominantly White NCAA Institutions* (New York: Palgrave Macmillan), 45.

4. Richard Lapchick with John Fox, Angelica Guiao, and Maclin Simpson (2015) "The 2014 Racial and Gender Report Card: College Sport. The Institute for Diversity and Ethics in Sports," March 3, http://nebula.wsimg.com/308fbfef9 7c47edb705ff195306a2d50?AccessKeyId=DAC3A56D8FB782449D2A&disposit ion=0&alloworigin=1

5. William C. Rhoden (2006) *Forty Million Dollar Slaves: The Rise, Fall, and Redemption of the Black Athlete* (New York: Three Rivers Press), 176.

6. Lori Latrice Martin (2015) *White Sports/Black Sports: Racial Disparities in Athletic Programs* (Santa Barbara, CA: Praeger), 82.

7. Rhoden, *Forty Million Dollar Slaves*, 175.

8. Taylor Branch (2011) "The Shame of College Sports," *The Atlantic*, 308(3): 80–86, 88, 89, 93, 94, 96, 98, 100–102, 104, 106, 108, 110.

9. Brando Simeo Starkey (2014) "College Sports Aren't Like Slavery. They're Like Jim Crow," *New Republic*, October 31, http://www.newrepublic.com.

10. Rhoden, *Forty Million Dollar Slaves*, 171–98.

11. "NCAA Revenue Breakdown," NCAA, http://www.ncaa.org/about /resources/finances/revenue.

12. Ibid.

13. "Beckman Fired as U of I Football Coach" (2015) Pantagraph, August 28, http://www.pantagraph.com/sports/college/football/beckman-fired-as-u-of-i -head-football-coach/article_f25eb515-4e4b-5f2c-ae0d-8b9c24a935fb.html.

14. Kenya LeNoir Messer (2006) "African American Male College Athletes," in M. J. Cuyjet and Associates (eds.), *African American Mmen in College* (San Francisco, CA: Joesey-Bass), 155.

15. Sara Ganim (2015) "University of Illinois Fires Head Football Coach after Player Complaints," CNN, August 29, http://www.cnn.com/2015/08/28/us /university-illinois-coach-fired/.

16. R. A. Bennett, S. R. Hodge, D. L. Graham, and J. L. Moore (eds.) (2015) *Black Males and Intercollegiate Athletics: An Exploration of Problems* (Bingley, UK: Emerald Books), xii.

Chapter 5: Commodification of Black Bodies

1. D. C. Hine (2010) *African American Odyssey* (New York: Pearson), 22.

2. Ibid.

3. Ibid., 33.

4. Ibid., 34.

5. Ibid., 36.

6. Ibid.

7. Ibid.

8. Henry Watson (1850) *Narrative of Henry Watson, a Fugitive Slave* (Boston, MA: Bela Marsh).

9. Henry Walton Bibb (2001) "Narrative of the Life and Adventures of Henry Bibb, an American Slave," in S. L. Bland (ed.), *African American Slave Narratives: An Anthology, Vol. II* (Santa Barbara, CA: Greenwood), 393.

10. Ibid.

11. Ibid.

12. Yuval Taylor (1999) "The Narrative of William W. Brown, A Fugitive Slave," in Y. Taylor (ed.), *I Was Born a Slave: An Anthology of Classic Slave Narratives* (Chicago, IL: Lawrence Hill Books).

13. "Enslaved Ancestors Abstracted from Granville, County, North Carolina Deed Books, 1746–1828," Afri Geneas Library. Retrieved from http://www .afrigeneas.com/library/ncdeeds/1746-1828[o-z].html.

14. David Horsey (2014) "History of Economic Exploitation Still Hinders Black Americans," *Los Angeles Times,* September 9, http://www.latimes.com/opinion /topoftheticket/la-na-tt-history-hinders-black-americans-20140908-story.html.

15. Ibid.

16. D. Burris-Kitchen and P. Burris (2011) "From Slavery to Prisons: A Historical Delineation of the Criminalization of African Americans," *Journal of Global Intelligence & Policy*, 4(5): 1–16.

17. Ibid., 2.

18. Ibid.

19. Ibid.

20. Ibid.

21. Ibid., 3.

22. Ibid.

23. Ibid., 1–16.

24. Hollis Lynch, "Americans of African History," International World History Project, http://history-world.org/black_codes.htm.

25. Ibid.

26. Ibid.

27. Ibid.

28. Ibid.

29. Ibid.

30. Ibid.

31. Ibid.

32. Ibid.

33. Ibid.

34. Ibid.

35. Ibid.

36. Ibid.

37. Ibid.

38. Ibid.

39. Ibid.

40. Richard Zuczek (ed.) (2006) "An Act to Regulate the Relation of Master and Apprentice, as Relates to Freedmen, Free Negroes, and Mulattoes," in *Encyclopedia of the Reconstruction Era: M–Z and Primary Documents, Vol. 2* (Santa Barbara, CA: Greenwood).

41. Devon Douglass-Bowers (2014) "Slavery by Another Name: The Convict Leasing System," The Hampton Institute, October 30, http://www.hampton institution.org/convictleasesystem.html#.VzqEuiMrI1I.

42. Ibid.

43. Ibid.

44. Ibid.

45. Ibid.

46. Ibid.

47. Ibid.

48. Calvin R. Ledbetter Jr. (1993) "The Long Struggle to End Convict Leasing in Arkansas," *Arkansas Historical Quarterly*, 52 (Spring): 1–27.

49. Ibid., 2.

50. Ibid., 6.

51. Ibid.

52. Ibid.

53. Ibid., 27.

54. Burris-Kitchen and Burris, "From Slavery to Prisons," 9.

55. Ibid.

56. "Lynching in America: Confronting the Legacy of Racial Terror," Equal Justice Institute of America, http://eji.org/reports/lynching-in-america.

57. Ibid.

58. Ibid., 13.

59. Ibid.

60. Ibid., 18.

61. Ibid., 19.

62. Robin D. G. Kelley (2007) "The Case of the Scottsboro Boys," http://www.writing.upenn.edu/~afilreis/88/scottsboro.html.

63. Ibid.

64. Burris-Kitchen and Burris, "From Slavery to Prisons," 12.

65. Ibid.

66. Ibid.

67. Ibid.

68. Ibid., 13.

69. Ibid., 1–16.

70. Ibid.

71. Naomi Murkawa (2014) *The First Civil Right* (New York: Oxford University Press).

72. Ibid.

73. Gerald Shargel (2004) "Ronald Reagan's Tough Legal Legacy," *Slate*, http://www.slate.com/articles/news_and_politics/jurisprudence/2004/06/no_mercy.html.

74. Ibid.

75. Ibid.

76. Lori Latrice Martin (2015) *Big Box Schools: Race, Education, and the Danger of the Wal-Martization of Public Schools in America* (Lanham, MD: Lexington Books).

77. Ibid.

78. Ibid.

79. Ibid.

80. Ibid., 67.

81. Ibid.

82. Ibid., 43.

83. Ibid.

84. Ibid., 45.

85. Ibid.

86. Ibid., 46.

87. Ibid., 49.

88. Ibid.

89. Lori Latrice Martin (2014) "Been There Done That," in *Trayvon Martin, Race, and American Justice: Writing Wrongs* (Rotterdam, The Netherlands: Sense Publishers), 17.

90. Ibid.

91. Martin, *Big Box Schools*.

92. Martin, *Big Box Schools*, 51.

93. David J. Leonard (2012) "Jumping the Gun," *Journal of Sport and Social Issues*, 34: 254.

94. Ibid.

95. David Pilgrim (2012) "Brute Caricature," Jim Crow Museum of Racist Memorabilia, Ferris State University, http://www.ferris.edu/jimcrow/brute/.

96. Ibid.

97. Ibid.

98. Ibid.

99. Salim Muwakkil (2002) "Blacks, Sport and Lingering Racial Stereotypes," *Chicago Tribune*, June 17, http://articles.chicagotribune.com/2002-06-17/news/0206170135_1_tennis-stereotypes-black-athletes-dominate-sports.

100. Samuel Hodge, J. Burden, L. Robinson, and R. Bennett (2008) "Theorizing on the Stereotyping of Black Male Student-Athletes," *Journal for the Study of Sports and Athletes in Education*, 2(3): 203–26.

101. Ibid., 217.

102. Ibid., 218–19.

103. A. Arnett (2015) "Media Fuels Negative Perceptions about Black Athletes," *Diverse Education*, June 4, http://diverseeducation.com/article/73591/.

104. Ibid.

105. Ibid.

106. Ibid.

107. A portion of this chapter appears in L. L. Martin (ed.) (2015) "Toward a Unifying Perspective on Race, Racism, and Sports," *White Sports/Black Sports* (Santa Barbara, CA: Praeger), 9–19.

108. Ibid.

109. Ibid.

110. G. A. Sailes (1991) "The Myth of Black Sports Supremacy," *Journal of Black Studies*, 21(4): 480.

111. A. Bejan, E. C. Jones, and J. Charles (2010) "The Evolution of Speed in Athletics: Why the Fastest Runners Are Black and Swimmers White," *International Journal of Design and Nature*, 5(3): 199–211.

112. Z. W. Brewster and S. N. Rusche (2012) "Quantitative Evidence of the Continuing Significance of Race: Tableside Racism in Full-Service Restaurants," *Journal Of Black Studies*, 43(5), 359–84; J. R. Feagin (1991) "The Continuing Significance of Race: Antiblack Discrimination in Public Places," *American Sociological Review*, 56(1): 101–16; P. Y. Warren (2010) "The Continuing Significance of Race: An Analysis across Two Levels of Policing," *Social Science Quarterly*, 91(4): 1025–42.

113. L. Forster-Scott (2011) "Understanding Colorism and How It Relates to Sport and Physical Education," *The Journal of Physical Education, Recreation and Dance*, 82(2): 48–52; K. Hylton (2010) "How a Turn to Critical Race Theory Can Contribute to Our Understanding of 'Race', Racism and Anti-Racism in Sport," *International Review for the Sociology of Sport*, 45(3): 335–54.

114. D. A. Bell (1995) "Who's Afraid of Critical Race Theory?" *University Of Illinois Law Review*, 1995(4): 893–910.

115. C. Herring, V. Keith, and H. D. Horton (eds.) (2004) *Skin Deep: How Race and Complexion Matter in the "Color-Blind" Era* (Chicago: University of Illinois Press).

116. H. D. Horton (2002) "Rethinking American Diversity: Conceptual and Theoretical Challenges for Racial and Ethnic Demography," in Stewart Tolnay and Nancy Denton (eds.), *American Diversity: A Demographic Challenge for the Twenty-First Century* (Albany, New York: SUNY Press); H. Horton and B. Allen (1998) "Race, Family Structure and Rural Poverty: An Aassessment of Population and Structural Change," *Journal Of Comparative Family Studies*, 29(2): 397–406.

117. H. Horton (1999) "Critical Demography: The Paradigm of the Future?" *Sociological Forum*, 14(3): 363; H. D. Horton and L. L. Sykes (2008) "Critical Demography and the Measurement of Racism: A Reproduction of Wealth, Status, and Power," in T. Zuberi and E. Bonilla-Silva (eds.), *White Logic, White*

Methods: Racism and Methodology (Lanham, MD: Rowman & Littlefield); D. S. Massey (1999) "What Critical Demography Means to Me," *Sociological Forum*, 14(3): 525.

118. A. Onwuachi-Willig (2009) "Celebrating Critical Race Theory at 20," *Iowa Law Review*, 94: 1497–1504.

119. R. Closson (2010) "Critical Race Theory and Adult Education," *Adult Education Quarterly*, 60(3): 261–83; K. J. Fasching-Varner (2009) "No! The Team Ain't Alright! The Iinstitutional and Individual Problematics of Race," *Social Identities: Journal for the Study of Race, Nation and Culture*, 15(6): 811–29.

120. L. M. Burton, E. Bonilla-Silva, V. Ray, R. Buckelew, and E. Freeman (2010) "Critical Race Theories, Colorism, and the Decade's Research on Families of Color," *Journal of Marriage & Family*, 72(3): 440–59.

121. M. Romero (2008) "Crossing the Immigration and Race Border: A Critical Race Theory Approach to Immigration Studies," *Contemporary Justice Review*, 11(1): 23–37.

122. C. L. Ford and C. O. Airhihenbuwa (2010) "Critical Race Theory, Race Equity, and Public Health: Toward Antiracism Praxis," *American Journal of Public Health*, 100(S1): S30–S35; L. Graham, S. Brown-Jeffy, R. Aronson, and C. Stephens (2011) "Critical Race Theory as Theoretical Framework and Analysis Tool for Population Health Research," *Critical Public Health*, 21(1): 81–93.

123. S. Arai and B. D. Kivel (2009) "Critical Race Theory and Social Justice Perspectives on Whiteness, Difference(s), and (Anti)racism: A Fourth Wave of Race Research," *Journal of Leisure Research*, 41(4): 459–70; B. Carrington (2013) "The Critical Sociology of Race and Sport: The First Fifty Years," *Annual Review of Sociology*, 39(1): 379–98; Hylton, "How a Turn to Critical Race Theory Can Contribute to Our Understanding of 'Race', Racism and Anti-Racism in Sport," 335–54.

124. Bell, "Who's Afraid of Critical Race Theory?"

125. Burton, Bonilla-Silva, Ray, Buckelew, and Freeman, "Critical Race Theories, Colorism, and the Decade's Research on Families of Color."

126. Bell, "Who's Afraid of Critical Race Theory?"

127. T. Zuberi (2011) "Critical Race Theory of Society," *Connecticut Law Review*, 43(5): 1573–91.

128. Onwuachi-Willig, "Celebrating Critical Race Theory at 20," 1502.

129. Arai and Kivel, "Critical Race Theory and Social Justice Perspectives on Whiteness, Difference(s), and (Anti)racism."

130. Bell, "Who's Afraid of Critical Race Theory?"

131. A. Treviño, M. A. Harris, and D. Wallace (2008) "What's So Critical about Critical Race Theory?" *Contemporary Justice Review*, 11(1): 7–10.

132. Onwuachi-Willig, "Celebrating Critical Race Theory at 20," 1502.

133. K. Hylton (2008) *Race and Sport* (New York: Routledge).

134. B. Louis (2004) "Sport and Common Sense Racial Science," *Leisure Studies*, 23(1), January, 31–46, quoted in ibid.

135. Hylton, *Race and Sport*.

136. Ibid.

137. Ibid.

138. Treviño, Harris, and Wallace, "What's So Critical about Critical Race Theory?" 7–10.

139. J. N. Singer (2005) "Addressing Epistemological Racism in Sport Management Research," *Journal of Sport Management*, 19(4): 464–79.

140. Ibid.

141. Ibid.

142. Ibid., 473.

143. Ibid., 475.

144. D. Hartmann (2007) "Rush Limbaugh, Donovan McNabb, and Little Concern," *Journal of Sport and Social Issues*, 31(1): 45–60.

145. Ibid.

146. Ibid., 50.

147. Ibid., 56.

148. Ibid., 58.

149. J. N. Singer (2009) "African American Football Athletes' Perspectives on Institutional Integrity in College Sport," *Research Quarterly for Exercise Sport*, 80(1): 102–16.

150. Ibid.

151. Ibid., 104.

152. Ibid., 102–16.

153. Ibid., 106.

154. Ibid.

155. Ibid., 102–16.

156. Ibid.

157. A. R. Carter and A. Hart (2010) "Perspectives on Mentoring: The Black Female Student-Athlete," *Sport Management Review* 13(4): 382–94.

158. Ibid.

159. Ibid.

160. A. Y. Bimper, L. Harrison, and C. Langston (2013) "Diamonds in the Rough: Examining a Case of Successful Black Male Student-Athletes in College Sport," *The Journal of Black Psychology*, 39(2): 119–42.

161. Ibid.

162. Ibid.

163. M. Regan, A. R. Carter-Francique, and J. R. Feagin (2015) "Systematic Racism Theory: Critically Examining College Sport Leadership," in L. L. Martin (ed.), *Out of Bounds: Racism and the Black Athlete* (Santa Barbara, CA: Praeger Publishers), 34.

164. Ibid., 35.

165. Ibid., 37.

166. Ibid., 38.

167. Ibid., 45.

168. C. Herring (2004) "Skin Deep: Race and Complexion in the 'Color-Blind' Era," in C. Herring, V. M. Keith, and H. D. Horton (eds.), *Skin Deep: How Race and Complexion Matter in the "Color-Blind" Era* (Chicago: University of Illinois Press), 3.

169. Ibid.

170. See, for example, Edwards, Carter-Tellison, and Herring, "For Richer, for Poorer, Whether Dark or Light: Skin Tone, Marital Status, and Spouse's Earnings"; Herring, "Skin Deep: Race and Complexion in the 'Color-Blind' Era"; and M. S. Thompson and V. M. Keith (2004) "Cooper Brown and Blue Black: Colorism and Self Evaluation"—all in C. Herring, V. M. Keith, and H. D. Horton (eds.), *Skin Deep: How Race and Complexion Matter in the "Color-Blind" Era*, 65–81, 1–21, and 45–64, respectively.

171. Burton, Bonilla-Silva, Ray, Buckelew, and Freeman, "Critical Race Theories, Colorism, and the Decade's Research on Families of Color."

172. A. P. Harris (2008) "From Color Line to Color Chart?: Racism and Colorism in the New Century," *Berkeley Journal of African-American Law and Policy*, 10(1): 52–69.

173. Ibid.

174. Ibid.

175. V. M. Keith (2009) "A Colorstruck World: Skin Tone, Achievement, and Self-Esteem among African American Women," in Evelyn Nakano Glenn (ed.), *Shades of Difference: Why Skin Color Matters* (Los Altos: Stanford University Press), 25–39.

176. J. Robst, J. VanGilder, C. E. Coates, and D. J. Berri (2011) "Skin Tone and Wages: Evidence from NBA Free Agents," *Journal of Sports Economics*, 12(2): 143–56.

177. J. Hersch (2008) "Skin Color Discrimination and Immigrant Pay," *Emory Law Journal*, 58(2): 357–77; M. Hunter (2008) Teaching and Learning Guide for "The Persistent Problem of Colorism: Skin Tone, Status, and Inequality," *Sociology Compass*, 2(1): 366; V. M. Keith and C. Herring (1991) "Skin Color and Stratification in the Black Community," *American Journal of Sociology*, 97: 760–78.

178. H. Horton and B. Allen (1998) "Race, Family Structure and Rural Poverty: An Assessment of Population and Structural Change," *Journal of Comparative Family Studies*, 29(2): 398.

179. R. Carter (2005) "NBA's New Dress Code: Racist or Just Smart Business?" *New York Amsterdam News*, November 17, 10–41.

180. A. L. Sack, P. Singh, and R. Thiel (2005) "Occupational Segregation on the Playing Field: The Case of Major League Baseball," *Journal of Sport Management*, 19(3): 300–18.

181. E. Cashmore and J. Cleland (2011) "Why Aren't There More Black Football Managers?" *Ethnic & Racial Studies*, 34(9): 1594–1607.

182. C. Hallman (2012) "Colorblind Racism: Language of Sports Filled with Barely Disguised Bigotry," *Minnesota-Spokesman Reporter*, June 27.

183. L. L. Martin (2013) *Black Asset Poverty and the Enduring Racial Divide* (Boulder, CO: First Forum Press).

184. Hunter, Teaching and Learning Guide for "The Persistent Problem of Colorism," 366; Keith and Herring, "Skin Color and Stratification in the Black

Community"; L. Martin (2009) "Black Asset Ownership: Does Ethnicity Matter?" *Social Science Research*, 38(2): 312–23.

185. Martin, *White Sports/Black Sports*.

186. Ibid.

187. Ibid.

188. Ibid.

189. Ibid.

190. Ibid.

191. Horton, "Critical Demography," 363.

192. Ibid.

193. Ibid.

194. H. D. Horton (n.d.) "Critical Demography and Racism: The Case of African Americans. Perspectives," http://www.rcgd.isr.umich.edu/prba/perspectives/springsummer2000/hhorton2.pdf.

195. D. Fogarty (2011) "Are White People Losing Interest in the NBA Because None of Its Superstars Look Like Them?" SportsGrid, February 21, http://www.sportsgrid.com/nba/nba-white-people-interest; M. Schneider-Mayerson (2010) "Too Black: Race in the Dark Ages of the National Basketball Association," *International Journal of Sport and Society*, 1(1), 223–33.

196. M. Wilbon (2011) "The Foreign Flavor of This NBA Draft," *ESPN*, June 25, http://sports.espn.go.com/espn/commentary/news/story?page=wilbon-110624.

197. Martin, *White Sports/Black Sports*.

198. Ibid., 9.

199. Ibid., 10.

200. Ibid.

201. Ibid.

202. Ibid., 15.

203. Ibid.

204. Lapchick, Hippert, Rivera, and Robinson, "The 2013 Race and Gender Report Card," http://www.tidesport.org/racial-and-gender-report-cards.html (accessed 6/22/2014).

Chapter 6: Current Controversies: An Analysis of the Northwestern and O'Bannon Cases

1. Lori Latrice Martin (2015) *Big Box Schools: Race, Education, and the Danger of the Wal-Martization of Public Schools in America* (Lanham, MD: Lexington Books).

2. Ibid.

3. Ibid.

4. N. Burleigh (2015) "Politicians Try to Union-Bus Their Way to the White House," *Newsweek*.

5. Ibid.

6. Ibid.

7. Ibid.

8. Ibid.

9. Ibid.

10. R. Zullo (2011) "Right-to-Work Laws and Fatalities in Construction," Irlee .umich.edu.

11. Ibid.

12. Ibid.

13. Ibid., 2.

14. Ibid.

15. Martin, *Big Box Schools*, 58.

16. Ibid.

17. "Sports Unions Work to Level the Playing Field" (n.d.) American Postal Workers Union, Labor History Articles, https://www.apwu.org/labor-history -articles/sports-unions-work-level-playing-field.

18. H. Bloom (2014) "NFL Revenue Sharing Model Good for Business," Sporting News, http://www.sportingnews.com/nfl/news/nfl-revenue-sharing -television-contracts-2014-season-business-model-nba-nhl-mlb-comparison -salary-cap/gu0xok7mphu01x3vu875oeaq6.

19. L. Bien (2015) "The 2015 Salary Cap Explained," SB Nation, March 2, http://www.sbnation.com/nfl/2015/3/2/8134891/nfl-salary-cap-2015-franchise -tag-explained.

20. "Pro Sports Lockouts and Strikes Fast Facts," CNN Library, May 4, 2016, http://www.cnn.com/2013/09/03/us/pro-sports-lockouts-and-strikes-fast-facts/.

21. "Understanding Life Outcomes of Former NCAA Student-Athletes," Gallup Purdue Index Report, https://www.ncaa.org/sites/default/files/2016_Gallup _NCAA_StudentAthlete_Report_20160503.pdf.

22. Ibid.

23. S. R. Harper, C. D. Williams, and H. W. Blackman (2013) *Black Male Student-Athletes and Racial Inequities in NCAA Division I College Sports* (Philadelphia, PA: University of Pennsylvania, Center for the Study of Race and Equity in Education), https://www.gse.upenn.edu.

24. Ibid.

25. Martin, *White Sports/Black Sports*.

26. A. Gimino (2013) "Arizona Basketball: All about Mark Lyons," *Tuscon Citizen*, March 27, http://tucsoncitizen.com/wildcatreport/2013/03/27/arizona -basketball-all-about-mark-lyons/.

27. B. Joravsky (1996) *Hoop Dreams: A True Story of Hardship and Triumph* (New York: HarperCollins).

28. Martin, *White Sports/Black Sports*.

29. A. C. Jones and M. Naison (2011) *The Rat That Got Away* (New York: Fordham University Press).

30. Martin, *White Sports/Black Sports*.

31. Ibid.

32. Jones and Naison, *The Rat That Got Away*.

33. V. M. Mallozzi (1990) "Basketball; Legend of the Playground," *New York Times*, November 11, http://www.nytimes.com/1990/11/11/sports/basketball -legend-of-the-playground.html?pagewanted=all&src=pm.

34. Ibid.

35. Ibid.

36. Martin, *White Sports/Black Sports.*

37. Ibid.

38. Ibid.

39. Ibid.

40. Lapchick et al., "The 2012 Racial and Gender Report Card: Major League Baseball," http://nebula.wsimg.com/c338db497f95b8758669c703c9e60de1?Access KeyId=DAC3A56D8FB782449D2A&disposition=0&alloworigin=1.

41. H. Edwards (1979) "Sport within the Veil: The Triumphs, Tragedies and Challenges of Afro-American Involvement," *The Annals of the American Academy of Political and Social Science*, 445, 117.

42. Ibid.

43. Ibid.

44. Ibid., 119.

45. Ibid., 121.

46. Ibid., 124.

47. Lapchick et al., "The 2011 Racial and Gender Report Card," 5, http://aaes ports.org/documents/2015/7/28//2011_College_Sport_Racial_Gender_Report_ Card.pdf?id=19.

48. Ibid.

49. E. Buzuvis (2015) "Athletic Compensation for Women Too? Title IX Implications of Northwestern and O'Bannon," 41 J.C. & U.L. 312.

50. Ibid., 313.

51. Ibid., 315.

52. Ibid., 316.

53. Ibid.

54. United States Government before the National Labor Relations Board Region 13, https://www.insidehighered.com/sites/default/server_files/files/NU% 20Decision%20and%20Direction%20of%20Election.pdf.

55. Ibid., 2.

56. Ibid.

57. Ibid., 3.

58. Ibid., 4.

59. Ibid., 5.

60. Ibid.

61. Ibid.

62. Ibid., 6.

63. Ibid., 9.

64. Ibid.

65. Ibid., 9–10.

66. Ibid., 10.
67. Ibid., 11.
68. Ibid.
69. Ibid, 13.
70. Buzuvis, "Athletic Compensation for Women Too?"
71. Ibid., 299.
72. Ibid.

Chapter 8: Rules for Transforming Amateur Athletics

1. S. Siebold (2015) "College Sports Programs Compensate Coaches Well—and Now It Is Time to Pay the Players," *The Huffington Post*, May 26, http://www.huffingtonpost.com/steve-siebold/college-sports-programs-c_b_6944176.html.
2. Ibid.
3. Ibid.
4. "Care Statement in Support of University of Missouri Black Football Players" (2015) CARE-FC, November 9, http://care-fc.org/.
5. Ibid.
6. Ibid.
7. Ibid.
8. Ibid.

Bibliography

"1890 Land Grant History." *Prairie View A&M University.* Retrieved from http://www.pvamu.edu/library/about-the-library/history-of-the-library-at-prairie-view/1890-land-grant-history/.

Albright, Evan. (Winter 2007). "Blazing the Trail." *Amherst Magazine.* Retrieved from https://www.amherst.edu/aboutamherst/magazine/issues/2007_winter/blazing.

Alexander, Errol D. (2015). *The Rattling of the Chains.* Bloomington, IN: Xlibris Corporation.

"The Athletes Who Paved the Way." (June 5, 1997). *The Morning Call.* http://articles.mcall.com/1997-06-05/features/3143223_1_african-american-african-american-all-american-african-american-football.

Bates, Christopher. (2015). *The Early Republic and Antebellum America.* New York: Routledge.

Blassingame, John W. (1979). *The Slave Community.* New York: Oxford University Press.

"The Culture of the Corn Shuck." Retrieved from http://www.history.org/history/teaching/enewsletter/volume2/september03/primsource.cfm.

Henderson, E. B. (1939). "The Negro in Sports." *Associated Press.* Washington, DC.

Hine, D. C. (2010). *African American Odyssey.* New York: Pearson.

"Integration on the Court: College Basketball in the South." (2012). Retrieved from http://www.sportsinblackandwhite.com/2012/10/21/integration-on-the-court-college-basketball-in-the-south/.

Lapchick, Richard. (2008). "Breaking the College Color Barrier: Studies in Courage." ESPN.com: Black History 2008. Retrieved from http://sports.espn.go.com/espn/blackhistory2008/columns/story?id=3254974.

Lindholm, K. (1998). "William Clarence Matthews." *Harvard Magazine.* Retrieved from https://harvardmagazine.com/1998/09/vita.html.

Magriel, Paul. (1951). "Tom Molineaux." *Phylon,* 12(4): 329–336.

Martin, L. L. (2015). *Big Box Schools: Race, Education, and the Danger of the Wal-Martization of Public Schools in America.* Lanham, MD: Lexington Books.

Martin, L. L. (2015). *White Sports/Black Sports*. Santa Barbara, CA: Praeger.

Naze, D. (2014). "Jackie Robinson Day: The Contemporary Legacy." *Out of Bounds: Racism and the Black Athlete,* edited by L. L. Martin. Santa Barbara, CA: Praeger.

Pennington, B. (2012). "In 1956, a Racial Law Repelled Harvard's Team." *New York Times*. Retrieved from http://www.nytimes.com/2012/03/15/sports/ncaa basketball/in-1956-a-racial-law-soured-harvard-on-a-trip-to-new-orleans .html?_r=0.

Pennington, R. (n.d.). "Racial Integration of College Football." Retrieved from http://richardpennington.com/index.php/publications/entry/racial -integraton-of-college-football-in-texasracial-integraton-of-college.

Reed, R., and Kinney, G. (n.d.). "Celebrating George Jewett: A Look at the Achievements of Michigan's First African American Football Letterman." Bentley Historical Society, University of Michigan. Retrieved from http://bentley .umich.edu/features/celebrating-george-jewett/.

Runstedtler, T. (2012). *Jack Johnson Rebel Sojourner*. Berkeley, CA: University of California Press.

Sparks, Randy. (1992). "Gentleman's Sport: Horse Racing in Antebellum Charleston," *The South Carolina Historical Magazine*, 93(1): 15–30.

Sumner, J. (2011). "College Basketball Pioneers in North Carolina." *Tar Heel Junior Historian*, 51(1).

Tuttle, Dennis. (May/June 2005). "Famous Early African American Track Stars," *Footsteps*, 7(3): 10.

"Why Black Colleges?" *The Black College Football Museum*. Retrieved from http:// www.theblackcollegefootballmuseum.org/why.html.

Wiggins, D., and Miller, P. (2003). *The Unlevel Playing Field: A Documentary History of the African American Experience in Sport*. Chicago, IL: University of Chicago Press.

Winkler, Lisa K. (2009). "The Kentucky Derby's Forgotten Jockeys." Retrieved from http://www.smithsonianmag.com/history/the-kentucky-derbys-for gotten-jockeys-128781428/?no-ist.

Woullard, Jason. (October 4, 2013). "George Jewett: College Football's Original Renaissance Man." *The Shadow League*. Retrieved from http://www.the shadowleague.com/articles/george-jewett-college-football-s-original -renaissance-man.

Index

About the Authors

Lori Latrice Martin is associate professor of sociology and African and African American studies at Louisiana State University. Recent publications include *Big Box Schools: Race, Education, and the Danger of the Walmartization of Public Schools in America; Out of Bounds: Racism and the Black Athlete; White Sports/Black Sports; and Black Asset Poverty and the Enduring Racial Divide*. Dr. Martin was born and raised in Nyack, New York. She earned a doctorate degree from University at Albany, State University of New York.

Kenneth J. Fasching-Varner is the Shirley B. Barton Endowed Associate Professor of Education and director of the Higher Education Administration Program at Louisiana State University. Dr. Fasching-Varner's recent publications include *Racial Battle Fatigue in Higher Education; Working Through Whiteness; Occupying the Academy*; and *Understanding, Dismantling, and Disrupting the Prison-to-School Pipeline*. Dr. Fasching-Varner earned his doctorate degree from The Ohio University.

Nicholas D. Hartlep is assistant professor at Metropolitan State University, School of Urban Education. He holds a doctorate degree from University of Wisconsin-Milwaukee.

Sidney Silverman Library
and Learning Resource Center
Bergen Community College
400 Paramus Road
Paramus, NJ 07652-1595

www.bergen.edu
Return Postage Guaranteed